THE
HONEYMOONERS'
COMPANION

3/7/80
I love you.
Sar.

THE HONEYMOONERS' COMPANION

THE KRAMDENS AND THE NORTONS REVISITED

DONNA McCROHAN

WORKMAN PUBLISHING, NEW YORK

Library of Congress Cataloging in Publication Data

McCrohan, Donna.
  The Honeymooners' companion.

  Includes index.
  1. The Honeymooners. I. Title.
PN1992.77.H623M3   791.45′7   77-93033
ISBN 0-89480-022-1

Workman Publishing
1 West 39 Street
New York, New York 10018

Manufactured in the United States of America
First printing May 1978
10 9 8 7 6 5 4 3 2 1

Permissions:

Workman Publishing thanks the following for permission to include copyrighted material:

Broadcasting, Honeymooners review, Oct. 10, 1955. © 1955 by *Broadcasting magazine.* Reprinted by permission.

Crown Publishers, Inc., excerpt from *The Longest Street,* by Louis Sobol. © 1968 by Louis Sobol. Used by permission of Crown Publishers, Inc.

New York Daily News, "They Create a Musical a Week," Dec. 28, 1969. © 1969, New York News, Inc. Reprinted by permission.

Delacorte Press, excerpts from *Milton Berle: An Autobiography* with Haskel Frankel © 1974 by Milton Berle. Reprinted by permission of Delacorte Press.

Lyn Duddy and Jerry Bresler, lyrics from the songs "Raccoon Alma Mater" and "There's Nothing That I Haven't Sung About." © Lyn Duddy and Jerry Bresler.

Good Housekeeping, "How to Tell a Story," by Jackie Gleason, March, 1956. © 1956 by the Hearst Corp. Reprinted by permission.

International Creative Management, selections from *The Golden Ham,* by Jim Bishop. © 1956 by Jim Bishop. Reprinted by permission of International Creative Management.

Miami Herald, "Gleason Starts Second Honeymoon," Sept. 17, 1977; "The Honeymoon Isn't Over Yet," Nov. 2, 1975. Reprinted by permission of the Miami Herald Publishing Co.

National Comics Publications, Inc., *Jackie Gleason and The Honeymooners* comic books. © 1956, 1957, 1958 by VIP Corporation. Reprinted by permission of the publishers, D. C. Comics, Inc.

New York Post, "Gleason Return to the Screen Is Just Special," by Bob Williams, Nov. 14, 1977. © 1977. New York Post Corp. Reprinted by permission.

New York Times, "TV: It's Business," by Jack Gould, Dec. 25, 1954; "Bi-Focal Camera," by J. P. Shanley, Sept. 4, 1955. © *The New York Times.* Reprinted by permission.

Newsweek, "Battle of the Giants," Sept. 26, 1955; "Why Favorites Faded," May 28, 1956. © 1955 and 1956, respectively, by Newsweek, Inc. All rights reserved. Reprinted by permission.

Saturday Night Live, transcript of the parody of *The Honeymooners.* Written by the writers and cast of *Saturday Night Live.* Reprinted by permission.

SongSmiths, Inc., "Melancholy Serenade," music by Jackie Gleason, lyrics by Duke Enston. © 1952, 1953, and 1954, SongSmiths, Inc. All rights reserved. Reprinted by permission. "You're My Greatest Love," music by Jackie Gleason, lyrics by Bill Templeton. © SongSmiths, Inc. All rights reserved. Reprinted by permission.

TV Guide, "Psychiatrist's Explanation," by Frank De Blois, Oct. 1, 1955; excerpt from "Finally Out of the Cave," by Edith Efron, Sept. 23, 1967; "It Was Chaos. Crazy," by Al Stump, Jan. 24, 1976. © 1955, 1967, Walker and Company, Inc., excerpts from *How the Golden Age of Television Turned My Hair to Silver, Time,* "Second Honeymoon," Oct. 14, 1966. © Time, Inc. Reprinted by permission.

Walker and Company, Inc., excerpts from *How the Golden Age of Television Turned My Hair to Silver,* by Kenneth Whelan. © 1973 by Kenneth Whelan. Reprinted with permission of the publisher.

To Harry and Mildred James,
the youngest, wisest, dearest
Honeymooners I know.

FOREWORD

While I am not the first to indulge in this particular book-length literary form, I can still be the first to name it. I call it "The Great American Fan Letter."

The Honeymooners' Companion is a cult object, lovingly crafted, for the innumerable Honeymoonies who populate our cities and hamlets from coast to coast and abroad.

It is for the steadfast fans who will not permit their local stations to take *The Honeymooners* off the air, no matter how many times they have seen each episode.

It is for the recent converts, who came to *The Honeymooners* late in life, and now can't imagine what life was like before the Kramdens and the Nortons.

It is for everyone who works late, and rushes home to see *The Honeymooners;* for everyone who works days, and stays up to watch *The Honeymooners* and for all the families whose dinner plans have been rescheduled around *The Honeymooners*.

It is for the serious students of television and for TV "trivia" addicts.

It is for the Ralphs and Eds of the world, for their long-suffering Alices and Trixies, for their drinking buddies and their understanding pals.

It is for all the creators of a show almost too good to be true, and so true that it has become timeless.

It is for everyone who believes, or wants to believe, that genius is another word for magic. When a TV show runs for twenty-eight years with the same eight basic pieces of furniture, what else can you call it?

Donna McCrohan

ACKNOWLEDGMENTS

Many years ago, it came to me that something I really wanted to do was to stand, actually, in the kitchen of the Kramdens' apartment. To do that it would be necessary to research and write about *The Honeymooners*. I didn't though, until Judy Fireman asked me to contribute an article about my *Honeymooners* passion to her *TV Book*. She then suggested expanding the article to manuscript length, and in doing so, she became not only the hand of providence, but my indefatigable editor too. For this I thank her wholeheartedly.

Somewhat providentially, I first met The Great One in the Kramdens' kitchen, during rehearsals of the most recent *Honeymooners* special. To Jackie Gleason, and to all the others who have made this book possible with their diligence, enthusiasm, and support, both on and off the set, I am deeply indebted.

Special thanks to W. John Abramson, John Behrens, Morey Bernstein, Ken Bomar, Jerry Bresler, Art Carney, Imogene Coca, Bob Cummings, Phil Cuoco, Lyn Duddy, Denise Ehdaivand, Ray Fisher, Teddy Gilanza, Richard Green, Dutch Hardie, Jim Harrison, Lydia Hernandez, Bob Hope, Jane Kean, Terri King, Barry Kluyger, Penny Lambeth, Norman Lear, Sam Levenson, Sheila Madigan, Julia Dennehy Marshall, Pete McGovern, Audrey Meadows, Hank Meyer, Johnny and Penny Olsen, Joseph Parente, George Petrie, Jack Philbin, Jerry Plunkett, Dan Ragan, Joyce Randolph, Ruth Regina, Joan Rivers, Duke Rick, Howard Rogofsky, A. J. Russell, Betty Schafer, Barry Secunda, Sydell Spear, Walter Stone, Matt Tepper, Joe Tiernan, Ed Waglin, Patricia Wilson, Syd Zelinka, and Alan Zweibel.

And finally, my gratitude to those whom I have never met or spoken to, whose contributions to the show have shown me what talent is all about.

CONTENTS

I. GLEASON AND COMPANY

II. KRAMDEN AND FRIENDS

III. BEHIND THE SCENES WITH THE HONEYMOONERS

IV. THE HONEYMOONERS PLOT SYNOPSES

V. THE HONEYMOONERS HIGHLIGHTS

VI. THE HONEYMOONERS BIOGRAPHIES

VII. THE CHAUNCEY STREET IRREGULARS GLOSSARY

I. GLEASON AND COMPANY

GLEASON BEFORE TELEVISION

*Gleason was to television what P.T. Barnum was
to the world of the big top.*

KAY GARDELLA, *NEW YORK DAILY NEWS*

Ralph Kramden and Jackie Gleason grew up together in the Bushwick section of Brooklyn. In many ways, they have always thought alike. They both like to do things in a big way or not at all. They're both born showmen. And they both have very definite ideas about television.

Take Kramden's efforts to sell the Handy Housewife Helper during a commercial break between segments of a Charlie Chan movie. Or his careful preparations to win big money on *Beat the Clock* and *The $99,000 Answer*. Granted he's still driving a bus, but nobody can accuse him of thinking small. And no one will ever accuse him of giving up.

Gleason, who did everything from prizefighting and exhibition diving to playing gangsters in Warner Brothers movies, tried TV as its first Chester A. Riley, in *The Life of Riley,* and then took a turn as guest emcee on DuMont's *Cavalcade of Stars.* It wasn't his style. Everything about it was small. It was time for Gleason to think about television in a big way— or forget it.

Fortunately, he didn't give up. Television is through thinking small. Gleason doesn't have to be a prizefighter anymore.

In 1953, Gleason said: ''I did my act, as much of an act as I ever had. There was a planned start and a finish, and what went on between was strictly impromptu. Even the start and end were subject to change without notice. I don't think I was very good.''

TELEVISION BEFORE GLEASON

In 1947, when antennas began to bloom on rooftops,
Gleason couldn't afford a TV set.

JIM BISHOP, *THE GOLDEN HAM*

The end of World War II brought America's manpower home. This, in turn, produced postwar babies and television—the longest-running symbiotic collaboration in show business history. Little did anyone know where it would lead. But then, little did anyone know about TV. Wartime television had been restricted by the government to four hours a week. The scientists, engineers, industrialists, and equipment necessary to develop the infant industry were needed for the war effort. It wasn't until the war was over that commercial TV as we now know it began. A millionaire known as Earl W. "Madman" Muntz was turning a profit selling sets at $10 per screen inch—$170 for a seventeen-inch screen, and, as Stan Opotowsky observes in *TV: The Big Picture:*

> The eagerness with which the American public grabbed at the opportunity to become hollow-eyed zombies is graphically demonstrated by television's growth. It took sixty-two years for electric wiring to reach 34 million homes. It took eighty years for the telephone to reach the same number of homes. It took the automobile forty-nine years and the electric washer forty-seven years. But it took television only ten years. In 1950 there were 104 TV stations in operation. By 1960 there were 531. Between 1948 and 1950 alone the amount of money spent by advertisers in TV leaped 229.2 percent, from $8,700,000 to $90,629,000.

Even so, it was almost impossible to attract headliner celebrities to TV in those early days. Established stars of the movies and radio had so little incentive to risk overnight failure in full view of millions, especially when success on the tiny tube seemed to offer so little in return. True, TV offered exposure, but what major star lacked exposure? If anything, success was synonymous with using up good material faster than it could be replenished. For stage performers, it meant using up, in one appearance, an act that might have lasted for years in nightclubs or vaudeville.

"History knows no [other] era when laughter was fed to whole populations for hours at a time, steadily, night after night, month after month," wrote Steve Allen in *The Funny Men*. "People get tired of you a lot quicker on TV than they do on the radio. They pick you up faster, but they drop you faster, too. On the radio it took a long time to become a star, and if you made it you could stick around for maybe ten or fifteen years right at the top."

In the 1950s, when Bob Hope had switched from a 90-minute show to a 60-minute show and then to a 30-minute show, he joked with *TV Guide*, "I think they're grooming me for spot announcements." Once TV caught on, performers would agree, "There's no place left to be bad anymore." Most stars with anything to lose did not fancy losing it on network television.

The first programs—*Meet the Press, Kraft Television Theatre,* and *Howdy Doody,* all making their debuts in 1947—could get along fine without big box-office names. In 1948, with the TV advent of *Arthur Godfrey's Talent Scouts,* Ted Mack's *"Original Amateur Hour,"* and Ed Sullivan's *Toast of the Town,* the emphasis was changed only slightly, since the talent used on these showcase offerings was expected to be amateur or newly discovered.

Contrary to widely held belief, Elvis Presley was not one of the vast array of performers to make his TV debut on Ed Sullivan's show (Presley was first on Gleason's *Stage Show*). On the other hand, Gleason *was* one of that vast array. Even before *The Life of Riley,* while he was still appearing in *Along Fifth Avenue* on Broadway, he appeared on Sullivan's *Toast of the Town.*

But TV had a lot to offer up-and-coming celebrities ready to take the plunge—Sid Caesar, Steve Allen, Jack Paar, Red Buttons, George Gobel, Lucille Ball, and Jackie Gleason among them. The networks were prepared to create their own star system: their first great star was Milton Berle (who actually took a cut from his radio salary to try his hand at television). It was an inspired gamble by the man destined to become "Mr. Television" and the "Uncle Miltie" of a nation. Before long, it was possible to hear a whole broadcast of Berle's *Texaco Star Theatre* just by walking down the streets of most neighborhoods in America on a Tuesday night.

In 1948, Jackie Gleason—of Broadway, Hollywood, radio, and the night-club circuit—had scarcely been heard at all. Even so, TV didn't interest him—yet. It would. They were made for each other. They were part of the same American dream.

THE DUMONT DAYS

No one in television ever rose so fast so soon.

LEO ROSTEN, *LOOK*

"**A**lmost anyone who knew Jackie Gleason in the 1940s would tell you The Fat Man would never make it," wrote Robert Metz in *CBS: Reflections in a Bloodshot Eye*. By 1952 he would be regarded as one of television's few authentic geniuses, a veritable Orson Welles at his own brand of showmanship. Everything he had done before that—every job he had taken, every audience or camera he had faced, every memory of his life—would complement his instinctive brilliance in every aspect of TV production. But before he came to TV, his brilliance had nowhere to shine.

Of course, friends from his old neighborhood might have told you he'd make it. They were there when he got his first audience laugh; when their school principal picked up a fallen microphone and Jackie ad-libbed, "That's the first thing you've ever done for us kids." They were there at the Halsey Theater in Brooklyn on amateur night when he won his first five-dollar prize. They were there, and so was he, and laughter was plentiful but money was not. If he was going into show business, it would have to pay his keep. That meant water shows, carnivals, and prizefighting when he wasn't doing what he did best—working with live club and theater audiences. It meant working in the movies for Warner Brothers at the age of twenty-five playing gangster roles, or the sailor-type who said to Jack Oakie, "It's time to get back to the ship."

"They paid me two-fifty a week, but I had to provide my own ammunition," Gleason recalled in a *Cosmopolitan* interview. "It was awful. The only fun I had on the Coast was hanging around with Phil Silvers and Rags Ragland. We used to register at hotels as Mr. Eberhard, Mr. Faber, and Mr. Ticonderoga."

Dissatisfied with Hollywood, he agreed to try television in 1949 (his first actual TV appearance was a few years earlier on Ed Sullivan's show), in the Chester A. Riley role created on radio in 1944 by William Bendix, who was unavailable that year due to previous commitments, although legend has it that an appliance manufacturer was willing to sponsor the show only if its star did not have the name of a rival washing machine. In fact, Pabst beer was the sponsor. *The Life of Riley* won an Emmy in 1950. Gleason did the best he could in a role that did not suit his smart-aleck style; he was unnaturally boxed in by a schlub of a character already established before he came to the scene. After twenty-six episodes for NBC, Pabst, unimpressed, dropped the show to sponsor the fights. For Gleason, for the moment, it was back to nightclubs and other live shows.

By now there were four networks in New York—CBS, NBC, ABC, and the smaller, short-lived DuMont. Milton Douglas, a singer with an idea, approached the Whelan Drug Company with plans for a one-hour weekly variety show. He would produce it. DuMont, large enough to reach major cities but small enough to be affordable, would air it. Production costs, nearly $400,000 for a year of programming, would be borne by the stores of the Whelan chain. They called it *Cavalcade of Stars*.

In *The Golden Age of Television,* television writer Max Wilk recalls:

Cavalcade was a noisy affair; the format was trite and true. An eager, on-the-way-up comedy hopeful as master of ceremonies, a troupe of hardworking girl dancers, some hokey sketches, and here and there an occasional "guest star." (Since the show was sponsored by Whelan's Drugstores, the rumor was that everybody got paid off in toothpaste.) The sets were shabby, the camerawork was nervous and under-rehearsed, and the band played loud, not good. By today's elegant nighttime variety show standards, *Cavalcade* was strictly El Cheapo. But then, even in its own time, the show was considered Poverty Row—with music. However, as George Burns once remarked, "All comics need a place where they can be lousy." That was truly the function of DuMont's Saturday night show.

The "star" in the title *Cavalcade of Stars* didn't fool anybody. It was another showcase of sorts. Different hosts from week to week would use the show as a stepping-stone if they got lucky. Jack Carter, Larry Storch, and Jerry Lester were a few who made it. By July 1950, the producer was ready for a host who could unify the show, a performer who could move back and forth from emcee to sketch-comic and keep the audience with him every step of the way. Someone approached debonair Peter Donald (who later turned up as host on *Masquerade Party*) who declined, but suggested Jackie Gleason as the right man for the job.

By now Gleason was attracting some attention on his own; whether it heralded stardom was anybody's guess. One week he'd get $150 for a radio program like *Edelbrau Hour,* another week he'd get $3,000 at the Roxy. Some weeks he wouldn't work. He was at Slapsie Maxie's, then the most famous nightclub in Los Angeles, when the call came from DuMont. The offer was two weeks at $750 per week. He wasn't interested. He didn't see much point in going East for a couple of weeks when he already had a job. They offered him four weeks. He took it for the money, but still didn't see the point. His first taste of television, with *The Life of Riley,* had not been encouraging. When he left Slapsie Maxie's for New York, he fully expected to return within the month.

Yet, according to DuMont's initial publicity release, his hour had arrived:

June 30, 1950, New York—Arriving from California aboard the Super Chief Friday morning, Jackie Gleason promptly set to work on plans for his debut on *Cavalcade of Stars* Saturday, July 8 (9 to 10 P.M. EDST) over WABD and the DuMont Television Network. Jackie is taking over the comic-emcee duties for the star-studded variety show which were formerly conducted by Jerry Lester and Jack Carter.

Born in Brooklyn thirty-four years ago, the attractive, dark-haired comedian is one of the few who can "be funny" just because it comes naturally. Having recently completed *Desert Hawk,* [starring Richard Greene, before his days as TV's Robin Hood, with Gleason and Rock Hudson in minor roles] a Universal picture to be released soon, Jackie is enthusiastic about his new DuMont network program. He feels the *Cavalcade* format will give him more opportunity to do the kind of comedy he enjoys and is best suited for—ad-lib, situation skits, and generally zany fun.

Among the guests to greet Jackie on his debut, July 8, will be Rose Marie, the petite, now-grown-up child singing star, and Evelyn Farney with her Morrison Dancers.

In 1930, when sound was revolutionizing the movie industry, it was "all talking, all singing, all dancing" pictures that lit up the silver screen. In 1950, when a home audience brought up on radio suddenly had voices and music *plus images* on their living room screens, it was again "all talking, all singing, all dancing" that best showed off the new medium.

This kind of TV needed Gleason. *Cavalcade* was broadcast live; it was performed before a live theater audience. It had show girls and comics, extravaganza numbers and skits. He had the feel for it. Since he first got into show business, no matter how small his own part in a stage show, he would hang around to watch the other numbers go on, observing every detail of lighting, staging, costuming, props, and the rest, until he knew production from every angle.

Today, watching him on the set or talking to the people who work with him, there is little doubt that he has the knowledge to back up the standards he sets for them and their equipment. In 1951, he was expected to confine his interests to the front end of the camera.

That didn't stop him from wanting to do it all or not at all. The first day he walked onto the set of *Cavalcade,* the producer and director took him around to show how things would be done—their way. He straightened them out in no uncertain terms. After all, he only planned to be around four weeks. "If we do it, we'll do it my way," he told them. "If I fall on my face, I want it to be my fault and no one else's. And gentlemen, if you think I'm only doing this to be altruistic, you're mistaken. If we're a success, I want the credit."

He has had firm control of his shows ever since. He has almost always gotten the credit.

Gleason's version of *Cavalcade* combined comedy with elegant production numbers and beautiful women whom he personally selected. June Taylor (whose June Taylor Dancers would later make her the Busby Berkeley of television) provided a chorus line of six girls at $50 a week each, charged $85 for her own services, and made a good show of things despite the fact that they could only afford seventy-five-cent orchestral arrangements to dance to. Once in a while, Milton Douglas, original mastermind of *Cavalcade,* would go on as a singer.

Gleason treated his audiences, both the one in the theater and the one at home, like ticket holders at a stage show. "Oh, boy, you're a dan-dan-dandy group tonight," he'd begin. He'd continue to play to them throughout the evening. Rather than employ "name" guest stars, and aware that no single personality is strong enough to sustain an hour-long show week after week, Jackie chose to develop his own repertory of characters: The Poor Soul; Joe the Bartender; Charlie Bratton, the Loudmouth (inspired by his real-life "Uncle Fat" who flashed wads of big bills to impress folks); Rudy the Repairman; Reginald Van Gleason III; Stanley R. Sogg, TV pitchman for Mother Fletcher's Pastafazool between segments of the late-late-late show—and Ralph Kramden, a Brooklyn version of Everyman.

But there was no Ralph Kramden, no *Honeymooners,* the first night Jackie Gleason did *Cavalcade.* As Jim Bishop tells it in *The Golden Ham,* his biography of Jackie Gleason,

> On the opening night of *Cavalcade of Stars,* Jackie went through two rented sketches and a satire on an Italian movie named *Stromboli.* He was so funny that even the writers laughed. In one sketch, there was a Dutch half-door Gleason was supposed to exit through. The door got stuck. Gleason climbed over it. The audience giggled. When he had to make another entrance, Jackie climbed over it as though that was the way a Dutch door was intended to be used. The audience roared. He went in and out and over that door so many times that people were weak from laughter. Even the camera crews roared. The network wondered if Gleason could be that funny twice in a row.

The second week, he used an impressionist/announcer who had been spotted playing a waiter on Morey Amsterdam's *The Silver Swan Cafe* (a show produced and directed by Irving Mansfield, whose wife, Jacqueline Susann, appeared in the cast as a cigarette girl). This actor, Art Carney, who has since been recognized as a consummate "actor's actor" by the likes of Katharine Hepburn and Alfred Lunt, first appeared on *Cavalcade* as a disapproving, inhibited, fussbudget commercial photographer—what today we would call a Felix Unger type after the role he created on Broadway in *The Odd Couple.* In the sketch, Carney was assigned to photograph Reggie Van Gleason III as "Man of Distinction" for a liquor ad. Reggie was Gleason's own creation, from his top hat, flowing opera cape, and dilettante mustache to the exaggerated mannerisms of a worthless "swell." Reggie would take a swig of the sponsor's prop liquor, burp, behave badly; the photographer, disgusted, would take a swig and try to get on with the shooting. By the end of the sketch they were both smashed on the sponsor's firewater.

For the third show, Gleason and his writers decided to develop a basic sketch that relied not on caricature but on familiar domestic situations. It would be a husband-wife routine; the couple would be poor. This would be good material—flexible, funny, extremely recognizable since just about everyone watching television in the 1950s had been poor or at least strapped at one time or another. It would be a vignette; it would rotate with other basic bits to give them the three sketches needed to fill out the hour show. Its creation, as reconstructed by Jim Bishop in *The Golden Ham,* went something like this:

> One afternoon writers Joe Bigelow and Harry Crane were trying to write a sketch with the star, and Gleason said that he had an idea for a sketch that would revolve around a married couple—a quiet, shrewd wife and a loud-mouthed husband.
>
> "You got a title for it?" asked Bigelow.
>
> "Wait a minute," said Crane. "How about 'The Beast'?"
>
> Jackie got to his feet. "Just a second," he said. "I always wanted to do this thing, and the man isn't a beast. The guy really loves this broad. They fight, sure. But they always end in a clinch."
>
> Bigelow shrugged. "It *could* be a thing."
>
> "I come from a neighborhood full of that stuff. By the time I was fifteen, I knew every insult in the book."
>
> "Then let's try it," said Bigelow.
>
> "But not 'The Beast,' " said Jackie. "That's not the title."
>
> "Why not?"
>
> "It sounds like the husband is doing all the fighting. We need something a little left-handed as a title. You know, this kind of thing can go and go and go."
>
> "How about 'The Lovers'?" said Harry Crane.
>
> "That's a little closer, Harry." Gleason paced the floor. "A little closer, but it could mean that they're not married. We need something that tells everybody at once that they're married."
>
> "The Couple Next Door."
>
> "No. How about 'The Honeymooners'?"
>
> "Aw, no. That sounds like they're lovey-dovey."
>
> "All the better. This dame is very wise and very tired. She knows this guy inside out, see, and he's always got a gripe. Maybe he's a—no, a cop wouldn't do. They got a little flat in Brooklyn. Flatbush Avenue, maybe. Cold-water flat. Third or fourth floor. Hell, I lived in these joints. I know where the sink should be, the icebox—and don't forget the drip pan underneath—the sideboard and the round table. The little gas range. You know? Maybe we got something."
>
> "I got the opening line," Bigelow said. "The guy comes home tired. He worked all day. He's beat. He walks in, mad at the whole world, and his wife says, 'Don't take your coat off. Go downstairs and get me a loaf of bread,' and the guy gives her a look that would split a grapefruit and he shakes his head sarcastically and says, 'I'm not getting anything. I worked all day. What did you do?' and they're off to the races."
>
> "That's the general idea," Jackie said. "Make it real. Make it the way people really live. If it isn't credible, nobody's going to laugh. The guy at home has got to be able to look at it and say, 'That's the way my old lady sounds.' "

"This can be a thing," said Crane. "A real thing."

"I even know who can play the wife," said Gleason, enthused. "Pert Kelton." He held out both hands for the verdict. "Is anybody more natural than Pert for this bit? Did you guys ever see her in a part where she gets mad at a guy? Holy smoke!"

The first *Honeymooners* episode was only a few minutes long. There wasn't any Norton yet, only Ralph and Alice. Ralph comes home from driving a bus, Alice asks him to get the bread. "You mean," he rages, "after a hard day at work, you expect me to go to the store?" Within three minutes, they're both worked into a lather. She reminds him that she's been busy too, and shows him the pie she baked. He tosses it at her, she ducks and it sails out the window. They argue. There's a knock at the door and a neighborhood cop appears, wearing pie. The cop is played by Art Carney! The scene ends—though probably not the fight—when she gets her leg out the window and threatens to jump. "Go ahead and jump," says Ralph. Alice replies, "I wouldn't give you the satisfaction."

A later *Honeymooners* episode was done with no script at all. Gleason still hates to be overrehearsed; in those days he wouldn't look at the script till the morning of the show. Because he has a photographic memory, he was able to memorize the whole thing between 7:00 A.M. and 9:00 A.M. One morning no script was delivered. He was not concerned enough to do anything about it until early evening. At about 5:30 P.M. he, Pert, and Art went over to his hotel to see what they could put together. Pert figured she could work a typewriter if she really put her mind to it. All three figured to have a drink before they really got down to work. Drinks over, they couldn't get anything down on paper. So they had another round. Hours later, they still had nothing down on paper (and only 20 minutes till curtain time), but they were feeling no pain. They formulated a game plan—Ralph and Alice would start bickering, and when they had it going good, Norton (the role of Ed Norton, Ralph's neighbor and closest pal, had been developed for Carney by then) would come in and make it worse. And that's all they went on with, live, before a TV audience of millions, despite the sponsor's disbelief and disapproval. When the show was over, the three went off to a dressing room and waited to get fired. Which, of course, didn't happen, since the sponsor thought it had been their funniest yet.

Some mornings, Gleason wouldn't like the scripts that were delivered. They would have to be rewritten in a few hours' time, either by the writers, or by Gleason as he went along. He was demanding, he was a perfectionist, and he had one of the fastest turnover rates for writers in the industry. Arne Rosen and Coleman Jacoby were his first writers, joined shortly by Joe Bigelow and Harry Crane. Harry Crane remained as a head writer, Joe Bigelow would return briefly a decade later as script supervisor, the others moved on. *Cavalcade* would have a new writing staff each week. At the time, Walter Stone, who had written for Robert Q. Lewis' daytime radio show, for Jack Carter on *Cavalcade*, and for Paul Winchell, was not working. Marvin Marx, who had met Stone when they were both working with Jack Carter, was about to be one of Jackie's writers-of-the-week. Marx asked Stone to try it for a week, what did he have to lose? Stone said, "Nothing doing. I heard about how that guy works," then decided to do it anyhow. By the time Stone got to *Cavalcade,* Marx was gone, another casualty of new-week-new-writers syndrome.

A few weeks later Marvin Marx was brought back to write with Walter Stone. Jackie Gleason signed himself into Doctors Hospital to lose weight. He was bored, so the writers would visit him some four or five hours a day. When they weren't shooting the breeze they'd do scripts, with Gleason as contributor and captive audience. They managed to write two shows in one week—three sketches plus a monologue for each show—something that had never happened before. This made Gleason take notice. The team stuck for the remainder of the DuMont contract, and even when the show moved to CBS. Although there have been other writers along the way, and although Marvin Marx died a few years back, Walter Stone still writes for *Honeymooners* specials.

Needless to say, the show was a hit. There was no question of Jackie's going back to Slapsie Maxie's. The other networks were looking for shows to cut into his Friday 10:00–11:00 P.M. ratings. *Cavalcade of Sports*—"the fights"—was one of them. Considering Gleason's audience, this was stiff competition. At Proce's bar

George Petrie with Van Gleasons II (Art Carney) and III.

Says Petrie, "*The Jackie Gleason Show* was the highlight of my professional life. It meant working with a couple of giants—two extremely talented men, professionals all the way."

in Brooklyn (the neighborhood bar from Jackie's childhood that inspired the Joe the Bartender skits), they had to install two television sets.

Anytime they did the *Honeymooners* on *Cavalcade,* the ratings went up; by the time the DuMont contract ran out, the show had gone from a 9 percent to a 25 percent share of the audience. The contract, which began as a $5,000-dollar *loan* to Gleason, had become a $1,500-per-week check (with deductions of $450 per week against the loan). Actually, after Jackie's manager, agents, and staff had gotten their percentages, it was not unusual for him to finish with $90 a week. And one week, when a toothache and resulting swollen jaw prevented him from speaking or performing, the sponsors would not pay him a cent.

Jackie was a big star now. The modestly proportioned DuMont network was enough to make a small man claustrophobic. When he was a guest on other shows, he could ask as much as $12,500 per appearance. (Although when he was on Frank Sinatra's show, he waived his fee in memory of the days when they were both dirt-poor and working together on their careers.) *Cavalcade of Stars* was no longer the showcase where neophyte performers had a chance to be bad. With maybe six minutes of product advertisement in an hour, it left a full fifty-four minutes for quality stage-show entertainment. All of Gleason's characters had caught on to some extent with the public; at least four—The Poor Soul, Reggie Van Gleason III, Joe the Bartender, and Ralph Kramden—were household words. *The Honeymooners,* which was never expected to develop beyond an ongoing husband-wife quarrel, now included sewer worker, Ed Norton and his ex-burlesque-queen wife, Trixie, played only once by Elaine Stritch, and afterward, for years, by Joyce Randolph.

Joyce Randolph had done her share of TV variety shows in the early 1950s, working with Martin and Lewis and Fred Allen among others. Her first role on *Cavalcade* was in a serious vein. She and Gleason played former sweethearts, once separated by show business, who were now reunited in their hometown in a dressing room scene that was poignant, moving, and not at all what the audience expected from the wisecracking Jackie Gleason. When, weeks later, Gleason needed someone in a hurry to play Ed Norton's Missus, he said, ''Get me that serious actress.'' Trixie was in.

In July of 1952, the DuMont contract running out, the Gleason troupe embarked on a personal appearance tour of major cities that broke records everywhere it went. The crowds roared, inside the theaters and out.

The cast was doing four shows a day, a tiring schedule by any standards. When they weren't performing, they were partying. Pert Kelton wasn't keeping up. One day she went on in her Alice role, left the stage to get sick, and reappeared to pick up her squawk with Ralph. The audience loved it; they couldn't know, any more than the people in the cast and crew, that Pert Kelton would collapse by the end of the day. What had passed for a hangover turned out to be coronary thrombosis. Any efforts to keep up the grueling pace of a weekly TV show after that, and Pert would literally work herself to death. When they returned to New York in August, they would have to find a new Alice.

CBS: ROUND ONE

Self-confidence is a quality Gleason possessed in amplitude

LEO ROSTEN, *LOOK*

DuMont's *Cavalcade of Stars* had been Gleason's vehicle for a little under two years when he made a switch to CBS. In September of 1952, he signed with CBS after negotiating a contract that dwarfed his earlier one: to own, produce, and be solely responsible for the delivery of a weekly hour-long Saturday night variety show; he would hire the writers, the dancers, the orchestra, the cast; he would be ultimately accountable for every technical and professional detail of *The Jackie Gleason Show*.

"What else can you say about a man who produces, directs, edits, lights, stars in and otherwise masterminds a musical comedy a week. . . . He does pass on the gowns his dancers wear, and on the longstemmed beauties who wear them;

The principals read through the script a few times, making changes as they go along, before rehearsing on stage—where they will doubtless make more changes as they go along.

and he did write the haunting theme song of the show, plus half a dozen other ballads,'' wrote Leo Rosten in a 1954 *Look* magazine article.

His new contract was impressive: a weekly budget of $120,000 for each of 39 weeks, to be sponsored by Schick, Sheaffer, Nestlé, and others who would join the ranks as the show gathered force. The show would have to increase each sponsor's sales picture by over a hundred million or they would lose money. If jackie gleason enterprises (always with the small *j, g,* and *e*) brought an hour in for less than the designated production costs, ''enterprises'' and the network would split the difference; however, by contract, this difference could not amount to more than $5,000. In addition to his earnings through jackie gleason enterprises as producer, he would draw another $7,500 weekly as the show's host and star.

New members were added to the team: CBS director Frank Satenstein, who immediately conceded to Jackie's desire to do his own directing; and announcer Jack Lescoulie, who would do *The Jackie Gleason Show* for years on CBS while continuing to do Dave Garroway's show on NBC. June Taylor thought TV was ready for a sixteen-girl chorus line; including salaries, costumes, and other necessaries, the costs would soar to $3,000. On Broadway, these dancers could expect about $100 a week for several long nights' work plus matinees; from Gleason they could get up to $225. Getting them for the show would be no problem. Getting a sixteen-girl line on a seventeen-inch screen was something else. That was when Gleason developed the idea of overhead shots for the June Taylor Dancers—those wonderful kaleidoscopic patterns that became their trademark.

Gleason also brought Art Carney and Joyce Randolph from the DuMont show. Bill McCaffrey, Carney's agent, was prepared to hold out for $750 per show. Gleason had a better idea: ''He gets a thousand dollars or forget it.'' McCaffrey's further negotiations freed Carney for three weeks out of every thirteen to pursue his acting career on noncompetitive shows like *Studio One* and *Kraft Television Theatre.* Joyce Randolph, who had gotten $160 from DuMont for each show that used her—on a we'll-call-you-in-plenty-of-time-for-air-time basis—was signed at $200 a week.

They still needed someone to play Alice Kramden. Any number of actresses went after the role, but none of them measured up to Pert's briny prototype. Audrey Meadows, already known for her work with Bob and Ray, was particularly interested. She was also one of the most beautiful women in New York. Gleason didn't even want to consider her. She went to pains to unbeautify herself, but she still looked too classy for the role. In desperation, she had a photographer wake her first thing in the morning with his camera in hand; when Gleason saw the resulting photographs, she got the part. She was hired for two *Honeymooners* a month since, as on DuMont, it had not yet become a weekly feature.

Everyone should have been happy—Ralph, Alice, Ed, and Trixie were together again, along with Reggie, Charlie, Joe, Rudy, Stanley, and the Poor Soul—but the sponsors wanted to get the most for their investment. They had too much riding on the venture to take a casual attitude. Each wanted the best slots on *The Jackie Gleason Show*. Each wished Jackie would pay more attention to rehearsing the very expensive, fleeting product commercials. He just couldn't be bothered. He argued against rehearsing the show any more than he absolutely had to. When the debate looked as if it could go on forever, he came up with "Portrettes," beautiful girls in picture frames, who smiled seductively as they introduced the various products. The commercials, *live* commercials, were rehearsed no more than before.

On NBC, opposite *The Jackie Gleason Show,* was the *All-Star Revue,* which was one of the few programs on the air that could legitimately back up the "star" in its title. The first week Gleason went on CBS, Jimmy Durante beat him two-to-one in ratings on *All-Star*. Despite subsequent competition from Tallulah Bankhead and Margaret Truman, Gleason began to gain ground. The week of a blockbuster *All-Star* featuring Milton Berle, Groucho Marx, Ethel Barrymore, and Martha Raye, he managed to beat them at the ratings game. His audience may have reached 60 million by the end of his first year on CBS.

"The results were felt in many ways," wrote Jim Bishop in *The Golden Ham*. "In some cities, police noticed that there was less traffic than usual on the

Scene from an unfilmed *Honeymooners* episode.

Week after week, Ralph selfishly spends good money to go bowling while Alice sits home alone. Yet at times his bowling ball becomes a symbol of the absolute self*less*ness of which he is capable, as when he hocks it to buy Alice a Christmas present. Or when, in an early unfilmed episode, he and Alice quarrel over fifteen dollars he has saved to buy a bowling ball; a priest comes by to ask Ralph why he hasn't been to church . . . and Ralph gives him the money.

roads Saturday evenings. Theater managers reported a drop in business on Saturday nights. Supermarkets had a decline in dollar volume on Saturdays.''

The first year at CBS, *The Honeymooners* was confined to sketches in the larger variety show. It would be another year before they attempted the half-hour and even occasional hour-long expanded *Honeymooners* format. But already, Norton was an integral part of the show. (Later events remind us that Carney's Norton may have been more integral than anyone's Alice. To date, Gleason has worked with four Alices. But when Carney isn't available, *The Honeymooners* doesn't go on.) Audrey Meadows was fast mastering the intricacies of Alice Kramden. She devised a hard, frumpy hairdo and, once in the kitchen of 328 Chauncey Street, could hold her own against Ralph's most exasperating schemes and accusations.

Jackie's flair for condensing rehearsal time might have posed problems for a lesser team. Sure, *he* could memorize sixty pages of lines in a Saturday morning. But, didn't everybody know he was unique? Everything was live, yet he considered one onstage rehearsal sufficient for their purposes. Sometimes they ran through lines in his penthouse at the Park Central Hotel. Sometimes the rest of the cast honed up in a dressing room before the show. ''I kept showing up each day, expecting to rehearse, but nothing happened,'' says Audrey Meadows of her first night. ''By the time of the show, I was psychopathic with fright.'' Fortunately, there was always a chemistry above and beyond any script or rehearsal. Whatever the mishaps, it was natural for the team to bring it off onstage.

Kenneth Whelan, associate director of the show, remembers it well in *How the Golden Age of Television Turned My Hair to Silver:* ''When I walked into the studio on Saturday morning, I had no more idea of what was on tap than the Greek guy who delivered the coffee. I wasn't the only one who started from scratch on Saturday morning. The technical crew very seldom knew what was going to happen. . . . The most informed people in the studio were the stagehands, because they knew what sets had been delivered to the studio the night before.

Here is Whelan's description of a typical *Honeymooners* broadcast:

ME. (Eyes on script) ''Everything's fine! They're sticking right to the script! . . . Pat! [cameraman] Pull a little wider. Audrey's going to make a move to the bedroom door.''

PAT. ''*When* is Audrey going to the bedroom door?''

ME. ''She just did it!''

PAT. ''Aw, c'mon, Ken! . . . I almost missed it!''

ME. ''Oh, oh, Pat, I've lost them. . . . They've gone out of sequence! . . . They're not saying the dialogue I've got on this page!''

PAT. ''Try another page.''

ME. ''What the hell do you think I'm doing? Do you think I *always* read this fast? . . . Wait a minute! Here we go. . . . I've found them! . . . They skipped to page eight.''

PAT. ''Thanks a lot, Whelan . . . . Is it a good-looking page? . . . For God's sake, give me some information, will ya! (It was at times like this that I got the feeling I mentioned before. The feeling that Gleason, Art, and Audrey didn't spend *too* much time rehearsing in Gleason's penthouse.)

    ME. "Watch it, Pat! . . . Gleason's going to do the pain bit! . . . Follow Carney and Gleason to the icebox. . . . Carney will close the icebox on Gleason's finger. . . . Then carry them back to the table for the pain bit." (The round kitchen table that you saw in the *Honeymooners* sketch was the most important prop in television. It was our insurance policy. All action scenes involving the three characters were performed at that table. Whenever they got in trouble, they headed for the table like bird dogs. The reason was simple. If they were close together, around the kitchen table, they were easier to cover with the cameras.)

    ME. "Hold it! . . . Hold it! . . . They've gone back to page six! . . . Pull back, Pat! . . . They're going to spread all over the place! . . . Get back, Pat! . . . Go wide! . . . Go wide!"

(Reading Whelan's recollections, you learn a very important thing about the people who worked on *The Honeymooners*. They usually talked in exclamation points.)

Scene from an unfilmed *Honeymooners* episode.

"The louder Ralph yelled at Alice, the more you knew he was yelling at himself."—Syd Zelinka, *Honeymooners* writer

Back from Doctors Hospital after his leg injury, Gleason rehearses with Audrey Meadows for the April 1954 *Honeymooners* episode, ''The Next Champ.''

You can't say the audience was confused by the chaos. For one thing, a performance never looked chaotic unless a prop wall fell or something equally unsalvageable occurred. Otherwise, the principals would work their way out of it, in character. But more important, the spontaneity of the sketches worked as a plus. Gleason has always said the first time he delivers a line is the funniest. The fact that the cast had only walked through the moves and read through the parts before show time allowed them to react to the action and each other, for the first time, live on stage.

On January 30, 1954, in a satire on the silent movie *The Wedding,* Gleason was playing a bad little boy in a prissy suit when he accidentally slipped and fell on one of his own pranks. The audience, used to his incredible pratfalls, thought it was howlingly funny. Trouper that he was, he left the stage as casually as possible and headed straight for Doctors Hospital—with a dislocated right foot, torn ligaments, and a fractured leg. The next week, Ed Sullivan was guest host of the show in Gleason's absence. Sullivan also appeared in one of the sketches as a newspaperman trying to find out how "Mr. Saturday Night" got himself in such hot water in the "Peck's Bad Boy Episode" of the previous week.

Until Gleason's recovery, a series of guest shots, including Garry Moore, Red Skelton, Eddie Fisher, and Jane Froman took their turns at the show's helm. Carney had *The Honeymooners* pretty much to himself on February 13, when he and Robert Q. Lewis did a takeoff on Edward R. Murrow's *Person to Person.* It was the first show ever to take place in Norton's apartment, from which he was to be interviewed for the enlightenment of the waiting world.

Jackie's "homecoming" program, on March 23, combined a *Honeymooners* sketch with his own "romantic jazz" arrangements of "My Blue Heaven" and "You Can't Pull the Wool Over My Eyes." For this very special occasion, Jackie conducted the forty-piece Ray Bloch orchestra himself.

In July of 1954, he came in third in the American Research Bureau's ratings of once-a-week programs. CBS' *I Love Lucy* came in first, with a 56.8 rating to his 41.4; *Dragnet* was second at 41.9. By January 1955 he was first in the Nielsen Ratings, bringing in 53.4 percent of homes reached to *Lucy*'s 51.2 percent. Audrey Meadows was receiving hundreds of curtains and aprons in the mail from viewers who wanted Alice Kramden to lead a spiffier life. A woman sent her ten cents to buy a curtain rod because it would have been too hard to mail one. A bank sent her pot holders, and told her if Alice would bank with them, Ralph would never have to know. Gleason's walk was now so famous that you could hardly escape the party joker who flapped his arms and did an "away-we-go" for you, like it or not. The threats, "One of these days, pow, right on the kisser" and "bang-zoom, right to the moon" were on hundreds of lips at any given moment. Whole families would come to the theater for the late-night show. At least eleven hundred tickets were given out for every performance. People would line up starting at 11:00 A.M. for a show that began at 8:00 P.M.; the line would run from Broadway to Eleventh Avenue, across Fifty-second Street and up to Fifty-third. The folks on line would be laughing out loud before they got through the doors.

Soon it would be contract-renewal time. And time to up the ante again.

21

CBS: ROUND TWO

*When the contract was drawn up in its
final form, it was the biggest ever negotiated for a performer
in the history of show business.*

JIM BISHOP, *THE GOLDEN HAM*

TV: IT'S BUSINESS

Jackie Gleason's New Contract Follows Involved Sequence of Negotiations

Jackie Gleason's new contract, effective next fall, is a good example of the complex business that is television. Riding the crest of his popularity, the comedian has provided for his future about as well as a man possibly could in video. His deal also helps explain why television is traveling in some of the directions that it is.

To calculate what Jackie will gross from his new commitments is virtually impossible at the moment; not even the comedian himse!f knows. His present contract is only a prelude to further economic gains that actually may mean more to him personally.

In a neat sequence of negotiations, Jackie in effect declared a split of his present program running from 8 to 9 o'clock on Saturday evenings over the Columbia Broadcasting System.

Out of the current show he is taking his most popular feature, the sketch known as *The Honeymooners,* and turning it into a series of films of half-hour duration. The films will run from 8:30 to 9:00 Saturdays on CBS. The Buick division of General Motors Corporation will pay out $65,000 for each of the initial thirty-nine films. In other words, Jackie will gross for this half-hour what he now grosses for his full hour show. But this is only the beginning. During the summer of 1956 [remember the TV season runs September–August]—the first year of his contract—thirteen of these films will be shown a second time. On each of these occasions Mr. Gleason will receive an additional $32,500.

In the second year of the contract, Buick will pay increased fees: $70,000 for each original film plus $35,000 for each rerun.

The total amount Buick will pay Mr. Gleason in a two-year period will be $6,142,500. The automobile company also has an option on a third year. If picked up, the option would enrich Mr. Gleason by another $3,412,000.

To get back to Saturday night, Jackie, meanwhile, has the other half-hour—from 8:00 to 8:30—to help make ends meet. This will be handled by his producing concern, jackie gleason enterprises, inc., which in all probability will insert *Stage Show,* the program seen last summer as a replacement for the comedian. This will mean that the June Taylor girls will be around as usual, as well as the assorted chorus beauties and other celebrities. And what more natural than that Jackie should be a guest star now and then to give continuity to the entire hour—*Stage Show* and *The Honeymooners?*

What Jackie has done, in short, is to assure himself as much as anyone can of the advantages of live television, with its spontaneity and immediacy, and also capitalize on a film series. And in so doing he probably will at least triple his gross income.

The ramifications of the deal still do not stop. The figures bandied about in the headlines last week involved the total price of the films. Out of the $65,000 he will receive for the first films Jackie must pay all the production costs—the salaries of Audrey Meadows and Art Carney, musicians, shooting crew, etc. With Mr. Gleason's well-known propensity for doing things his way, his own share may not prove so staggering as it might seem.

But the films ultimately will mean the most economically. A film is a tangible piece of property that can be sold. When Jackie has completed seventy-eight or 117 films in two or three years' time he will be in a position to achieve the comedian's dream—a lucrative capital gains deal. He can sell out the whole batch of films and pay only a 25 percent tax. With a live show, a star not only is dissipating his personality but must pay the normal personal income tax. In Jackie's bracket the personal tax is virtually confiscatory.

If by now further details are not too much, Jackie also has negotiated a new understanding with CBS. The network, reasonably enough, wants exclusive call on his services. So, at the expiration of his Buick contract, CBS will assure him of an income for probably a fifteen-year term, whether he works or not. In exchange, Jackie will promise not to make eyes at other networks.

By no means the least interesting aspect of the whole chain of Gleason's events last week was the fact they were set in motion by Kudner Agency, Inc., representing Buick. To make the Gleason deal, Kudner elected to dispense with the present Buick comedian, a gentleman named Milton Berle, who is seen from 8:00 to 9:00 P.M. on Tuesday evenings over NBC. For a comedian once known as "Mr. Television," it must have been a psychological blow to be so unceremoniously dropped in favor of another. However, no one expects Berle to have difficulty in picking up another sponsor.

What is bound to come next in TV—indeed some of Mr. Berle's spokesmen have already so promised—is a flurry of complicated deals. Not too many stars are in Mr. Gleason's fortunate position; at the moment he happens to be "hot." But it is a sure thing the accountants and lawyers will be working overtime to think up new angles. Quite possibly the trend to film, with its attractive tax features, will become even more pronounced.

The hard fact, of course, is that a star of television no longer is assayed merely as a performer. In the eyes of sponsors he is also, if indeed not primarily, a salesman. Prices that may seem extravagant for the entertainment received are often economical business from a merchandising standpoint.

The advent of television has meant a new relationship between the world of theater and the world of commerce. To many businessmen, involvement in the backstage life of TV has been a strange, bewildering experience. But it sure hasn't taken the showfolk long to catch on to the business life. Weep not for the hungry actor who must take a temporary Christmas job at Macy's; it may be the most important part of his training.

This article by Jack Gould appeared in *The New York Times*, December 26, 1954.

So Jackie was in and Uncle Miltie was out. In his autobiography, Milton Berle tells how it was from his side of the fence:

I went into the 1954–55 season feeling good. Maybe there were newer faces than mine coming up on television, but I had a twenty-six-week vote of confidence in my pocket from Buick. The Nielsen ratings for the end of September put us in second spot with 50.1, just behind the leader, *Dragnet*, with 51.2.

Fall had just set in. I was walking over to the Center Theater to begin the day's rehearsals for the fourth show of the season. I stopped at a corner newsstand and picked up one of the trade papers, and there it was: "Buick Signs Gleason."

Audrey Meadows and Jackie Gleason with
Milton Berle and Phil Silvers at Toots Shors'.

I had been axed. The man swinging it was Myron Kirk, good old Mike Kirk, who had "discovered" me for Gillette in 1936, and "discovered" me for television in 1948.

It's one thing to fail, but not before you take the test. And what hurt most of all was that Myron Kirk didn't even have the decency to tell me to my face. I had to buy a paper to find out that I was going off television for Buick at the end of the year.

How the hell do you get through the rest of your season knowing that? The answer is, you do.

The last show took place on June 14, 1955—even the Center Theater was scheduled to come down after we vacated—and while I felt depressed, at least the edge was off it. I had already signed with RCA-Whirlpool and Sunbeam to do the first color series from California over the cable for the 1955–56 season.

Gleason and Berle were no strangers, although there were times when they didn't exactly behave like friends. As Joe McCarthy wrote in *Cosmopolitan* in 1953:

> Gleason is more than a match for any headliner who tries to steal a scene from him. Milton Berle has a trick of grabbing a person by the arm with apparently friendly intimacy and pushing him out of the spotlight. One night Gleason was to do an act with Berle at a testimonial dinner. When Berle grabbed Gleason's arm, he recoiled, wringing his hand in pain, and saw, too late, a row of pins bristling from Jackie's dinner-jacket sleeve.
>
> Another night, Phil Silvers and Gleason were performing at the Copacabana. Berle began to heckle them from a ringside table. Gleason pinned Berle to the floor and knelt on his chest, and a friend of Gleason's rushed up with a pitcher of water and poured it on Berle's head.

But "Mr. Saturday Night" never underrated the achievements of "Mr. Television." As Gleason later told a group at Toots Shor's, according to Louis Sobol in *The Longest Street:*

> This guy Berle was up there for seven long years, the Number One man. Seven years! That's a couple of lifetimes in this TV racket. How many guys you think there are now—name any of them, me, too—who will be up there, blasting away with the funny stuff and holding on to the top like Berle did. I'm not in love with the guy, but he's got it, and he's still Mr. Big in my book.
>
> Tell you something else. Wasn't for Berle, a lot of us wouldn't have got a break either. When he became Mister Television, those network guys began saying: "We gotta get comics. They want funny stuff. Let's get funnymen." Whatever else you say about Berle, don't forget that. And don't count him out, don't ever count him out. He'll be in there pitching for a long time.

In any case, the deed was done. Berle found other sponsors. Gleason's former sponsors found other shows to back. (Berle was not the only party to show

Gleason's production featured a total of ninety-one performers, the most ever assembled in a Broadway movie house.

During their hectic two-week schedule of live stage shows at the Paramount Theatre in 1954, the entire *Honeymooners* cast (plus the June Taylor Dancers and a fifty-piece orchestra) continued to do their regular weekly broadcasts of *The Jackie Gleason Show*. When, during the engagement, someone asked Audrey Meadows if they could bring her anything, she replied, "Yes, a cake with a file in it."

displeasure at not being consulted when the switch was made.) One of the supercontracts in TV history was in the bag, and Gleason had come out the winner in half a dozen ways. The contract provided for two separate shows: live half-hour *Honeymooners* episodes that would be performed for a live audience and simultaneously taped for rebroadcast and live half-hour variety shows, to be called *Stage Show*, that would precede the *Honeymooners*. Furthermore, Jackie Gleason and jackie gleason enterprises would produce the shows' summer replacement programs.

Jackie had done well for himself and his team. Art Carney was up to $3,500 a week, Audrey Meadows to $2,000 (which *TV Guide* reported as a one-million-dollar contract), Joyce Randolph to $500 (she would be in approximately three quarters of the filmed *Honeymooners* episodes). Two vital forces from behind the scenes of *The Jackie Gleason Show*, Jack Hurdle (as producer of *The Honeymooners*) and Jack Philbin (as executive producer of the whole package), also continued with Jackie under the new Buick contract. And Tommy and Jimmy Dorsey (who on May 23, 1953 on *The Jackie Gleason Show*, had made their first public appearance as well as TV debut since combining their history-making bands as "The Fabulous Dorseys") contracted to join the June Taylor Dancers on *Stage Show*.

In another contract with CBS, Jackie was guaranteed $100,000 annually for the following fifteen years whether he worked for them or not, provided he did not work for any competing network. It was a memorable aspect of the deal, but certainly not unique as things then went. Berle had a similar network contract for thirty years; Eddie Fisher, Jimmy Durante, and Martha Raye had exclusive network arrangements for from fifteen to twenty years.

The media wasted no time in reporting that Gleason had signed an $11-million contract with Buick. As sole owner of all the stock of jackie gleason enterprises which, in addition to supplying *Stage Show, The Honeymooners,* and the summer replacement series, controlled music publishing and oil drilling ventures, Jackie was (before taxes and professional and production expenses) going to be earning $3 million a year.

The results of the entire transaction were many and varied. Not the least of them was the filming of those thirty-nine *Honeymooners* that have been run and rerun countless hundreds of times in the U.S. and abroad for over twenty years. Considering the way *The Honeymooners* developed from one of a half-dozen skits of a variety show, with originally about the same weight as something like "The Family" segment of the *Carol Burnett Show,* it may rank as TV's first spin-off.

Filming *The Honeymooners* took more than the vast sums of money made available by Buick. It also required a technical advance over the kinescope process, one that provided high-quality film that looked as close to "live" as possible. The "Electronicam" system, which had been developed by DuMont Laboratories, was the answer. It had been discussed in connection with *Captain Video* and a "film university on the air." Now Jackie would bring the "live on film" cameras to situation comedy.

BI-FOCAL CAMERA

"Electronicam" Said to Cut Costs and Improve Quality of TV Films

In the Adelphi Theatre on West Fifty-fourth Street, one night last week, it looked as if a conventional live telecast of Jackie Gleason's show, *The Honeymooners*, were taking place.

On the stage, Mr. Gleason, Art Carney, Audrey Meadows and other members of the cast were performing before a familiar setting, the kitchen of the bleak apartment occupied by the Ralph Kramdens (Mr. Gleason and Miss Meadows).

Cameras were focused on the action from each side of the apron of the stage. Another camera was in operation on a ramp extending from the center of the stage about one third of the way out into the orchestra.

Pictures of the proceedings were being watched by members of the show's staff on monitor screens in a control room at the rear of the theatre and on other monitors in the orchestra pit. A studio audience of more than one thousand persons laughed and applauded as Mr. Gleason and his confederates became involved in a series of misunderstandings.

The audience had been given a standard "warm-up" before the show by Jack Lescoulie, the announcer. On the surface it looked like any of the live shows in which the group had appeared in the past.

The differences, however, were fundamental and significant. The program at the Adelphi was not being transmitted to an outside audience. Instead, it was being filmed by means of the new DuMont "Electronicam" process and will not be telecast until sometime this autumn. Then it will be seen over the Columbia Broadcasting System network as a Saturday night half hour show from 8:30 to 9:00 o'clock.

Developed by James L. Caddigan, now in charge of marketing the device, and a staff of DuMont engineers, the Electronicam system may have far-reaching effects on television and motion picture production. Here is the way it operates:

A television camera head and a film camera, having a common lens apparatus, are mounted side by side on the same base. When light passes through the lens, it splits in two parts. One part goes to the film and the other to the pickup tube of the unit's television section. Focus is controlled for both cameras by means of control buttons on the back of the device.

Mr. Caddigan says that the system can provide a high quality motion-picture film of a program in black-and-white or in color and simultaneously can give the broadcasting staff a "live" image of the same quality as would be available on a normal live telecast.

The device enables a director to overcome a formidable handicap. By using a conventional motion-picture camera he was never able to see the action before him in the same way that the camera saw it at the moment of shooting. The only one who could see it in this way was the man operating the camera. He watched it through the camera's viewfinder.

With the "Electronicam" system, not only the director, but the editor, choreographer, lighting, makeup and wardrobe experts can follow the action from monitor screens during rehearsals as well as during the actual filming.

Advocates of the system also maintain that because of the speed that is possible with it, considerable expense can be saved. George ("Bullets") Durgom, Mr. Gleason's manager, put it this way:

"If we did a half-hour *Honeymooners* show by the conventional filming process it would take us at least three full days. This way there is just an hour and a half of rehearsal. The actual shooting of the show takes less than forty minutes. It would be done in the actual time that it will take on the air except for a pause halfway through the show for changing of film magazines.''

Mr. Durgom said that ''spontaneity'' was one of the factors that had convinced Mr. Gleason that the new process could successfully enable him to make the transition from live shows to film.

''Jackie knew that people didn't like most of the shows they have seen on film made by the conventional process,'' he said. ''They felt they were being tricked. But with Electronicam we get a motion-picture product with a television reaction.

''We have the same kind of large audience that we had for the live shows. The shows are directed just as if they were live. And there are no retakes. If somebody skips a line or ad-libs there is no stop to do part of the scene over again.

''Three, or occasionally four cameras run simultaneously during the show. The total product of all the cameras is edited into the final half-hour program. It's worked beautifully. Jackie is a stickler. If Electronicam hadn't worked, he'd be back to live shows.''

Ted Bergmann, director of the broadcast division of the DuMont Laboratories, said that the new system was an answer to complaints about poor quality in kinescope films that have been in use since the beginning of television. Filmed from the face of a picture tube, their quality has been noticeably inferior to the average motion-picture film.

One of the reasons for the improved quality in Electronicam films was the use of motion-picture lighting of great intensity during filming, Mr. Bergmann said.

The battery of lights used at the Adelphi is situated on a specially built batten, just outside the proscenium arch. Located high above the stage, it does not interfere with the studio audience's view of the proceedings.

The only parts of the actual broadcasts that are not introduced simultaneously with the filming are the commercials and music. But, to enhance the illusion of ''live'' telecasting an orchestra plays in the Adelphi pit before and during the filming sessions.

Thirty-nine of the filmed shows are scheduled to be made this year on a two-a-week basis. A similar number may be done in the following two years. After the first thirty-nine shows are televised, it is planned to repeat thirteen of them next summer.

An obvious advantage to doing a television show on film is the factor of permanence. A good show can be repeated many times and reap profits far greater than a one-shot live presentation.

Last week's show at the Adelphi looked fine on the television monitor screen. It has not yet been shown from film. If the filmed version is as good as the system's advocates maintain it is, Electronicam could be one of the most important developments in video's history.

This article by J. P. Shanley appeared in *The New York Times*, September 4, 1955.

THE CLASSIC THIRTY-NINE

The star has to work so hard that he makes the people in the audience say, "I wouldn't do that for a million bucks."

JACKIE GLEASON

When the Buick deal was signed, it got huge publicity. Big headlines were still breaking in the papers the day of the first show. Jackie knew that the audience, as much as they had always been for the show, might resist him this time. After all, they'd be looking for $11-million worth of funny. He knew he couldn't feign indifference, so before the show began, he told the audience,

---

Jackie Gleason, Audrey Meadows, Art Carney

"Nobody on TV comes close to these three top pros."—Ed Sullivan, *New York Daily News,* December 19, 1953

"Okay, it's true. But I'm telling you, I'm funny." That broke the ice. Once again, the audience was his.

First came *Stage Show,* with Jackie, the Dorseys, the June Taylor Dancers, conductor Ray Bloch, and guest stars Dick Haymes and Jane Russell. *The New York Times* didn't like it: "An event not likely to worry Frank Sinatra or Dinah Shore," the paper said on October 3, 1955. "It was a labored sketch, by no means up to Jackie's best. . . . It would seem just possible that the biggest problem for Jackie the showman may be Jackie the businessman."

Broadcasting and Telecasting Magazine didn't care for the show either, in their review of the new season.

> The Jackie Gleason show died October 1. Services haven't been held yet, but the body's cooling. Barring some hasty rejuvenation by CBS-TV, it's only a matter of time.
>
> As just another situation comedy it isn't bad. But the TV nation has come to expect much more than that. It's used to having an exciting hour starting off with bursts of fireworks and beautiful girls proclaiming "and away we go!" It's used to seeing the June Taylor Dancers pace through their expertly executed numbers and then see the comedy master stride out to kid Ray Block [sic.] and tell the audience it is a dan-dan-dandy group. It's used to a lot of things it will never find in the 30-minute *Honeymooners.*
>
> True, *The Honeymooners* skit was always the hit of the show. But it wasn't all the show. Essentially it remains the same in the new version, but, because it's filmed, is without the spontaneity that made it great in seasons past.

One wonders why anyone had to miss the June Taylor Dancers and Ray Bloch when they were just where they always had been, in the half-hour preceding *The Honeymooners.*

Among the boosters for the new episodes were *TV Guide,* which reported that the new method "doesn't seem to have affected *The Honeymooners* in the slightest. It is still a rollicking, slapsticky, fast-paced situation comedy, played for the big reaction."

And Steve Allen, in *The Funny Men,* wrote: "*The Honeymooners* is as wonderfully funny as ever—in fact, even more so, since Gleason films a few more minutes of entertainment than he needs and can therefore always edit the portions that do not come up to expectations." (This is true, but misleading. It is a hallmark of Gleason's shows that he plays them live, straight through; they virtually never reshoot. If there is any editing at all, it is to make a show fit the time slot, never to delete "the portions that don't come up to expectations." Of course, in such cases, it stands to reason that the most expendable material will be dropped first.)

No matter who liked it or didn't like it, the premiere Electronicam *Honeymooners,* wherein Ralph and Ed jointly purchase a television set, is now

Alice and Trixie set the scene, with Trixie running in to discuss the latest news with Alice.

By 1956, Audrey Meadows' earlier reputation as the comedienne on *The Bob and Ray Show* was almost totally eclipsed by her fame as Alice Kramden. Joyce Randolph, formerly known for her guest shots on TV crime shows ("the most murdered girl on television"), had become Trixie Norton to the world.

regarded as a classic.

Production costs for that first *Honeymooners* were reported at $75,000—twice the cost of *Alfred Hitchcock Presents* (30 minutes), approximately twice the cost of *I Love Lucy* (30 minutes), seven and a half times the cost of *The Mickey Mouse Club* (60 minutes), less than half the cost of Bob Hope's *The Chevy Hour* and a "Heidi" special (90 minutes) reported for the same season.

The money was bigger, the equipment was more elaborate, but rehearsals were unchanged. Rehearsal time was still minimal, despite the fact that these episodes would last on film forever and ever. Cast, writers, and crew generated programs on a rarely altered schedule of two a week—as always, before a live theater audience. (The first two weeks, Gleason actually did eight shows—five *Honeymooners* plus *Stage Show;* a dramatic guest spot on *The Red Skelton Show;* and a *Studio One* production based on an original Jackie Gleason story.)

After thirty-nine episodes of filmed *Honeymooners* Jackie surprised the world by pulling out. His Buick contract called for seventy-eight at least, with an option for thirty-nine more. With some $7 million still owing on the contract, Buick was sure he was not playing square with them. They refused to let him out of the deal, until they realized he had no intention of taking the comedy series elsewhere. "The excellence of the material could not be maintained," says Jackie, "and I had too much fondness for the show to cheapen it."

The end of the Christmas 1955 episode. As the curtain closes, Gleason steps out of character and calls Meadows, Randolph, and Carney back for a curtain call.

Ralph is really worried. He spent all his money on a Christmas present for Alice, but now he's too embarrassed to give it to her. Norton is more interested in tossing tinsel on Ralph's Christmas tree. To spare his pal's feelings, he is doing it while Ralph isn't looking.

It was not the end of *The Honeymooners*. (Although 1955 did mark the demise of at least one familiar institution from Gleason's past. The DuMont network, unable to compete any longer, folded in September of that year.) For one thing, in three years ownership of the filmed episodes would revert to Gleason, who would subsequently sell them outright to CBS and later wish he hadn't. Art Carney would receive residuals for a while, but like Jackie Gleason and Joyce Randolph, he certainly does not receive them now. Only Audrey Meadows, whose manager fought for hers long before anyone took TV residual rights seriously, continues to collect when *The Honeymooners* airs. By today's standards, the cast sold out cheap. Yet nobody involved with *The Honeymooners* in 1955 expected them to be so completely deathless. (TV stars are not entirely sophisticated about such matters, it seems, if one is to believe what is said of the *Star Trek* cast. They reportedly stopped getting residuals after the series had run seven complete cycles.)

For viewers who still berate the stations running the original* *Honeymooners* for showing the same thirty-nine over and over again, this is the answer: there will never be more than these thirty-nine available. And there must be a great, great deal to be said for their excellence—they have rarely been off the air since that October evening in 1955.

*To distinguish them from the later Trip-to-Europe series starring Jackie Gleason, Art Carney, Sheila MacRae, and Jane Kean.

BATTLE OF THE GIANTS

Perry Como, who just stood there and sang for a little, and made a fortune that way, broke out all over last week with high-priced comedy and guest stars. He used to sing for fifteen minutes, three nights a week, for CBS-TV; he now sings and acts and generally makes himself agreeable for an hour, for NBC-TV. This is, NBC hopes, the ultimate answer to CBS's Jackie Gleason.

In a way, CBS has already taken to thinking of Gleason as an answer to NBC's Perry Como. From time to time, after NBC hired Como away last spring and announced plans for a new show, CBS has changed the Gleason show's hour. Soon after it set one hour, NBC announced that hour for the Como show. CBS moved the hour; NBC was right there. CBS moved again; so did NBC. Exhausted, the two shows have finally settled down together on the Saturday 8:00 to 9:00 spot, where Gleason will be competitively on view beginning next week.

The fatalities at NBC at the hands of Gleason have been impressive. He has knocked over, among others, Ezio Pinza, Tallulah Bankhead, and Jimmy Durante. If money is any defense, Perry Como will remain standing upright. The production cost of the new show is more than $100,000—a good $30,000 more than Gleason has been spending. Como himself has signed a twelve-year contract reportedly paying him $15 million.

One big slice of the new show's budget goes to Goodman Ace who is the highest-paid comedy writer in the business and should give Gleason a run for his money. Como, no comedian, can handle bits all right, and the new show is built around sketches, in each of which Como will appear, assisted every week by the best available guest comedians.

None of this appears to be worrying Gleason. Fearless of the comedy element in the Como show, Gleason predicts: "We'll keep the people who want jokes, and Perry will get those that want to hear him sing. NBC has been trying to knock me off for a long time."

If the giant appears to be dozing, however, he is dozing with one bright eye open. The new Gleason show is going to have a lot more razzmatazz than the old one. Divided into two half-hour segments, it will consist of song and dance and variety acts in the first half and the familiar *Honeymooners* situation comedy in the second. A permanent fixture of the first half will be the brotherly band of Tommy and Jimmy Dorsey. Helping kick off the new series next week—besides Jane Russell—will be Dick Haymes, whose presence strongly suggests in itself a healthy respect for the opposition.

"I don't like being in competition," Como says, "but if they want to play potsy, that's up to them." Gleason says: "I hope Perry does well."

This article appeared in *Newsweek*, September 26, 1955.

AND BACK TO LIVE

*About one third of the population of the United States
watches his antics every Saturday night. More people see him each week
than see a top-rank movie star in a year.*

JIM BISHOP, *LOOK*

When the Gleason-Como match was one year old, the all-live one-hour Jackie Gleason show returned.

The last of the "live on film" episodes of *The Honeymooners* was performed September 22, 1956. It was the one where Ralph, to impress an old friend with whom he is accidentally reunited, has to pretend that he runs the bus company when in fact he is only a lowly driver.

September 29 marked the return of *The Jackie Gleason Show,* sponsored by Old Gold cigarettes and the Bulova Watch Company. *The Honeymooners* continued, with the flexibility of the pre-tape days, since it was again possible to expand it to an hour-long format whenever the material justified the leap. The other part of the show, the variety segment, would in time be responsible for the TV debuts of Elvis Presley (*before* Ed Sullivan—and not merely from the waist up as Sullivan presented him, but head-to-toe), Bobby Darin, Connie Francis, Frankie Avalon, and Wayne Newton.

Businessman, showman, and comedian, Jackie Gleason was still on top in a year when the industry's own business sense found TV compulsively devouring its young. As *Newsweek* noted in an article in 1956:

It may be impossible to curb the high mortality rate among TV comedians. TV's coverage is distressingly ubiquitous. The frequency of a star's appearance is hard on both the star's personal appeal and his deadline-nagged writers' sense of humor. The demands of the medium are immeasurably sterner than those of the old vaudeville-Broadway-Hollywood circuit, on which a star could get interminable mileage out of the same old can of gasoline and a rasp-voiced Pat Rooney could seemingly go on forever with his "Rosie O'Grady" soft-shoe number so long as he came through each town only once a year.

Yet, some TV comedy attractions have set impressive records for durability. What makes them so is a matter of widely varying opinion. NBC executive, Leonard Hole, attributes it to "a certain chemistry between writer and talent." Sid Caesar's answer is simple, if not very rewarding: "Work and dedication. You have to grow. You must be stimulated." Herb Shriner, a six-year veteran variety show general (with five different ones to date), says helpfully: "To be a success in television you have to figure some way to stay on."

"They like my character," allows Jack Benny, as durable in TV as he was on radio. "It holds up. The moment I walk on, the viewers know the character. It stays the same; the shows are different."

There are not many Bennys for hire, however, and the networks admit to searching ceaselessly for new comedy faces. Once a face is found, the TV bosses show a new caution in exhibiting it. CBS now feels it was premature in presenting lanky Johnny Carson (1955's only new comedian to get a live night-time show). Johnny folded ignominiously after twenty-six weeks. ("He needed another month out of town"). Next fall Carson will be simmering hopefully on the back of the stove with his own daytime half-hour. Another CBS hopeful, Dick Van Dyck [sic], after a few weeks as major domo of the ill-starred *Morning Show,* will preside over next season's *Cartoon Carnival* while waiting for a big chance.

In 1954, Audrey Meadows was voted TV's Best Supporting Actress. She is shown here accepting her Emmy Award from Dave Garroway.

The article goes on to describe NBC's year-old multimillion-dollar "Comedy Development Plan," which had signed nine promising comedy writers selected from several thousands, who had already contributed substantially to programming although not one had worked his way up to a regular assignment. (Among the nine signed was a "sad-faced redhead with big ears named Woody Allen, who's only eighteen years old. He's so young that his father, a waiter in lower Manhattan, had to sign his contract. It pays Woody $160 a week while he is being groomed to become a full-fledged comedy writer," according to a magazine article by NBC's Leonard Hole, who headed up the search.) Aspiring young comics that season—Jonathan Winters and Don Adams, for instance—had appeared with only moderate success, though were "being watched" by the networks.

While the comics who were to dominate TV of the 1960s were waiting in the wings, the scoreboard for established comedians, as reported in the *Newsweek* article, shows that a "durable dozen" still had more than enough vitality to keep them going:

Listed here are the old-timers who will be back on the air next season. Their starting dates and a few reasons why they're still around:

Martin and Lewis (1948)—Eternal adolescence and a pleasant baritone.

Sid Caesar (1948)—A cordon bleu blend of satire and slapstick, ever new.

Life of Riley (1949)—Family-type laughs. Nice viewers identification.

Herb Shriner (1950)—TV's widest open face and friendliest drawl.

Bob Hope (1950)—Proof that if you keep talking long enough you're bound to say something funny.

Burns and Allen (1950)—Other people's stupidity is always amusing.

Jack Benny (1950)—If you pose as a defender of enough of mankind's minor vices (cupidity, vanity, cowardice), you eventually become lovable.

Lucille Ball (1951)—Bounce.

Red Skelton (1951)—TV's most expert practitioner of the venerable art of pantomime.

Jackie Gleason (1952) [*Newsweek* in error here. The correct date is 1950.]—The classic proportions of a clown. He can act, too.

Ozzie and Harriet Nelson (1952)—The American home again—always good for some laughs.

Steve Allen (1953)—Low-gear for the long haul.

The 1956–57 season would be the last New York season to feature *The Honeymooners*. Art Carney, except for occasional guest appearances, had decided to leave the show to devote more time to his other acting engagements. Buddy Hackett would join the Jackie Gleason show in 1958; the show itself would evolve into *You're in the Picture* (1961) and *Jackie Gleason and His American Scene Magazine* (1962–66) before *The Honeymooners* would return to the air on a regular basis. Only during the first few weeks of *The American Scene Magazine* was there any attempt to re-create *The Honeymooners,* when, briefly, Sue Ane Langdon moved into the role of Alice Kramden (September 29 to October 27, 1962), Patricia Wilson played Trixie, and Art Carney joined the show as a guest star to be Ed Norton. In 1966, Carney would again be appearing as Ed Norton, but Sheila MacRae would be the new Alice and Jane Kean would be the new Trixie. And viewers wouldn't be seeing the familiar Kramden apartment for long—the perennial losers would finally get lucky enough to win a trip to Europe!

HONEYMOON THAT RERAN FOR 10 YEARS

Alice, so help me, one of these days—*pow!* Right on the kisser!

Alice Kramden of the battling Brooklyn Kramdens has just annoyed Ralph, her spouse, for the 80 millionth time, and *The Honeymooners* are at it again. You folks can have your *McHale's Navy, F Troop* and *Get Smart* and all those other passing fancies. Our family's favorite TV show is still the same old one we've been watching—on reruns—over and over, week in and week out, winter and summer, for the last nine years, starring Jackie Gleason and Audrey Meadows as Ralph and Alice, with Art Carney and Joyce Randolph as Ed and Trixie Norton, the couple upstairs.

We are not alone. *The Honeymooners'* domestic market may have worn down from 152 to 26 areas, but it is still going strong in Los Angeles, Dallas and Davenport, Iowa—where it is shown *every* night from Monday to Friday—Australia, Dutch Guiana, Iran, Nigeria, Saudi Arabia and, most especially, New York where WPIX, which has run it since 1958, just upped it from once to twice a week on prime evening time and signed it up through 1970.

The astonishing thing about *The Honeymooners'* longevity is that it consists of only thirty-nine half-hour shows. Gleason stopped it at thirty-nine himself—breaking a three-year, $11 million contract because he felt his sources of material were running dry, a nicety that has never flustered *I Love Lucy* or *Sergeant Bilko,* each of them with scores of half-hour rerun segments. So anybody who, like the addicts around our house, has watched *The Honeymooners* over the past ten years has seen *each* show about fifteen times.

How come? If you've been in America (or Dutch Guiana) in the last ten years, no *Honeymooner* plot would hold any surprise for you; *Honeymooner* fans know the ending of every skit. Its continuing appeal is based solely on its enduring characters: Gleason's irate bus driver, Ralph Kramden, impulsive, overbearing, scheming, then filled with humble remorse ("Me and my bee-eeg mouth!") and Carney's breezy, naive Ed Norton, the sewer worker who wears a battered hat with upturned brim, even in bed. Somewhat reminiscent of Laurel and Hardy, but far more real and earthy, they bring a new warmth to the TV screen no matter how often that scene has been on before.

What happens in the Kramdens' dingy tenement doesn't sound like much outlined on paper but neither, as P. G. Wodehouse once said, does the plot of *Hamlet*. Ed Norton cowers from Ralph's wrath but patient Alice stands up to him calmly as he pounds the kitchen table and shouts, "You mean to say we got only $3.31 in the bank? Alice, what do you *do* with all our money?" "I put it into the bank," says Alice, getting in the infuriating last word.

The big news, of course, is about plans for revival. Last January Gleason persuaded Carney (who has drifted off to Broadway in recent years) and Miss Meadows to come back for a one-hour musical version of the old show—a touching episode about the Kramdens trying to adopt a baby. A short time later Gleason signed Carney for twenty appearances next season. Kramden and Norton will soon be back in business and, thank goodness, doing something new. Even for the faithful, watching Ralph Kramden threatening to send Alice to the moon fifteen times can get a bit repetitious.

This article by Joe McCarthy appeared in *Life* magazine, March 25, 1966.

Jackie Gleason and June Taylor watch a rehearsal of one of the original black-and-white (unfilmed) Trip–to–Europe episodes. (Audrey Meadows, Joyce Randolph, and Art Carney are onstage.)

AND ON TO MIAMI

SECOND HONEYMOON

When Jackie Gleason suddenly up and announced his retirement from CBS television last winter, he got a wire of "appreciation" from an NBC vice president. The telegram was ill timed. In the first place, the Gleason show had become so lackluster in recent seasons that he already seemed semiretired. In the second place, Gleason turned right around and signed an $8 million deal with CBS for one more season. It would be, he proclaimed, "something different" and "something better."

It is not a good deal different, but Gleason's new *Honeymooners* is a lot better—better, in fact, than any other comedy series on the air. Dressed up now and then with music and dancing, the adventures of gullible Brooklyn bus driver Ralph Kramden (Gleason) and goofy sewer worker Ed Norton (Art Carney) rock with a screwball spontaneity that puts the team in a class with the Marx Brothers and Laurel and Hardy. At the same time, they are never so far out that the audience has the slightest trouble identifying them as a couple of ordinary likable slobs. "This is a nudge act," explains Gleason. "Somebody's always out there in the audience nudging his partner, saying, 'There's Uncle Charlie.' "

Gleason admits that *Honeymooners* was long overdue for rehabilitation. "Some of the shows I did last year," he concedes, "looked like they had been made on the way to the men's room. But you don't kid an audience." He discovered that last year when the ratings at times showed a greater preference for *Flipper* and *I Dream of Jeanie*. This season *Flipper* and *Shane* oppose him, but so far *Honeymooners* has out-rated them both.

Legendary in show business as the "Great Non-Rehearser," Gleason now works six days a week, has cut down on his golfing (though he still manages to break 80 frequently). Otherwise, nothing has changed. Lots of pool in "Gleason's Pool Hall," a 40-by-60-foot air-conditioned annex to his house. More J & B Scotch than ever, though he shifts to champagne on taping day. The same omnipresent "executive secretary," Honey Merrill, who has been with Gleason for ten years. No nostalgia for New York City that he can't appease with daily phone calls to his friends and three visits a year. And no more talk of retirement. "Why should I quit?" asks he, "when I can get a laugh on 'Aw, shut up!' "

This article appeared in *Time*, October 14, 1966.

Gleason has become Florida's number—one tourist attraction.

MIAMI BEACH DAILY SUN, February 15, 1966

Television historians will tell you that the Kramdens got lucky before 1966— that many of the musical trip-around-the-world episodes had been performed, albeit in black-and-white, when Audrey Meadows and Joyce Randolph were still in the cast. For that matter, the historians may be the ones who got lucky if, indeed, they were able to see those live, forever-lost-to-posterity episodes. To-day's Honeymoonies are lucky to find the ''around the world'' episodes on TV at all; up until a few years ago, nobody had considered them for syndication.

But then, the decade between 1956 and 1966 saw many a change for *The Jackie Gleason Show*. In format, in casting, and, much to the delight of the Miami Chamber of Commerce, in location. Jackie had been complaining about the New York winters so long that Hank Meyers, the public relations man then represent-

The Miami Nortons and Kramdens: Art, Jane, Jackie, and Sheila.

ing Miami, approached Miami and Gleason, with the result that a train was chartered, a ten-day cross-country p.r. bash arranged, and Gleason brought *The American Scene Magazine*—later, again, *The Jackie Gleason Show*—to Miami to stay. (Today Hank Meyers' firm represents Jackie Gleason.) "The Great Gleason Express" made headlines in 1962 with the show's principals, the dancers, the production staff, Phil Napoleon's six-piece Dixieland jazz band, and members of the press aboard. The effect all this had on Miami was an estimated $9 million in free publicity, industry, and tourism annually. And that is not counting the television facilities created around Gleason, intended to draw big shows from all three networks to Miami, and pronounced by Bing Crosby and others as the best TV installation in the country. So successful was "The Great Gleason Express" that it was brought back in 1964 and again in 1965.

The new *Honeymooners*—slated to comprise ten out of thirty-two shows for the first season (the other twenty-two were to be variety format) would be breaking a lot of new ground along with the old. Gleason had lost so much weight that people might not recognize him as Ralph Kramden, or, in any case, might not laugh at the "fat jokes" now that he was thinner. Beyond that, viewers would have to get used to the idea of Ralph, Ed, Alice, and Trixie breaking into song. Art Carney, scarcely looking older and otherwise unchanged, was returning to his *Honeymooners* role after stints on *Batman* as The Archer and a successful Broadway run as Felix Unger in *The Odd Couple*. Would Ed Norton remain the same? Alice and Trixie would certainly be different, since neither Audrey Meadows nor Joyce Randolph—both happily married and enjoying the change of pace—were prepared to relocate to Miami. According to a September 23, 1967 *TV Guide* interview with Sheila MacRae:

She had to dye her hair orangey-red, by contract, and had to crop her nails, refrain from wearing bracelets, earrings or slacks. It was easy enough for her to comply with the surface requirements of "my Alice." She boggled mightily at some of the others.

"I just couldn't *get* Alice Kramden at first. Does she have nothing to do all day but yell at Ralph? I figure that she sits on the fire escape with plants and reads philosophy books which she hides when Ralph comes home. I try to think she really *loves* Ralph—or she'd never have stuck around for seventeen years."

It's this love notion that has caused some of her difficulties. "It's the antagonistic quality against men I can't get. I'm a worshiper of men. Audrey could look Ralph in the eye and give him hell. I can't *do* that. To me, the male image is not to be torn down. I have a hard time saying some of those lines. There's one—it sticks in my throat. Jackie says to me, "Hey, Alice, how'd you like to bag an elephant?" And I'm supposed to answer, "I already have." It just stuck in my *throat*. It's tough for me to tear him down. *My* Alice is sweeter. *My* Alice cries."

Her Alice, in consequence, has been criticized for being "over-sweet" and "without bite." Lucille Ball told her, "You *like* Jackie too much. You have to be tougher with him. You have to have the upper hand.'' Another friend of Sheila's, comedian Alan King, says: "I was a little worried about her Alice. She's not raucous, kinetic, like Meadows. It's a much softer Alice. But she's coming along fine." Jackie professes himself pleased with Sheila's Alice: "The very fact that I've rehired her means that I like her very much. She can continue to play Alice as long as she wants to.''

Jane Kean, who had worked with Gleason back on the old DuMont show and, on Broadway, in *Along Fifth Avenue,* got the Trixie part without audition. Like Sheila MacRae, she wasn't trying to duplicate the role of her predecessor. "I found my own Trixie," she says. "I didn't want to copy Joyce Randolph. Otherwise it would be impersonation, not acting."

The originally scheduled ten *Honeymooners* episodes were so well received that they became nineteen, and eventually forty-two, over the next few years. They took the Kramdens and Nortons to France, Italy, Ireland, England, Spain, Germany, and Africa before returning them to 328 Chauncey Street in time for Christmas. Back in Brooklyn, Ralph and Ed settled down to their usual dilemmas with the landlord, the tax collector, and their own high-flown notions of wheeler-dealing.

On March 4, 1967, Pert Kelton, the first Alice Gibson Kramden, returned to *The Honeymooners* as Mrs. Gibson, Alice's mother. For once, Gleason had delegated some of the casting. The choice of Pert came as a surprise to Gleason, who thought it a shade insensitive. But Pert threw herself into the role with gusto, breaking into the jazz waltz "That's What Comes of Marrying for Love" which Lyn Duddy and Jerry Bresler had written especially for her. In the song, she criticizes Alice's choice of a husband (ironically since, as Ralph's first Alice, she ought to know). Throughout the show she criticizes Ralph every chance she gets (just like the good old days). And she ends the show by beating up a crook whom Ralph has almost, inadvertently, helped to escape justice.

In 1970, Gleason and CBS agreed to disagree over the future of *The Jackie Gleason Show.* Jackie had not limited himself to hour-long *Honeymooners* over the past four years; he had interspersed them with the regular variety show formats, so that some weeks you would get one hour of *Honeymooners,* others you would get forty-five minutes of stage show with fifteen minutes of *Honeymooners,* and some weeks there would be no *Honeymooners* at all. CBS wanted all full-hour *Honeymooners.* Gleason didn't. Gleason went off the air.

Robert D. Wood, president of the CBS television network, explained the 1970 departure of *The Jackie Gleason Show* in a statement issued at the time of the decision:

It was obvious, of course, why our audience skewed toward the C and D counties [rural counties of less than 120,000 people, constituting only 31 percent of the country's population] and attracted a greater share of the older generation than the young. We were the victims of our own success.

One of our programs had been a hit for twenty-two straight seasons—

His table piled with groceries (notice the Flakey Wakey diet breakfast cereal boxes), Ralph debates entering the Flakey Wakey contest as Ed and Alice look on.

The Kramdens and Nortons about to embark on their Flakey Wakey trip to Europe.
Trixie was so long in getting to the ship that everyone thought she was lost. But she was only delayed . . . inasmuch as she had to carry all the luggage.

For the moment, Ralph and Ed are safely aboard ship on their Flakey Wakey way to Europe.

Except for motion sickness, Ralph is having the time of his life—he even plays potsie on the shuffleboard court. But rough seas are ahead, and Ralph and Ed manage to go overboard in a lifeboat—and find themselves doubting that they'll ever come out alive.

Back home and broke.

Alice, Ed, Ralph, and Trixie have left Europe behind, to pursue their impossible dreams from 328 Chauncey Street, Brooklyn, U.S.A. Sheila MacRae (left) plays Alice and Jane Kean (right) is Trixie in this episode filmed in Miami.

was actually as old as the network. Another had been brought back, again and again, for eighteen consecutive seasons. Still another for seventeen years. Indeed . . . close to one third of our entire nighttime entertainment schedule was back—by popular demand—for the sixth consecutive season. But as these shows returned year after year they had tended to maintain their popularity leadership through the deep-seated loyalty of those who had been following them from the very beginning. On the other hand, many of them were unable to pick up as large a portion of the younger viewers who had come of age in the more recent past.

Because we had so little program failure, we introduced relatively few new series. While such new programs might not draw as many viewers as some of the old standbys, they had the advantage of being new, novel, more "with it" in terms of the tastes of the moment, and thus more appealing to the young and the more sophisticated big-city audience.

In short, as a result of our success, we were inadvertently discriminating against urban viewers as well as our affiliates in the big cities. It was this situation that drove us to the conclusion that we must do more than simply hold the kind of audiences we already had. We had to take the bit in our teeth, change the program mix by dropping some of our old stalwarts in a move to broaden our base. This, then, was the philosophy on which we based our program judgments as we built a schedule for this fall. . . .

Simply ticking off the titles will give you a rough idea of just how agonizing it was. The trio included Jackie Gleason, Red Skelton, and *Petticoat Junction*. Not only were the decisions difficult because all three had contributed so much to our past success, but also because each was still performing so well. . . . Yet we were driven to drop the shows in order to carry out our shift in programming strategy—that is to evaluate programs not only in relation to how many watch but also in terms of who watches.

As CBS dropped *The Jackie Gleason Show* in 1970, *All in the Family* made its TV debut, giving rise to the rumor that Archie Bunker and Ralph Kramden could not exist simultaneously on Saturday night for the same reason that Clark Kent and Superman could never sing a duet. Anyone who knows them both knows the rumor is pure bunk—and wishes Ralph would make an appearance, just once, at Archie's door, to prove it.

"When we went off, we still had a very large audience," said Gleason in a 1976 interview. "We were always in the first fifteen and very often in the first ten. But they couldn't find things to sell to the people who were watching. They seemed to think that the people who watched us didn't buy anything."

In the end, Gleason did not renew his fifteen-year work-or-no-work-$100,000-annually CBS contract when it ran out in 1972. He signed, instead, with NBC for a year, and when that failed to produce a suitable piece of programming, with ABC. There has been talk, but no evidence, of regular *Honeymooners* episodes since that time. There have been, thanks to a Dean Martin roast for Jackie Gleason that brought the stars and writers together again, three flawless specials.

AND NOW: ABC

GLEASON RETURN TO THE SCREEN IS JUST SPECIAL

His eyelids no longer droop so far they keep the Miami sun out of his eyes.

He can talk to you head-to-head, not with sidelong glances. And his once vast waist-band has withered away in abject surrender to his belt.

"Cosmetic surgery did it," said Jackie Gleason. "I'm down to my fighting weight—205 pounds." This is miraculous for the Mighty One, whose flab once suggested the need of a wheelbarrow.

He's due back on the homescreen at 8:00 on Nov. 28 as supermouth Ralph Kramden in an ABC resurrection of his old *Honeymooners* series, along with Audrey Meadows as long-suffering wife Alice, Art Carney as putdown pal Ed Norton and Jane Kean as Trixie, Norton's spouse.

It's Yuletide at the bus garage, time for the annual holiday frolics. And Ralph, mindful that the guy who last produced the bash married the boss' daughter and got a promotion, figures it just might be his turn.

He somehow persuades the boss (Gale Gordon from the Lucy years) to let him mount a production of Dickens' "A Christmas Carol," in which he decides on casting Norton not only as Scrooge but Tiny Tim.

"I'm not doing it for the money," said Gleason. "Hope's got all that."

Along with the revival of *The Honeymooners,* Gleason also has turned out a Valentine special for the network. As usual, they dangled handsome offers for him to return to the screen as a weekly regular.

"I'm ducking that," he said. "Here I am sitting with my feet up looking at a blue Florida sky with a few puffy clouds, just back from a round of golf and I ask you, why should I work?"

Why, indeed, when you consider the lush greenery of his vast multi-million-dollar golf plant, Inverarry, north of Miami Beach? Speaking of greenery, what's he worth, anyhow?

"Let's not talk about my money," he said. "Let's talk about Hope's. Everytime we do anything together, he always whispers to me beforehand not to mention the story about his $150 million. And it's always the first thing I say."

Is he glad to be on ABC, which is to say off CBS, where he had one of the last of the old TV dream contracts, collecting $100,000 a year for merely

The Twenty-fifth Anniversary *Honeymooners*.

Ralph has jumped to yet another of his famous conclusions. This time he thinks Alice is expecting a blessed event; Norton, in the true spirit of friendship, shows Ralph how to diaper a baby.

doing nothing on NBC or ABC?

"Everybody at ABC is wonderful," he said, "and why not? They're winning everything. I don't think happiness is CBS or NBC, not the way the ratings are running."

Does he look at TV?

"Very little," he said. "It's a chore, except for the sports. I tried looking at the situation comedies and they all seemed to be doing what we did twenty—or was it thirty?—years ago.

"You always know how they're going to end. Why bother."

Gleason thinks the preoccupation by networks and sponsors with winning young audiences is a farce.

"I'm not saying this because we always did well with the eight o'clock audience, but I have to say we never had to resort to shock treatment. You even take a show like 'Rhoda.' It's a one joke thing—sex."

This article by Bob Williams appeared in the *New York Post,* November 14, 1977.

II. KRAMDEN AND FRIENDS

Scene from an unfilmed *Honeymooners* episode.

Ralph and Alice visited by George Petrie in his frequent role as Freddie Mullin, assistant bus dispatcher.

BACK TO THE BEGINNING

"IT WAS CHAOS. CRAZY!"

His *Honeymooners* Costars Never Knew What to Expect from Jackie Gleason

[The February 1976 ABC special reunites Jackie Gleason, Art Carney and Audrey Meadows in "The Honeymooners–The Second Honeymoon."]

What an odd mixture they were—raffish, 250-pound Jackie Gleason, the hard-drinking Broadway Los Angeles club comedian; Audrey Meadows, the proper, privately educated daughter of missionary parents; Art Carney, the mild, struggling radio actor; Joyce Randolph, an unknown. None, in 1951, had much reputation in television. And as one CBS executive put it back then, twenty-five years ago, "They don't even speak the English language the same way."

But when the four came together, something rare happened and they were so funny as *The Honeymooners* that much of the country watched and whooped and they became the biggest thing in television comedy. *The Honeymooners* was undisguised slapstick much of the time; weekly plots varied little. Action was compressed, mainly, to a single 20-by-30-foot set—a shabby, depressing tenement livingroom-and-kitchen somewhere in Brooklyn. Yet that was all Gleason, Meadows, Carney and Randolph needed to draw laughs by the millions on Saturday nights.

"We'd been on the air for just three years," relates Art Carney, now white-haired and a film star, "when Jackie bounced into Studio 50 in New York, waving his arms madly, with a new contract. "The Great One" had signed a three-year *Honeymooners*-Gleason variety deal for $11 million—the highest price paid for any series until then."

That was 1954, and the story of a fat, windbag bus driver named Ralph Kramden; his suffering but scrappy wife, Alice; and their sewer-worker neighbor, Ed Norton, lasted for 320 episodes and—with an absence from TV view now and then—a memorable eighteen-year run. Recently the Kramdens have become familiar to a new generation, through syndication to local stations. And now, for auld lang syne and to celebrate the twenty-fifth anniversary of the original *Honeymooners* performance, ABC is returning them on February 2 in a 60-minute special. The Kramdens will go toe-to-toe once more, with Ralph threatening to send his soul mate ''on a trip to the moon'' via a left uppercut, and with Alice replying. ''You're one balloon that'll never go up—not at your weight.'' At the end they'll probably kiss and make up, as they did in the old days.

At the beginning, it seemed unlikely that the Kramden-household idea, a brainchild of Gleason's, would succeed. *The Honeymooners* was first seen in 1950 as a 12-minute sketch as part of *Cavalcade of Stars* on the limited DuMont Network, with Jackie starred and Pert Kelton in the part of Alice. ''It got a few yuks,'' says veteran writer Walter Stone, who co-authored many *Honeymooner* sketches. ''But it was seen only in a few cities on DuMont and we sort of forgot about it.''

However, one season later, Gleason revived the characters and Audrey Meadows arrived on the scene. As she tells it now: ''Jackie turned me down flat for the plain-Jane wife part (which Pert had given up), saying I was too young and pretty. I told him he was out of his mind. So I hired a photographer to visit my apartment at 5:30 A.M., wake me up and take pictures without makeup. Gleason looked at them and said: 'Jeez she really is a dowdy broad!' He then went out and celebrated with six drinks—or maybe it was sixteen— his 'solving' of the casting problem.''

Then came clashes. Audrey, now married to Robert Six, board chairman of Continental Air Services, reveals, ''Very few knew it, but I came close to walking out on Jackie before the show even got off the ground. I'd worked in the Broadway theater, been with Phil Silvers in *Top Banana*, and knew how productions were organized. *Honeymooners* had no organization. It was chaos. Crazy! As the boss, Jackie didn't believe in rehearsals. Or in having scripts ready before 10:00 P.M., on Friday, although we faced a live audience on Saturday. What he and his cronies did believe in was hanging around all day at Toots Shor's saloon.

''While Carney and I sweated to rehearse our dialogue, Gleason was boozing. Either that or studying his lessons in clairvoyance and the occult, which was another big hobby of his.

''Some of the things he did to us had me in tears. I felt totally unprepared and desperate. Standing in the wings, ready to go on, I'd tell him, 'You are a simply dreadful man!' ''

During one early *Honeymooners* segment, a scene had Alice serving Ralph a frozen steak, which he was supposed to whack angrily and knock to the floor. ''As usual, we hadn't practiced it. I hadn't been told the steak was made of wood,'' says Audrey with a sigh. ''When he hit it, the steak split in two and one piece sailed high through the air and clear off the set. About twenty million people were watching and I had nothing to cover such an

George Petrie, Jackie Gleason, Audrey Meadows, Art Carney.

In this January 1955 episode, Ralph has had Alice hypnotized so that she will give him the money he needs to go to the Raccoon convention in Chicago. The same story was repeated in September 1968, in color, with Richard Deacon, Jackie Gleason, Sheila MacRae, and Art Carney—with a new location for the Raccoon convention: Miami Beach.

"Unlike *I Love Lucy, The Honeymooners* wasn't a farce. Lucy would blacken her teeth and Ricky wouldn't know her. We never did that. We worked from a possible—though perhaps not probable—premise, like Ralph's weaknesses, and proceeded from there."—Syd Zelinka, *Honeymooners* writer

unbelievable situation. It didn't worry Gleason. He just sat there silently, glaring at me—leaving me to bail us out. All I could do was make up a line: 'There you are Ralph. Tonight I'm serving you *half* of a steak!' ''

Shortly before another show, Gleason hadn't been seen at CBS for several days. And again script delivery was ''delayed.'' Walking into Jackie's penthouse hotel suite, Audrey found him presiding over a party for eighty and well-buzzed on martinis. On the next *Honeymooners,* Gleason was to hit Audrey in the face with a pie. And few in the company gave him better than a 6-1 chance to do it with accuracy. ''I knew he'd miss by two feet,'' she says, ''so when he wound up, I stumbled, managed to get in front of his wild throw and saved another scene.''

One of Art Carney's memories concerns the time he and Audrey visited Gleason in Doctors Hospital in Manhattan. He wasn't ill—his purpose was to lose weight on a rigidly supervised diet. ''The room was empty,'' says Art. ''The nurses told us Jackie had paid his bill and gone home—because, as he said, he felt sick.''

In this early *Honeymooners* episode, Kramden takes Norton and the wives to the movies because it is Norton's birthday.

Norton's ticket wins a TV set as a door prize, but, because Ralph paid for the ticket, he feels the set should be his. Note the dishes on top of the TV set; in true 1950s fashion, free dishes are included in the price of admission. Notice also that the movie playing at Ralph's friendly neighborhood theater is none other than *The Desert Hawk,* starring Richard Greene, Yvonne DeCarlo, Jackie Gleason, and ''a cast of thousands.'' This same episode, with some revisions, was repeated in the 1960s with the Miami *Honeymooners* cast. The big changes were that Norton wins a color TV, and *The Desert Hawk* is no longer showing.

Gleason lived in a unique $800,000 structure at Peekskill, N.Y., which was an architect's conception of a flying saucer—round in shape, like Jackie. The house's large rooms contained something like twelve liquor bars. Marble toadstools sprouted in the garden. Microphones popped up from hidden floor slots. "Also," says Walter Stone, "there were horse pools and crap games and people named Slapsie Maxie, Bullets, Fast Fingers, and Crazy Sam. Jackie rarely slept—three hours a night was all he needed—and the place ran on an around-the-clock fun basis."

To pry the owner from his hideaway and return him to the city took much persuasion. The other players would be instructed by him, "Unravel, relax, don't worry about anything. We'll get down to New York pretty soon and shoot another of 'em—Civil War style." By that Gleason meant they could let preparation slide and follow him—the leader—when the cameras rolled. And, when in doubt, improvise.

When he forgot his lines, Gleason would pat his stomach—the signal to Carney, Audrey, or Joyce Randolph (playing Trixie, wife of sewer man Ed Norton) to think of something. "If you get any bigger, gasbag," Audrey snapped at him one night, "you'll just float away." The words weren't in the script.

Warm relationships developed as the years passed. Audrey, Art and Jack became so devoted to each other they skipped other engagements to wrap Christmas presents together, and entertained each other at home, back and forth. Jackie presented ruby-studded jewelry to the others. Audrey bought Jackie a pool table and "the world's largest martini shaker."

"As nutty as anything that happened was the night Gleason threw a chicken dinner at home for friends," says Audrey "I thought I was a guest, but upon arriving, Jackie handed me an apron made of real orchids, led me to the kitchen and pointed to twenty raw chickens. He had no cook. One hundred people showed up and I slaved over those damned birds until 2:00 A.M."

While their chief was a barfly and a procrastinator, he was fantastic in action—"Whatta inspiration!" marvels Carney. "He could plot a sketch while sitting in his barber chair, getting manicured, reading the *Police Gazette* and talking with experts on the occult world by phone."

It was while sitting in his private barber chair that Gleason thought up a *Honeymooners* episode in which Kramden found an abandoned baby on his bus—and brought it home. "While we were fixing up the dump we lived in, so that we could adopt the baby," says Audrey, "the live audience cried and laughed so much we ran out of time with the performance uncompleted. Maybe that was our greatest sketch." When, the next week, the baby's mother appeared to snatch her away, Americans grieved.

It is reported that Gleason now weighs only 210, so he may need padding for his return as Ralph in *The Honeymooners* next Monday. If so, it'll be the first time these artists ever needed any kind of help.

This article by Al Stump appeared in *TV Guide*, January 24, 1976.

ON THE SET TODAY

Television's most durable situation comedy.

JOHN HUDDY, *MIAMI HERALD*

There have been three hour-long *Honeymooners* specials since Gleason and ABC joined forces in 1973. (*Silver Anniversary Show,* February 2, 1976; *The Christmas Show,* November 28, 1977; *The Valentine Special Show,* February 13, 1978.) Each has preserved the character of the vintage *Honeymooners* episodes without sacrificing the advantages of contemporary subject matter as a source of humor. It has, therefore, been possible for the ranks of avid Honeymoonies to increase over the years, including now not only the original fans of the show but also the postwar babies who have grown up with the show. (And who, while they may have watched it as toddlers, did not actually connect with it until the reruns

Rehearsal for the 1953 Christmas show. Note the snow in the corners of the windowpanes which adds a touch of realism.

came on.) Today the specials reinforce the reruns and the reruns reinforce the specials. And people of all ages—urban, suburban, and rural—discuss Ralph Kramden like a guy from the old neighborhood whom everyone remembers even when he's not around.

It was good news to them all, though certainly not unexpected, when the papers announced that Ralph and Alice were going to celebrate their twenty-fifth wedding anniversary on February 2, 1976.

When the show aired—the Kramden apartment unchanged, the Raccoon Lodge as dopey as ever, Ralph and his mother-in-law still at each other's throats, and Ralph and Alice renewing their vows—it was reassuring to remember that people don't have to transform themselves or move up in the world to be completely happy.

Then, for the Christmas 1977 season, it was old times all over again for viewers who watched *The Honeymooners* play-within-a-play version of Dickens' *A Christmas Carol*—with Jackie Gleason as Ralph Kramden and Daddy Cratchit; Audrey Meadows as Alice Kramden and Mother Cratchit; Art Carney as Ed Norton, Scrooge, and Tiny Tim; and Jane Kean as Trixie and Tiny Tim's sister.

Like old times too were the behind-the-scenes complications that kept the cast and crew on their toes, but unstoppable.

GLEASON STARTS SECOND HONEYMOON

The old icebox with the old chicken leg was there. So were the old sink, the old cast-iron stove and the old cast.

It was as if nothing had changed in the five years since Jackie Gleason and *The Honeymooners* last took to the air. Only Gleason was a few dozen pounds lighter Friday night, and there was a new stage.

For the first time since "The Great One" and company came down here in 1964, *The Honeymooners* were not playing Miami Beach. They were taping the first of two television specials in Gusman Cultural Center, and no one, save the Tourist Development Authority, which refused to back Gleason, seemed to care.

"It's just like we never broke up," Gleason says, between long periods of silence. "Audrey Meadows and the others came in like they'd never been away."

Gleason waits backstage like a racehorse at the gate. He extends each arm across a chair, chain-smokes and keeps his face down. Art Carney walks by. The two say nothing.

Only Gleason's wife, Marilyn Taylor Gleason, breaks the silence, with a kiss.

"Jackie's so excited," she later explains. "It's a kind of rolled-up exuberance. It's like a driver waiting for the start of a race. . . . Even his stepson has been moving around him quietly for the last three weeks.''

The city of Miami didn't realize it when it agreed to help Gleason defray production costs, but the city will get more than its money's worth when the first of *The Honeymooners* specials airs on ABC Christmas week.

Gleason started the show, singing ''Moon Over Miami''; mentioned the city fifteen other times, the state three times and got in plugs for Calder Race Track, the Landmark Bank of Fort Lauderdale and the Miami Beach Kennel Club. The cast even managed to sneak in a quick rendition of the Burger King jingle.

The show must go on, but every once in a while there are some problems. Gleason's snow-effect maker broke down earlier in the day and had to be fixed. ''Must be from New York,'' one stagehand said.

Someone also lost the ethyl chloride, but the Miami Fire Rescue Squad sent an ambulance to Jackson Memorial Hospital and got some.

The crew had no trouble with one prop. They bought sixty boxes of cornflakes at a North Dade County grocery store. [Most of the crew will tell you that they used Styrofoam, not cereal, for snow, and that the weight of the Styrofoam jammed the mechanism of the box from which it was supposed to fall. Messy business when the snow finally fell, but fun.]

Neither cue cards nor master of ceremonies Johnny Olsen was really needed to lead the Gusman audience in cheers.

It gave Gleason a standing ovation.

*This article by Andy Rosenblatt appeared in the *Miami Herald,* September 17, 1977.

The ''Valentine 1978'' special was one of the most technically complex *Honeymooners* ever made, with major costume changes between scenes for Gleason and Carney, involving dresses, wigs, and the other ornaments necessary to get two grown men to look like two fun-loving females. The Kramden apartment underwent its first radical transformation. The show concluded with a series of staged electrical explosions. And as always, it was done without retakes before a live theater audience.

Rehearsal, as usual, was cut to the bone. Although the cast had read through the script together a few times before getting to Gusman Hall to run through it on stage, they had in effect only allowed themselves Wednesday, Thursday, and Friday to get ready for the hour-long Friday night show.

Everyone was either getting over the flu or getting it. Art Carney had been sick enough to spend time in the hospital, delaying rehearsals by a day. Thursday Gleason was too sick to come in, but another delay was out of the question, so the rehearsal went ahead on schedule with Dick Lynn standing in for the show's director, rewrite authority, and star.

All this time, the script that everyone had read through was evolving each time a scene was played. A reference to rum and Coke was changed to zombies (although Art Carney distinctly remembered that where he came from, they used to be called carioca coolers). A scene where Ralph looks up mushroom poisoning in a particularly heavy medical encyclopedia ("I hope it has some information about hernias," ad-libbed Gleason the first time he hefted it) was rehearsed repeatedly before it was dropped just hours before show time. Audrey Meadows, who had to take a list out of her apron pocket in the first scene, was reminding people either to settle on the apron she was going to wear or, at least, to put a list in the pocket of every apron that was being considered.

Friday afternoon, when an unseasoned observer would have sworn that no way could there be a show by evening, executive producer Jack Philbin wondered out loud, "Do you think we're overrehearsed?" And Art Carney replied, "Maybe I was better off in the hospital."

The Valentine special was another great show in the ongoing history of the most durable situation comedy on TV. One hopes it won't be the last. Once a Honeymoonie, always a Honeymoonie. May the Honeymoon never be over.

Christmas 1953 with *The Honeymooners*. The police officer is played by Frank Marth, one of the most familiar of the regular "Gleason Players."

THEY ARE US

TV's most successful comedy series.

BETTY ROLLIN, *LOOK*

It preceded *I Love Lucy* by a year, has rerun concurrently with *I Love Lucy* for over a quarter of a century, and, with the specials of late 1977 and early 1978, *The Honeymooners* has outlasted *I Love Lucy* (even considering *The Lucy Show* as an *I Love Lucy* extension) as the longest-running situation comedy in the history of television. Furthermore, Lucy has used three characters (Lucy Ricardo, Lucy Carmichael, and most recently, Lucy Whittaker) to accomplish this feat. Gleason's Ralph Kramden has endured throughout the years.

If the show were less than funny, if the cast were less than brilliant, this would not be the case. But the combination of funny and brilliant is rarely enough to assure immortality on TV. When a show has genuine staying power, the long-lasting fondness that fans develop for it can usually be traced to a sense of

Who needs a telephone? When Alice wants to chat with Trixie, all she has to do is holler out the window.

identification, an element of basic truth.

In the case of *The Honeymooners,* everything is immediately familiar, even if you've never seen the show before. Exposition is entirely unnecessary. It is, as James Wolcott remarked in the October 18, 1973 *Village Voice,* "the comedic sister to the Bronx-kitchen naturalism of Paddy Chayefsky." Just as it would not be *The Honeymooners* without funny business, it would not be *The Honeymooners* without this fond and knowing regard for human nature and daily life. The situations, the dialogue, the settings, even the names and addresses, have to convince us because we've known them, maybe lived them, ourselves. Certainly Gleason did. He actually grew up in an apartment on Chauncey Street, the Kramdens' street, and Mr. Dennehy, the unseen patron of the Joe the Bartender sketches, was his neighbor and friend. In fact, Gleason has often discarded scripts that he thought very funny because they were out-of-character for *The Honeymooners.*

Except for some of the mannerisms, Ralph in pain or Ed holding a pencil, for instance, there is very little exaggeration in *The Honeymooners.* If we don't quite go into business to sell wallpaper that glows in the dark, or to mine uranium in Asbury Park, we probably have friends or family who have tried worse. "Everything we did could have happened," says Gleason. "People like the show because we are them."

A significant, almost symbolic, corner in the Kramden apartment. The battered dresser, the lunch pail, and the ornamental candy dish that makes you wonder: was it a wedding present, or Alice's one big splurge to add a touch of class to her drab, curtainless surroundings?

I BELIEVE IN BENSONHURST

BY LEHMAN WEICHSELBAUM
PHOTOGRAPHS BY CATHY LEHRFELD

In the collective video consciousness of America, Bensonhurst is forever synonymous with the Honeymooners' home ground. It is the neighborhood of the Hong Kong Gardens, the Raccoon Lodge, and the crumbling tenement on Chauncey Street that sheltered the comic quartet of the Kramdens and the Nortons.

The hitch is that the real Chauncey Street never even so much as nudges Bensonhurst's borders. And Bensonhurst itself has long been a comfortable, middle-class Brooklyn community of one- and two-family homes, bearing scant resemblance to the humble, six-floor-walkup setting on TV.

Yet much of *The Honeymooners'* ambiance was drawn from Jackie Gleason's own early experiences. Most of his adolescence, in fact, was lived right on Chauncey Street in a small apartment he shared with his mother. But the territory was Bushwick, not Bensonhurst.

"Bensonhurst is a funny place," says A. J. Russell, a former writer on the show, justifying this bit of poetic license. "Like Brooklyn, it inspired applause whenever it was mentioned on the show. Bensonhurst *was* Brooklyn, like Flatbush. Bensonhurst would be known in Peoria."

More recently, Bushwick was lifted to at least an equal—although decidedly unfunny—national status, when it erupted into a battle zone of looting and arson during the July 1977 New York City blackout. Months later, many bombed-out storefronts still gape under the Broadway el. Bushwick, now as when Gleason was growing up there, is a pocket of the oppressed, though today its inhabitants are not Irish and Italian, but black. Ethnic and class lines are more bitterly divided than ever.

Yet, contrary to popular misconceptions, Bushwick today is far from a scene of unrelieved blight. To be sure, much of it is slum, rubble, and lots vacant but for the bountiful litter—a state of affairs long antedating the blackout. Gleason's own former block on Chauncey Street is now a wide, gutted shell. But just down the street from a site of devastation, the visitor can walk along a block of pleasant, well-kept brick or brownstone row houses. The net effect is a rather startling checkerboard of desolation and preservation. Life struggle is the constant in Gleason's old stomping grounds.

Jackie Gleason's grade school graduation, 1931.

"It was a warm neighborhood, in some ways a variation on *Studs Lonigan*, but without the bitterness," recalls Thomas C. Robinson, a boyhood pal of Gleason's, now a historian and vice-president of Pace University in New York. Robinson was a precocious youngster, dubbed "Bookshelf" by his friends (the name often came up later in Gleason's Joe the Bartender sketches). He was virtually the only high school graduate from the old crowd, much less the sole emissary to the world of higher education.

Times were hard in Bushwick well before the Depression, especially for the Gleasons. Jackie's father Herbert, an insurance clerk, disappeared when the boy was nine. His mother Mae, left alone to support herself and her son, died nine years later. In its various stages, the family lived in half a dozen locations before settling on Chauncey Street. The bare Kramden stage set is actually a distillation of Gleason's various boyhood homes.

Irene Wall *née* Wilson, Gleason's cousin and surrogate big sister, remembers one railroad flat on Marion Street, "a dreary, horrible-looking place." A storage company in the back blocked out what available light there was. Antiquated gas jets protruded from the walls. Mae's furniture, like Ralph and Alice Kramden's, was spartan, though Mrs. Wall does recall some token amenities, like a Tiffany-style lamp and a radio in the dining room. An adopted mouse shared the water dish with the family poodle.

Entrance of Gleason's
grade school, P.S. 73,
and the yard of P.S. 137
where he played,
as they look today.

The Chauncey Street apartment, where Mae died, was hardly more sumptuous. The superintendent was Thomas "Pop" Dennehy, the prototype of the "Mr. Dennehy" greeted ritually by Crazy Guggenheim in the Joe the Bartender sketches. (Those bits, a staple of *The Jackie Gleason Show*, were a virtual encyclopedia of real names from the old neighborhood. Joe's establishment itself was modeled on Jimmy Proce's saloon.) His daughter Julie was Gleason's first girlfriend. Today, Julie Dennehy Marshall recalls the Gleason digs: "A coal stove heated the kitchen. They had six rooms, but only three were heated. Some rooms had to be shut off because winters were really bitter in the thirties."

Through it all, Mae Gleason provided. "You may have holes in your shoes, but you'll have food in your stomach," says "Renee" Wall, testifying to her aunt's perseverance. "Mae loved life," she continues. "And she loved her son. The sun rose and set on him. He couldn't do wrong."

Jackie reciprocated that devotion—and shared that love for life. He wore the aura of promise from birth, when he arrived in the world with an extra "caul" of skin, a traditional sign of future attainment. The brilliant audacity that was to stand him in such good stead showed itself early. When he was two, for example, an older brother died. Little Jackie punctured the doleful solemnity of the occasion, if only for one anxious moment, when he was discovered underneath the hearse, striving to attach rubber bands around the horses' legs. He was trying, he explained, to hold up the beasts' white "stockings."

One night only a year or two later, he decided to visit his cousin Irene a mile away. Armed with a flashlight, he crept out his bedroom window, climbed up the fire escape to the roof and made his way down another fire escape to the street below. As the cop on the beat suddenly approached, the boy ducked behind a bush, then beamed his flashlight smack in the officer's face. The startled but luckily not trigger-happy cop carted the wayward tot home, where his absence hadn't even been noted.

Young Gleason was an inveterate ham. He gained an early reputation when he delivered a hilarious rendition of "Little Red Riding Hood" in Yiddish dialect, no less, at his elementary school graduation at P.S. 73. Later, Gleason found a captive audience in the Nomads, the neighborhood "club." Out of school and more often than not out of work, the Nomads found little else to do than hang out—shooting baskets in the P.S. schoolyard, taking it easy in Schuman's candy store, being regaled by Gleason in Saratoga Park. "He was funnier at fourteen than he is now," says Teddy Gilanza, ex-Nomad who later took care of Gleason's business in the salad days.

Young Gleason was a striking figure, a Robert Taylor double, astonishingly unlike the famous fat man he became in later years. "Jackie used to stand in front of Freitag's Deli (another name that would come up on *The Honeymooners*), swinging his key chain. He wore a derby, black chesterfield, white silk scarf—his mother dressed him very well—tall, thin, blue-black hair and blue eyes," says Julie Marshall. He was an expert swimmer and became a formidable pool hustler, keeping himself and his Nomad backers in spare change.

Show business remained his dominant attraction, however. "Jackie started in show business almost on a dare," says Teddy Gilanza, "at the Halsey Theater on Halsey Street. It was an amateur night from which he walked off with first prize, aided and abetted by his gang who screamed and applauded lustily." Gleason immediately became a Halsey regular at five dollars a week.

"Jackie was so good that Gilbert, the entrepreneur, took him all over New York," says Julie Marshall, his companion and secretary in those days. "Gilbert was a great believer in gams and gals, but he was so impressed by Jackie that Jackie emceed his shows. Sometimes he used to come on to the stage swinging from a rope."

Soon Gleason had moved up to the Folly Theater on Graham Avenue at fifteen dollars a week. From there he went on to other showcases locally and across the Hudson in Newark, before landing a big break at the prestigious Club 18. Not long after that, the call came from Jack Warner in Hollywood.

After his night of stardom at the Raccoon Lodge, Ralph Kramden, the stagestruck bus driver from Bensonhurst, utters the immortal credo: "Be kind to the people you meet on the way up, because you'll be meeting the same people on the way down." It is advice that Gleason himself has followed faithfully. Whether paying an uncle's medical bills, helping out an old pal with a job or drawing generously on yesterday's people and places for his TV material, he has always remained true to his roots.

And the old crowd has returned the sentiment. Julie Marshall, Tom Dennehy's girl, recounts one memorable reunion: "One day we visited Jackie at the Park Sheraton. Jackie had really made it. Pop Dennehy wasn't one to show emotion over anything, and Jackie was always knocking himself out trying to impress Pop. He had Pop shown around the place, but Pop said nothing. Finally, unable to contain himself, he asked, "What do you think, Pop?"

"Pop replied, ' 'Tis a great country, Jack, where anyone like yourself, with only half a brain, could get all this.' Coming from Pop, this was the best compliment of all."

Teddy Gilanza remembers the grand occasion when the Great One came home. "One day, all the guys came to the set, parked themselves at an old Italian restaurant next door and kept after him to go back to the old neighborhood. Finally, he canceled the show to oblige them and left cast, crew, and audience to run old material or fend for themselves. Crowds were all over him in the old neighborhood. They had to close doors all over town to keep them from wrecking the places Jackie visited."

Whether narrowed down to Bensonhurst or Bushwick, Brooklyn is as much a state of mind as a geographical label. And if it's carried forward with love, a raucous spirit of fun and an infallible eye for the human comedy, you've got the ingredients for a classic that people everywhere will recognize and take to their hearts. Ask the folks in Peoria.

Lehman Weichselbaum is a reporter who honeymoons in Brooklyn and Manhattan.

72

Saratoga Park in Brooklyn, a favorite hangout
of Gleason and his boyhood chums.

The real Chauncey Street building as it appears today.

ALICE GIBSON KRAMDEN AND RALPH

Baby, you're the greatest!

RALPH KRAMDEN

At the core of *The Honeymooners* is the domestic scrap. No writer had to invent it. For all the efforts of TV historians to trace its roots to radio's *The Bickersons* (which in turn can be traced to the original *Baby Snooks*), there is no reason to have to trace it beyond the fire escape; just hang your head out of practically any urban apartment window to find excellent sitcom material.

Ralph wants money for another scheme, Alice says no. Alice wants her mother to visit, Ralph says no. Ralph can be jealous; Alice can be secretive. They can both be nasty. As long as they're happy. . . .

Consider the title. In radio, you find *The Bickersons,* the prototypical husband-wife spat sitcom. But 1950s TV was *I Married Joan* and *I Love Lucy, A Date with the Angels,* and *Mr. Adams and Eve. The Honeymooners,* which preceded them all, suggests a marital affection that has little in common with the squabbling couple of radio comedy. It also suggests, almost ironically, a relationship that hasn't evolved much over the years. With each new incident, Ralph and Alice have to start all over again from scratch—doubting, fighting, scheming— and learning all over, again and again, that they're still very much in love. While their love is unquestionably genuine at the end of each episode, it is never any greater than it was at the end of any previous episode. It is not cumulative; they will always have a lot to learn about getting along with each other.

Of the two, Alice is the grown-up, but she is also stuck with Ralph. She cannot change him, so she cannot change their relationship or even her part in their relationship. Of her role Audrey Meadows has said, "You can get away with anything. If you can also convey love." And Sheila MacRae, as a quieter, less demonstrative Alice, explained, "Alice is direct. She has the courage to think that people will like her in spite of her ugly dresses and not having her hair fixed. She's secure, she's confident. She doesn't expect her man to leave her." Whether Alice is a dynamo or a doormat, Ralph is Ralph and marriage to him is one long, loud honeymoon.

Like honeymooners, Ralph and Alice have no children. It has been observed that they could have children if Ed would leave them alone long enough. But that conclusion is unfair to Ed, Alice, and particularly to Ralph, who is generally honest enough to realize that he could never handle fatherhood. Ralph and Alice don't have children for the same reason their mutual affection can never be cumulative: what would happen next week? Ralph with a kid becomes Chester A. Riley, a lummox cut down in the prime of life by premature adulthood; a menace to his family. "Alice can take care of herself," says *Honeymooners* writer Walter Stone. "But you'd feel sorry for the kid. Even when we did the adoption show, we couldn't keep the baby. When you think about it, Lucy didn't either. Once the comic material was exhausted, you didn't see much of Little Ricky. He would have gotten in the way of the plots."

Gilbert Seldes, in *The Public Arts,* comments on the "inappropriate name of *The Honeymooners,*" concluding that the show's "prime virtue" is that "it is almost totally unsentimental." When you think about it, though, the show is as sentimental or unsentimental as real life. It's not romantic—if it were, it would become soap opera—but it's sincere. Ralph never manages to say, "Baby, you're the greatest" without its sounding like a surprise to him. Like a revelation that will turn things around. Like things are going to start to change for the better.

Nothing will change, of course.

That's life.

The *Honeymooners* as newlyweds and on their twenty-fifth anniversary.

"Call me irresponsible . . . unpredictable . . . but I'm undeniably mad about you," sang Jackie Gleason in the movie *Papa's Delicate Condition.* The song was a natural for him; it fit not only his movie role but the role he'd been playing for two decades on *The Honeymooners.* The only things that *are* predictable about Ralph are his irresponsibility and his genuine affection for his Alice.

ONE OF THESE DAYS, ALICE...

Psychiatrists Explain Why TV Audiences Revel In Gleason's Battle of the Sexes on TV

Christmas 1955. "Baby, you're the greatest."

The big, fat, bug-eyed fellow walked purposefully across the dingy room and shook his fist under the nose of the redheaded girl.

"Alice," he said. "Alice, I'm gonna belt you one!"

Defiantly, the girl stepped up as close to him as she could without bumping into his stomach. This maneuver left them about a yard apart at shoulder level.

"Oh, you are, are you?" she asked, in a voice a fraction of a decibel below a screech. "Well, go ahead and belt me, Ralph."

She extended an inviting chin. The fat fellow began to make low animal cries. But he didn't swing. Instead, he looked at his fist pleadingly, then shrugged and swaggered away.

"One of these days, Alice," he muttered. "One of these days . . ."

Scenes like this one between Jackie Gleason and Audrey Meadows in *The Honeymooners,* which tonight (Saturday) makes its bow on CBS in its new half-hour film version, apparently had a compelling appeal for their 45 million followers last season. At least, that's what their fan mail indicated.

Why? Well, for one thing, viewers apparently keep dialing in to find out whether Ralph actually *will* crank up and let Alice have one "Pow! right in the kisser!" Male viewers in particular seem to get a vicarious satisfaction out of watching a man prepare to clobber his spouse. As for their wives, well, they just love to watch Alice make Ralph Kramden sizzle.

According to Mrs. Ruth Wassell, the chief psychiatric social worker at the University Settlement House, New York Psychiatric Clinic, this is a classic example of an expression of animal impulses to which many of us sometimes regress. These impulses are rarely carried out, but they are present nevertheless.

A prominent psychiatrist holds that imbedded deeply in the consciousness is the idea that wives are all-powerful and that husbands are mere pawns. Men subconsciously resent this state of affairs and, quite naturally, are delighted when Ralph Kramden threatens to release the pent-up hostility of his sex. Wives, on the other hand, are secretly delighted at what they interpret as visual proof of their superiority in the age-old war between men and women.

This is a war that has been going on for some time. Delilah won a skirmish for her side when she gave Samson a haircut. Othello evened the score when he wiped up the bedroom floor with Desdemona. In *The Taming of the Shrew,* we observed a woman brought to heel by her husband, and in *Agamemnon* Queen Clytemnestra won the main event by entangling the man of the house in the living room drapes.

"The aggressive reaction of the male-to-female domination," the psychiatrist says, "is, of course, symbolic rather than actual. No decent fellow really wants to hit his wife—he is indeed horrified by the thought—but in the average male heart is the desire to be supreme in the family circle."

The good doctor believes that *The Honeymooners* would never be popular in France, Germany, Italy, Scandinavia, or the Baltic States, where the man already is the undisputed boss of the home.

Apparently it is chiefly in the U.S., where women customarily occupy an equal (and sometimes superior) position, that the revolt of the male is a suitable subject for humor. The psychiatrist thinks that the American male has a feeling he is being submerged by his mate and that he recognizes his own submersion in Ralph Kramden's comic exasperation.

(Somehow, doctor, it doesn't seem so funny when you put it that way!)
Now back to Mrs. Wassell, who is a Gleason fan herself.

The appeal of *The Honeymooners,* she believes, exemplifies the expression of primitive instincts, as in the case of the very young child who, "to assert himself in an adult's terrifying world, hits, bites and scratches those he loves most dearly and yet expects continued acceptance and love in spite of this behavior."

Basically, Gleason's own analysis of the popularity of *The Honeymooners* agrees with that of the psychiatrists.

"I wonder if many a husband doesn't feel the same way Ralph does when Alice puts one over on him," says Jackie. "It's an evidence of the simple frustrations and suppressions we all have. And it's funny because, knowing Ralph's character, we realize Ralph really won't hit her at all."

Well, there you have it. Now you know exactly why you're supposed to start laughing the next time Ralph Kramden talks like this to his wife:

"This is the day! Today! This is the day you're gonna get yours, Alice!"

Ralph and Alice, it appears, are just doing what comes naturally.

This article by Frank De Blois appeared in *TV Guide,* October 1, 1955.

ED NORTON AND RALPH

Ed is the kind of person even dogs and cats like.

ART CARNEY

Ed Norton is to Ralph Kramden what Sancho Panza was to Don Quixote, only with the dimensions in reverse. Off the two go in search of some impossible dream, leaving their wives behind to shake their heads in disbelief while the dauntless duo defy enchanted windmills and defend schemes so grandiose that they are bound to fail ingloriously—schemes that sound so brilliant to them that anyone who doesn't agree must be crazy.

Ed and Ralph are a team, not straight man and comic but equally matched. They are exasperating in different ways, but they are equally exasperating. They deserve each other. The Ralph-Alice relationship may be the core of *The Honeymooners,* but Ralph Kramden, like Don Quixote, can't get into mischief without his gullible sidekick.

They have been compared, not inappropriately, to Laurel and Hardy, who were, incidentally, among *The Honeymooners* most ardent fans. They are, after all, a team composed of one rotund dope who thinks he knows it all and one thin, easily led dope who sticks by his arrogant pal like a loyal puppy. They look like Laurel and Hardy, especially when, for a bus company party, they go in costume as the famous pair. They even get into the sort of situations Laurel and Hardy tend to get into: petty disputes, botched deceptions, financial schemes, and fights with bullies. But they transcend the basic caricature that underlies Laurel and Hardy and move into real life, a railroad flat in Brooklyn.

Ed has had more than one Trixie Norton in his life, but Art Carney has worn

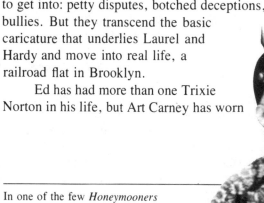

In one of the few *Honeymooners* episodes to appear on *The American Scene Magazine,* Ed and Ralph prepare for a nuclear holocaust with a bomb shelter in the basement.

the same battered felt hat, bought in his real-life high school days in Yonkers, through all those years on *The Honeymooners*. An Academy Award–winning serious actor, Carney has always been a terrific comic actor on *The Honeymooners* because Gleason and the writers have always made a point of giving him plenty to do that's funny. Throughout the years, Jackie has asked the writers to write Art's part bigger, or switch one of Ralph's bits to Ed so Art could get the laughs. "The boys at the Columbia Broadcasting System practically have had to invent a title for what Art Carney does," wrote *TV Guide* in 1953, "and what they've come up with is 'Second Banana.'"

"I guess I've always loved *The Honeymooners* more than the other Gleason skits," confess Jack Philbin. "Secretly, I think it's always been Jackie's favorite too. One of the great helps there were writers, Marvin Marx and Walter Stone, who were Ralph and Ed's counterparts. Marx thought like Ralph, Stone thought like Norton."

There are a lot of reasons why people watch Ralph and Ed with such pleasure. Not the least is that Gleason and Carney obviously get such pleasure out of playing the roles. But the reason given most often is as obvious as the drip pan under the Kramden's icebox. In *Look* magazine Betty Rollin once said, "In Situation Comedy City, shows that work are shows that come close to the people who watch them . . . the dreams and woes of big blowhard Ralph Kramden and his pea-brained sidekick, Ed Norton, are the dreams and woes of Everyman."

ARE YOU IN PAIN, OR CAN I LAUGH NOW?

By Ashton Trice

In one episode of *The Honeymooners,* Ralph gets Ed to invest in an illusionary corporation. The corporation consists of Ralph's assets (plus Ed's $20 contribution), and profits will be divided according to a percentage painstakingly arrived at by the principals. Days later, while Ed is complaining about corporate stagnation and the absence of dividends, Ralph is informed that he is mentioned in a will by a woman he has helped on and off the bus for years. The woman is worth many millions. Ralph assumes he will inherit all. Ed assumes *he* will be entitled to a percentage. The audience knows that by the episode's end Ralph and Ed's financial position will be unchanged.

The Honeymooners uses the two most characteristic psychological ploys, the disguise and the defeat, of sitcom television, but in a rather benign way. Berle used the disguise of transvestism; Lucy was constantly disguising her housewifery as stardom; *M*A*S*H* frequently disguises words as other words in rapid-fire punning. Disguises have been funny since the time of Aristophanes. Ralph disguises a loan as an investment. The loan then dis-

"Neither one of them was smart. But the difference between Kramden and Norton is that Ralph thought he was smart, Norton knew he wasn't."—Syd Zelinka, *Honeymooners* writer

guises itself as a windfall for Ed. By episode's finish the loan is just a loan again. In short, the characteristic disguise of *The Honeymooners* is the trivial deception. It is basically benign because no one but Ed or Ralph could be fooled by it.

Defeat is a more difficult comedic device. Today, the inevitable return of Lucy to her kitchen after her taste of a career, is not as funny as it was before the women's movement, and the current TV comedies, such as *M*A*S*H, One Day at a Time,* and *All in the Family,* have frequently defeated their characters, but with no comic intent.

But the current TV fare frequently uses truly adverse consequences to its characters' behavior to defeat them. Frank Burns' inept surgery endangers patients. Phyllis' husband dies, as do many characters on *Mary Hartman, Mary Hartman* (though by preposterous means, such as drowning in soup or being impaled on a fake Christmas tree). In psychology such behavioral consequences would have to be called punishment, and punishment is hard to make funny. True, the pie in the face is a punishment, or the seltzer bottle or the pratfall. But death and poverty are rarely funny. They are too real and too likely to punish the audience vicariously. Comedy rests on defeating the characters without, unlike tragedy, spreading the umbrella of defeat to the audience. The audience must feel superior to the characters: they could avoid the characters' defeat.

A safer technique is the use of penalty, or the removal of some positive condition. Bilko gets to be a consultant on a Hollywood movie, but he bungles the job and loses the prestige. This is safer than punishment. While Ed and Ralph fail to make their millions, they are no worse off at the end of the program than they were at the beginning. We can laugh at them. They have hurt no one and not been hurt themselves, except in their inflated concept of their own worth, which has been punctured and considerably brought down. We would never have made such a mistake.

Furthermore, *The Honeymooners* achieves its charm not only by making the defeat benign (failure to meet unrealistic goals) but it makes the characters benign. Ralph is less than appealing and honest, and considerably less than smart, but it was his courtesy to an old, ostensibly poor woman that caused him to be mentioned in the will. His wife has enough sense and street savvy to be in control and on top of most situations that arise. Ed is a good and loyal friend to the Kramdens.

The Honeymooners plod on. They resolve conflicts, hope for better times while adapting to the present conditions, and they have redeeming characteristics for their many flaws. They look forward with hope, however unrealistic, to the future, and they still seem able to laugh all around at their own clumsy amateurish style of living. Much of the affection for this show shown by its fans, I feel, must be in the same vein as the tolerant, good-natured humor derived by adults from the dead-serious antics of children and adolescents.

Ashton Trice is with the Department of Psychology at Johns Hopkins.

RALPH KRAMDEN

*Just because I've been married for twenty-five years
is no reason for me to stop being sexy.*

RALPH KRAMDEN

Almost always seen in a uniform (either a bus driver's or a Raccoon's) Ralph is the kind of guy who doesn't look good in a uniform. He's the last guy in the neighborhood to own an icebox, the only one who still doesn't have a phone. He's a big sport and a big baby, a loudmouth and poor soul, a fat man with an emotional age of sixteen—and your heart goes out to him. He's all the Gleason types (Charlie Bratton, Rudy the Repairman, The Poor Soul, all of them) rolled into one personality that transcends caricature. He's a walking amalgam of stock phrases and running gags—*har-har-har-dee-har-har; One of these days, right on the kisser; You're going to the moon; Baby, you're the greatest;* the mother-in-law bits; the ways he finds to look foolish throwing his weight around, in both senses of the word. He's Gleason's timing, vitality, expressiveness, sincerity, pratfalls, and fluctuating massiveness. He's a poor man scheming to get rich, and he can't win for losing:

> ALICE. Look, Ralph, maybe until you get something for yourself I could get a job and help out.
> RALPH. Oh, no, you don't. When I married you I promised you'd never have to work again.
> ALICE. But it won't be for long.
> RALPH. I don't care, Alice, I've got my pride. Before I'd let you go to work, I'd rather see you starve. We'll just have to live on our savings.
> ALICE. That'll carry us through the night, but what'll we do in the morning?

There was an early sketch in which Ralph and Ed build a hot-dog stand across from a big building going up. They've pooled their money and shot off their mouths about the fortune they are going to make selling hot dogs to the lunch crowds from this mammoth edifice. First day on the job, Ralph is boasting to his first customer, "Would you believe only yesterday I was driving a bus?" Then Ed says something typical about sloshing around in the sewer. But joy turns to sadness, and the tycoons must return to their former jobs when they discover that the building across the street is going to be a Howard Johnson's.

Ralph dreams big, but what poor man hasn't? If he didn't, what would he have? If you said to him, "Go slow, Ralph, and you'll get there," can you

imagine how long it would take him to get there, and how mediocre *there* would be?

"Everyone has known someone like Ralph or Ed," says Gleason. "It may be an uncle, a cousin, a next-door neighbor. They goof up, but they never give up. I don't know if I could do it, plugging away day after day, the way Ralph does."

As long as he can hope and scheme for his pot of gold—no-cal pizza or the KramMar Mystery Appetizer (dog food) that he feeds his boss—he is willing to fail, and bounce back, and try again. As long as he has his dreams, and his wife's love, and his best pal's friendship, his life is an adventure worth living. He never stops scheming, but I don't remember that he has ever really complained.

He's a happy man.

FROM RAGS TO RICHES AND BACK

T. NOGARO

Weary not thyself to be rich;
Cease from thine own wisdom.
Wilt thou set thine eyes upon it?
It is gone;
For riches certainly make themselves wings
Like an eagle that flieth toward heaven.

PROVERBS 23:4–5

Ralph Kramden, like all of us, dreams the American dream and hopes its hope of hopes: to be filthy rich. All his doomed schemes draw for us a picture of ourselves. His drive for fame and fortune, for the overnight success, is a common dream: to beat the Protestant work ethic and get rich quick. And we want acclaim nevertheless. We want to be recognized for competence and knowledge, deserved or not. These are the human frailties we wish to avoid but which also curiously add beauty and love to our lives.

The ambitious dreams that give focus to Ralph's life are, not coincidentally, those which sustain our TV viewing and the cultural values it contains. They predicate much of our present and past TV game show activity. There is something totally American, as well as plainly human, about Ralph's appearance on the *$99,000 Answer,* itself a takeoff on the *$64,000 Question* of the 1950s, the ancestor of contemporary shows like *Jeopardy, Concentration, Let's Make a Deal,* and *The New Price is Right,* where hysteria is the added element.

Ralph appears on stage just after the preceding contestant has successfully answered the question regarding the number of times the numeric or written form of "one" appears on the dollar bill. (What better way to point up the show's meaning.) Ralph comes on, dressed in his familiar conservative dark suit, striped tie, and dark round hat. Ralph's desire to wear his hat throughout the interview is significant. It bespeaks, among other things: the ephemeral, in-and-out character of his visit; his general lack of ease in this world of design and stage makeup; the unpolished character of live TV in the 1950s; and the general naiveté of the age, symbolized in the person of Ralph. Moreover, the hat illustrates another unforgettable truth: Ralph Kramden's character goes with him wherever he goes; it even supercedes TV's total artifice.

Ralph's nervous stuttering also reveals his lack of ease. He cannot escape himself, especially on TV. Only after the emcee describes a recent unpleasant rainy-day experience, wherein an inconsiderate bus driver splashed rainwater up from the street onto the emcee's new suit, is the code of silence broken. Ralph relaxes immediately and exclaims, without self-consciousness, "Was that you?"

Ralph choses popular songs as his category, but he must return the following week to receive his first question because the show has run out of time. This break in the action involves a beautiful technical device, i.e., postponement. That not even the first question is answered, let alone asked, allows the entire weight of tension of the Unknown to be suspended until the following week. The postponement allows Ralph to saddle himself, in the intervening week's span, with the "responsibility" of preparing to outrun the Unknown. Ralph is like a tightrope walker on the high wire, blindfolded and carrying a clothes bureau on his back, with the wire greased!

It is a characteristically hopeless and futile task. (Almost as ridiculous as trying to master golf in one evening in one's kitchen, or learning to box in one lesson!) Though he does have a rudimentary background in music, to try to eliminate chance altogether is obviously dangerous and ridiculously ambitious. (To think of testing oneself against the gods!) Alice knows this and tries to forewarn him; she bids him to take the whole matter in stride and be happy even to win the six hundred dollars for answering the first question correctly. He replies: "Six hundred dollars? Peanuts! What am I going to do with peanuts?"

In his first appearance on *The $99,000 Answer*, Ralph is a bundle of nerves.

Alice's answer to this is apt, direct, and profoundly funny: "Eat them. Like any other elephant." On the surface she seems to be commenting on his weight, and her remark bears direct resemblance to an ordinary put-down. She is telling him, in effect: "Take the money and use it, you need it; we need it; be grateful for whatever you may win, as an elephant in a zoo is for the peanuts thrown to him." But even in her insult we see common sense, the obvious but never-heeded remedy to most of Ralph's problems.

Ralph, however, disregards her good advice. His money fever is too blinding; he has been set in motion by the twenty-two times the number "one" appears on the dollar bill. He succeeds in infecting his friends and neighbors with his greed. Mrs. Manicotti pops up to the apartment late at night to challenge him with the Italian song "Take Me Back to Sorrento," while Norton is busy at the piano challenging Ralph with songs from the 1930s and 1940s. Alice is banished, along with all the other rational and sleep-oriented neighbors who try to quiet him down.

Ralph's mania to win impairs his ability to see those around him clearly. The action is focused on Ralph, yet it is clear that this episode's more subtle and primary problem is that of Norton. Who is Norton? Does Ralph really know Norton as well as he thinks?

Both men think they know every last detail of the other's life. After fourteen years of intimate friendship where they live and breathe together, and even once share a TV set, it is reasonable to assume that they know each other well. In "The Safety Award," Norton says of Ralph, "Why I know Ralph Kramden so well that I could answer the $64,000 question on Ralph Kramden." Probably he could.

But this episode, which deals ostensibly with Ralph's desire to win, is more seriously concerned with the issue of who Ed Norton really is. Ralph goes on the show to win money, but ends up revealing to himself and to the world his real ignorance of Norton and of what musical or other life he might be capable of living.

Garrity comes in to complain about the noise from Ralph and Ed's late–night practice session; Mrs. Manicotti offers help.

By the time of Ralph's second appearance on the show, he is all confidence. But the goal of great wealth, as he soon finds out, is still an impossible dream.

Omens of ignorance first appear in the practice session where we are surprised to learn that Norton can read music and play the piano very well. In the "Bensonhurst Bomber" episode, Norton's theretofore unrevealed boxing skills similarly come to light only when Ralph suddenly and immediately needs a sparring partner and boxing instructor. Norton's personal qualities and capabilities remain nonexistent, merely potential, until they are needed by Ralph. Norton's essence remains unfixed, in flux: it is determined by the particular requirements of each situation Ralph presents. The problem, in short, is, does Norton ever assert himself; is his character ever asserted in and of itself, or is it wholly brought into being by Ralph? Does Norton indeed have a life of his own?

Alice interrupts their late-night practicing with a plea to Ralph's rationality; she argues that it is too late at night to be playing the piano. Ralph immediately rejects this idea, whereupon she appeals to Norton by saying that she realizes he is more fair and reasonable than Ralph ("Ed, I *know* that you are a reasonable man, and *being a reasonable man*, realize that it is late!"). Ralph, for his own selfish reasons, immediately contradicts her: "Wait a minute! Wait a minute! He's just as unreasonable as I am!" Ralph attempts to justify his own behavior by implicating Norton; he "creates" Norton's unreasonableness by assertion.

Norton neither rejects nor accepts either claim. Certainly he is, as always, reasonable and fair; and certainly he is not, insofar as he is willing to help his friend prepare for the show and keep other people awake. Norton delicately sidesteps the issue by explaining it absurdly as a question of his genius: "Why, oh why, were these hands born with such great talent?" Predictably, his character remains a mysterious, amoral enigma.

It is now time for the showdown; Ralph must reveal his knowledge of music and his knowledge of Norton. Ralph quickly dismisses the idea of not going all the way to the $99,000 question. He is highly confident, and feels fully prepared for the Unknown. The timing is perfect; at the height of his confidence, the spotlight is on him. The entire world is watching him, and he is left with only himself and his Maker. And what is it that is resonated up "by chance" from below the great depths? The same tune which Norton has struck into Ralph's unconscious during their practice sessions. Only now Ralph is not bored and impatient. Now we see desperation, the desperation of having allowed the obvious to slip between his fingertips and out of reach.

In this highly dramatic moment, Ralph's pride and ego suffer a kind of death. He must publicly humble himself to the Unknown and the Unknowable. Despite everything, music still may not be his possession. Although he had sought to use music to gain fame and fortune, that very prize has "made itself wings" at his potential moment of glory. And how? Ralph, once again, has not seen the obvious. He never took the time to ask Norton who in fact did write "Swanee River."

Daringly, Ralph takes a stab in the dark. His only hope, as per usual, is Norton. He questions whether it might in fact have been Norton. Could his good friend Norton have written this, and once again bail him out? In the rejoinder to this "answer," Ralph must own up to the fact that he does not possess either Norton or the irreversibility of time. Norton too, despite his infinite willingness to be what is required at each moment, is also helpless against the fact of time. Norton is not here and will not come. Ralph is alone, before the world's eyes, and without Norton. In Ralph's potential hour of triumph it is Norton who might have received the glory. And even he doesn't.

The world of possibility, where Norton might have written the song, must be just as closely checked as the world of actuality, where everything about Norton is alleged to be known and mastered. Norton is alleged to be known and mastered. Norton neither wrote "Swanee River" nor would it be fair to say that he could never have done so; surprises are always possible. In Ralph's sudden and painful epiphany, the delicate balance between the actual and the possible is restored, and once again brought down to earth. Simultaneously, so is the question of the essence of Norton: he remains not-Ralph, while at the same time not necessarily the Stephen Foster who created "Swanee River." As he remains undefined, he is defined. He is simply Norton. And in realizing this, Ralph once again becomes simply Ralph.

Every national epic needs its bard: The Honeymooners *has T. Nogaro, poet, writer and Honeymoonie extraordinaire.*

III. BEHIND THE SCENES WITH THE HONEYMOONERS

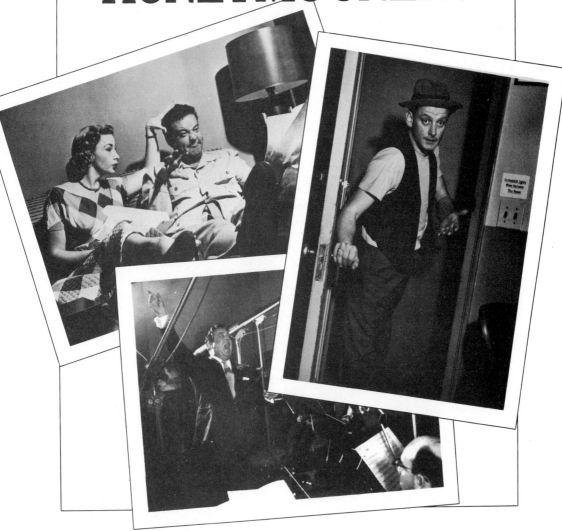

THE REHEARSAL THAT ALMOST ISN'T

*I have learned more from working with Jackie Gleason
in eleven years than I could ever learn
in a school of acting.*

JOHNNY OLSEN, *HONEYMOONERS* EMCEE

Unlike *All in the Family* or *The Mary Tyler Moore Show,* much like "The Family" segment of *The Carol Burnett Show, The Honeymooners* was initially one regular sketch out of several in the course of a one-hour variety show. It used the same core of people each time, but not exclusively in *The Honeymooners* part of the show (for instance, Zamah Cunningham, who was Mrs. Manicotti in *The Honeymooners,* was also Reggie Van Gleason III's mother; and Art Carney played, besides Ed Norton, Reggie's father and also Charlie Bratton's foil, Clem Finch). It was performed on a stage, as opposed to an elaborate set. (Whereas Ralph's apartment effectively suggests a rundown Brooklyn apartment, it is much less realistic than Archie Bunker's living room or Mary Richards' newsroom.) In short, throughout the twenty-five-plus years of *The Honeymooners,* it has always projected the quality of a live stage show.

Without this quality, *The Honeymooners* would be a very different, and perhaps very disappointing, show. The spontaneity and ad-libbing we have come to expect would disappear. We would be asked to accept tricks done with cameras on a show that has never employed any effect (including exploding water pipes and appliances, and even a life raft at sea) that could not be created live on stage.

The force behind this basic honesty of staging is Gleason himself. He is demanding in the extreme, but his team delivers. He is uncompromising in his expectations, but not unkind. He has something to say about every phase of production, from scriptwriting to performing to placement of microphones in the audience. He seems, instinctively, to know what he is doing. Ruth Regina, head of his makeup department, has worked with Groucho, Bing, Elvis, Garland, Hope, Benny, the Beatles, and seven presidents and presidential candidates. She says:"Jackie is the genius of all time. He knows what's going on in every department. He has a feel for everything—everything."

He will not use cue cards. Once he filmed twenty commercials in a row, reading each script once only before shooting, and finished all twenty, letter perfect, in under fifteen minutes. He takes pride in the "Gleason actors" who can "do a show in the middle of the Civil War." (Says Audrey Meadows, "The

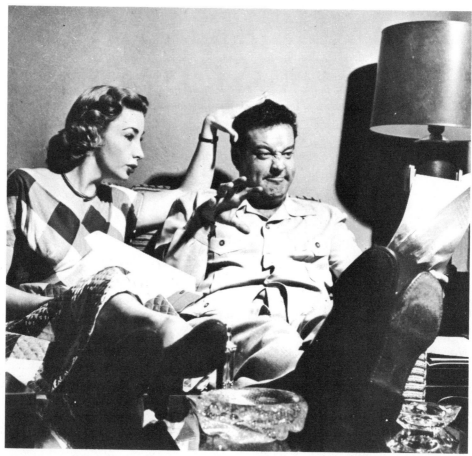

Gleason never did, never will, enjoy rehearsals or preliminary readings of the script. His attention span is short but his memory is photographic. He needs rehearsals like the Poor Soul needs dialogue. No wonder Audrey Meadows ("The Rock") has to focus his attention on the day's material.

Gleason actor is the kind of a guy who lets nothing bother him once he's on the air. If you're waiting behind a door and your cue doesn't come, you walk in anyway.") Without rehearsals, even the supporting players can come in prepared, on no more than last-minute notice. Frank Marth was a frequent "Gleason actor," and George Petrie could be counted on for any voice, any dialect. "Wear a scar, wear a beard, dye your hair," Gleason would advise; that way it was less obvious that the same few faces kept reappearing week after week in different roles.

When wireless microphones first came out, Gleason couldn't wait to try them, since players who wore them didn't have to be followed around by mike booms. But the attempt failed when it was discovered that a wall and only about ten feet of alley stood between Studio Fifty and a Con Edison power station. The only thing that the mikes picked up was the sound of Con Ed's generators. Gleason was not pleased; this technicality stood between him and the perfection he constantly strove for. On another occasion, reported in Kenneth Whelan's *How the Golden Age of Television Turned My Hair to Silver,*

He stopped the rehearsal, and asked the technical crew to assemble on stage. It was obvious that he was frustrated about something. Not angry, but very upset. He started out in a low, conversational tone. "Look, guys, I want to ask you a question. . . . Now, I know you have your job to do, and I have my job to do, and all that stuff. But, I still want to ask you a question . . . in fact, a couple of questions. . . . This is a theater, right? . . . It's got a stage, and twelve or thirteen hundred seats, right? . . . The people who sit in those seats are called an audience, right? . . . This live audience is very important to me. I play to this live audience. The whole show is designed for a live audience, right?" His voice shifted another gear. "Now, what I want to know is, when I'm on stage doing a sketch, why can't I see the audience, and why can't the audience see me? . . . When I look at the audience, all I see is cameras, mike booms, electrical cables, and you guys running all over the place! . . . And all the audience can see is your rear ends!"

On the set for the rehearsal of the Silver Anniversary special in 1975, John Huddy of the *Miami Herald* witnessed another example of Jackie in action:

> Nothing is missed. A portrait of Alice is on the wrong side of the chest. A ball of yarn is too ensnarled. A piece of paper needs to be flat and stiff. Microphones into the audience are improperly placed.
>
> But no one seems to mind the sharp, forceful direction. Jackie Gleason, television director? "Why not? Look at Chaplin," says Jane Kean during a break. "I like it. I think it's always been that way anyway. He really knows his cameras, just like Lucille Ball. During her shows, she knew exactly what you wanted, when she wanted it—and so does Jackie."
>
> "We've never had a fight, never as much as a cross word," says Carney. "I always felt I was closer working with Jack onstage than I was with him offstage. In working with him, there is a special kind of rapport, a meeting of the minds."
>
> "Fantastic instincts," says Meadows. "You can't look bad when you're in a scene with Gleason. He's that good."

Retakes are rare. The audience is not likely to laugh as hard the second time they hear a joke; and the purists behind *The Honeymooners* refuse to dub in laughter. Only mechanical failure and the occasional glaring incident (like the time Art Carney, singing about "Cain, the guy who slew his brother," slipped and came out with a word that rhymes with "slew") will bring cameras to a halt. Over the years, in the vast majority of cases, according to Jack Philbin, "We didn't know the meaning of stopping and going back."

Audrey Meadows, nicknamed "The Rock" for her ability to get people back on the script, and because she almost never fluffed her lines, slipped the night of the "Beat the Clock" episode. In this episode, Ralph and Alice go on Bud Collyer's popular game show (which, not so coincidentally, was broadcast from the studio next to the Gleason show), but time runs out before they can complete their stunt. They are invited to return the following week, so they spend the next seven days rehearsing—rolling lemons down a slide and catching them in saucers, and keeping a balloon in the air at all times. While Ralph, Alice, and Ed lunge and bolt frantically on stage, Jackie, Audrey, and Art are feeling the pressures of a strenuous schedule that at that time included up to six live shows a day at the Paramount Theater. So Audrey speaks one line that is barely coherent, and immediately turns it into a plus. She stamps her foot and says, "Ralph, you've kept me up so late doing this that I can't talk straight. I'm going to keep saying it until I get it right." Then she says the words slowly and deliberately—and hilariously.

One of the incidents Kenneth Whelan remembers in *How the Golden Age of Television Turned My Hair to Silver* might have spelled disaster on any other show, but not on *The Honeymooners:*

BACKSTAGE STORY: A MISSED CUE

I remember one Saturday night when Gleason made an exit through *The Honeymooners'* bedroom door, and forgot to come back.

Gleason went through the bedroom door, followed later by Audrey Meadows. According to the script, Audrey was supposed to return with Gleason, immediately. According to Eddie Brinkman, the stage manager, Audrey couldn't *find* Gleason when she went through the bedroom door. Being a little confused, and thinking he had a little more time, he had gone looking for a Kleenex to mop his sweating brow.

As a result, *no one* came back through that bedroom door, and Art Carney was left all alone on the stage. Now remember, this was live television. Millions of people were watching, and that ramp camera had nothing else to shoot but Art Carney. He was alone, and those millions of people expected him to do something funny.

Carney could have done many things. He could have looked at the camera, imagined all the people watching him, gulped and headed for the nearest bar. He could have become frozen with fright. He could have apologized to the viewers, explaining the situation, and asking them to understand. He didn't do any of those things. Instead, he wandered over to the icebox that was a permanent prop in *The Honeymooners* set. He made a funny bit out of looking through the icebox for something to eat.

We were holding our breath in the control room. The stage manager was running around backstage trying to find Gleason while Carney continued to bluff it out on stage. By some miracle of good luck, Art found an orange in the icebox, and for the next two minutes he sat at the kitchen table and peeled that orange. That's all he did, so help me God. He didn't say a word. He just sat there in front of millions of people, and peeled an orange. Of course, it was the funniest two minutes I've ever seen, but that's not important. What stunned me was the complete trust this man had in his own talent. He never faltered for a split second, and I doubt if anyone watching the show at home was aware that anything was wrong.

Jackie and Audrey made their entrance through the bedroom door before Art finished peeling the orange, but I was convinced that if they hadn't shown up when they did, Carney could have gone on for hours thinking of funny things to do.

Incidentally, that's the only cue I remember Gleason missing during the two years I worked on the show. It wasn't because he was such a hard worker, or that he rehearsed himself to death. (I always believed that he was basically lazy.) Gleason has a photographic memory. He could memorize an entire *Honeymooners* sketch in one hour, and be letter perfect three days later when he went on the air.

Art Carney, Joyce Randolph, Jackie Gleason, and actor-turned-advertising-exec Dick Charles. Today Joyce Randolph is Mrs. Dick Charles. Despite the fact that in this photo Gleason seems to be taking all the credit, they were in fact introduced by *Honeymooners* costume designer Peggy Morrison.

Joyce Randolph and Art Carney back stage.

"For years now, Mama, who lives in Detroit, has been sending scolding letters to her daughter, Joyce Randolph, a lovely young thing with green eyes, blonde hair and a luscious shape that the millions who see her on television don't even suspect, on account of the things she's been doing since she came to New York. The letters have changed in the past few years, however. 'They're still complaining letters,' says Joyce, 'but nowadays Mama is complaining about something else. Her chief gripe these days is because I play the wife of a sewer worker.'" — *Pictorial TView*, May 29, 1955

"Audrey's sister Jayne, a dramatic actress who has appeared on many television shows and is a permanent panel member on *I've Got a Secret,* can't bear to watch her sister rehearse. 'She came one afternoon,' Audrey explains. 'It was a frantic day, but Jackie was relaxed, as always. We had gone through our sketch, but at the dress rehearsal, such as it is, she heard Jackie call to me from the stage, "Hey, Aud, give me your line here," and I called the line from out front in the theater. He said his line and then trailed off into the rest of his dialogue by saying ad-*da*-da-*da*, not bothering to repeat all the words, only the action, and then he asked for my next line and went through the same sort of performance. Then he gave Ray Bloch, our musical director, the music cue that came at that point, and that was that. Jayne looked at me. "That's your dress rehearsal?" she asked. I nodded. She has never come to rehearsal since.' " — *TV Show,* April 1953

Announcer Jack Lescoulie and Gleason during a rehearsal break at CBS.

The magazine *TV Show* once said: "There's bedlam every minute when Jackie's around. Horns squawk, people yell, and Jackie carries on like crazy. Rehearsals are so mad it's a shame they aren't televised as well as the show itself."

The writing, and re-writing, of the scripts doesn't end in the writers' offices. Here Jack Philbin, Art Carney, Jackie Gleason, and Joyce Randolph re-work their lines during rehearsal.

When Gleason played a double role on June 4, 1955, as Kramden and a mob boss who looked just like him, the audience laughed so hard and so much that the show ran overtime. The following day, at least one New York newspaper reported the event, not on the television page, but up front with the major news events of the world. It seemed that the entire population watched the following week's show to know if the mob exterminated Kramden. Gleason didn't disappoint them. He began the June 11 show with a verbal wrap-up of Ralph's underworld saga.

In another early episode, Ralph and Ed were assisting Alice's brother-in-law-to-be (played by George Petrie) in an attempt to elope with Alice's sister (played by Patti Pope, Mrs. George Petrie). When Gleason started up the ladder, it shook precariously. Patti was starting down the ladder, tennis racquet and parrot in hand, when Gleason told her to go back through the window and come out the door. They lost time. The plot was virtually rethought on stage to make it come out right, with Gleason taking a few minutes at the end of the show to tie up remaining loose ends for the audience.

On one of the trip-to-Europe episodes, someone from the audience marched up on stage on an impulse. Art Carney, thinking it was a gag arranged by Gleason, played along. Gleason, knowing better, clowned around just long enough to get the man off stage.

Sets have fallen down. Doors have jammed (on one show, Art Carney had to enter the Kramdens' apartment through the window). Time and again, things gone wrong have been made right by the "dream team" of showmanship.

And Jackie, who has been known to nod off to sleep at major contract negotiations, throws his entire energy into each show. This may say something about his priorities. It says a lot about why *The Honeymooners* reruns—a combined total of less than thirty hours of television (thirty-nine half-hour episodes and ten hour-long trip-to-Europe episodes, or about 10 percent of the total number of Lucille Ball shows)—have held their own for so long.

328 CHAUNCEY STREET HITS THE ROAD

Phil Cuoco provides everything from a full-grown elephant to props in small, medium, and large for a circus of small, medium, and large fleas, and for acts that range far and wide in between, all for Jackie Gleason's "American Scene Magazine."

As chief set decorator and interior designer he is charged with all of the trappings and furbelows that appear onstage and used by the star of the CBS TV network program. It's a job he's been doing for Gleason for fifteen years.

Phil, it so happens, is the unsung behind-the-scenes hero of the Miami Beach reunion of the *Honeymooners,* that is to say Gleason, Art Carney, and Audrey Meadows who will be seen in a musical comedy version of that fabled TV series now in syndication.

When Gleason struck on the idea a few weeks ago of getting together with his versatile chums in their still-familiar Brooklyn tenement flat, and the visitation of Carney from Mt. Vernon, New York, and Miss Meadows from Beverly Hills, California, was established, the next order of business, even while the script was still being readied, was a duplication of that self-same major setting: the Ralph Kramdens' flat.

Cuoco not only had the answer at his fingertips, he had the original props!

Two years back when Jackie and his sizable entourage entrained for Florida it was the job of all the department heads making up the cadre of the hour-long comedy-variety program to ship to the southern clime all the necessary paraphernalia pertinent to their respective units.

Although knowing full well at the time that Gleason had long ago scrapped his *Honeymooners* image, and with little chance at the time of its being revived, Cuoco hesitated to give the order to "strike" the set permanently. He says today his only reason for not doing so was that after fifteen years he well understood the mercurial nature of his talented boss.

So without a second thought he had crated and shipped to a Miami storeroom the main ingredients, shy of the walls and windows, of the easily recognized Kramden kitchen: the old-fashioned wooden icebox with the drip pan beneath, the Kramden sink and stove, and the three-tiered bureau and the plain old round kitchen table with three chairs.

Just prior to the first rehearsal of the *Honeymooners Revisited*—which cast includes, besides its stars, Anne Seymour, Phil Bruns, Sid Fields, Jan Crockett, Monroe Myers, and George DeVries—Gleason called a production staff meeting. At this session Cuoco revealed that he could on a moment's notice not only duplicate but produce the original set props used back in 1950 by Gleason and company, a pleased Gleason smiled on Cuoco a most benign smile, an appreciation from the star to his old workhorse that was far more meaningful than mere words.

Remarked Gleason later: "And when Art, Audrey, and I walked out there for the first time at rehearsal, and walked around the set doing our lines, it was like we'd never been away."

And Cuoco added still another touch of current vintage. A line in the script calls for a leopard-shaped antique with a clock in its stomach. He came up with that too, made by his department—but with less trouble than Cuoco had producing the interior of Ralph Kramden's kitchen.

J.G. Enterprises press release. Miami

Phil Cuoco's set design for the final scene of the Valentine Special 1978: Ralph's fully electric kitchen, color TV, and stereo system, minus the electric cables that will be festooned around the set. Notice that the toaster has been repositioned, from the center table to a side wall; since it is going to have to explode live on stage, it makes good sense not to set it off where the stars are sitting.

THE SCRIPTS

Every night is an opening night.
There are no out-of-town tryouts.

GOODMAN ACE

Sit through an episode of *The Honeymooners* without watching it, and you'll find you've still experienced a first-rate show. That's because some of the best comedy writers in the history of television have written scripts so rich in content that viewing can almost get in the way. All the dialogue contributes to the net effect; the jokes are in rapid succession, nothing is wasted. And nothing is ever said merely to fill time till the next funny bit.

When Steve Allen wrote, in *The Funny Men,* "Television is such a terrible grinding machine that we occasionally have to be reminded of just how great our comedians are," his praise was not limited to onstage celebrities. Even a comedian like Gleason, with full control of his scripts and a penchant for substantial contributions, needs funny writers. Without a constant supply of new material, any personality can get stale.

Any writer who gets stale is out of work. In the early 1950s there were maybe two hundred and fifty practicing TV comedy writers in the country and only a few reruns to fill programming time. Everybody needed words, so those writers were much in demand. But tolerance has never been a virtue of TV audiences, and the turnover was staggering. One writer's formula for success in the field was: "Marry a rich girl; short of this, marry a funny girl who can write for you."

Leonard Stern, co-writer of many of the classic *Honeymooners* scripts, once remarked that the big TV comedies go through three distinct phases for the viewers: "In the first stage the comedian's act is all new and the viewer is charmed. In the second stage there's a feeling of pleasant anticipation. The viewer knows what's coming next, but he's proud of it—he likes to tell his wife, 'Now watch him do so and so.' Then in the third stage there is only boredom, and that's the end of the road." Happily for Honeymoonies, Stern's formula for success has been to lodge his episodes firmly in phase two.

But even for writers who managed to meet the demand for quality material, the 1950s were not the best of times. If a show was funny, the celebrity was credited with its success. If it wasn't, the writers were fired. Before the advent of Rob Petrie (*The Dick Van Dyke Show*), the profession of television comedy writer was unknown to the citizenry of TV-land. Goodman Ace, one of television's most successful comedy writers, wrote in *The Book of Little Knowledge: More Than You Want to Know About Television:*

I simply hold that writing the lines for a performer to read is as much a craft as the performer's rendition of those lines on television. In the theater the writer is accorded the same dignity as the actor. In radio and television the caricatural conception that a writer is a necessary evil to have around the show has grown too popular. This is not to say that a performer may not lend stature to a writer's dialogue. On the other hand, seeing the writer and discussing the show with him may lend stature to the performer.

The media has always given so much attention to the range of Gleason's talents that his writers have rarely shared the spotlight. In the early days, Gleason's writing staff was reputed to change more frequently than anybody's with the exception of Red Buttons', although a few, like Marvin Marx, and Walter Stone stayed with Gleason for years. By the mid-1950s, he had settled on a team system that rotated essentially the same writers for alternate shows, or for alternating sketches within a single show. At first they worked in groups, later paired off. When they had to turn out a weekly hour-long show, they often worked nights; when they did the half-hour *Honeymooners,* they split the work among three teams: Marvin Marx and Walter Stone, Syd Zelinka and Leonard Stern, and Andy Russell and Herb Finn. Rod Parker, now producer of *Maude,* joined *The Honeymooners* when Gleason moved the show to Florida.

The actual ideas for shows came from Gleason (who, for a while, was billed as the last writer in the credits), Jack Philbin, or the writers. From a basic idea, they progressed to a script that could be discarded, rewritten, or run through rehearsals (and then rewritten). Says Jack Philbin, "Our formal rewrite is very often on stage."

Syd Zelinka says: "You'd tell your idea to Gleason, and his first reaction

Walter Stone, Marvin Marx, Jackie Gleason, Syd Zelinka, and Leonard Stern putting together a show shortly after Gleason's on-stage fall.

was always 'no.' Then you'd explain it to him, he'd let you try it. It usually worked okay after that."

One summer, Zelinka remembers, the writers had finished ten scripts in advance. When Gleason saw them at the beginning of the fall season, he rejected all ten as being entirely unplayable. "He was like a kid who kept hoping the school would burn down before September." But once Gleason got into the routine again, the scripts were reconsidered and accepted. Among them was the award-winning "$99,000 Answer."

For their contribution to the face of TV comedy, Gleason's writers got money in lieu of fame—an average of $750 a week in the early days of CBS, $1,250 by the late 1950s, more yet as the years wore on. They were paid a weekly salary, no matter how long individual scripts took. They received residuals for the taped shows, but only for the first seven cycles. The residuals were paid off by the end of the first year.

Their shows had become legends by the time the money stopped. But, in the words of Walter Stone, "It's a good feeling to be in a strange place and hear people quoting and laughing over your jokes. Like the night after Ralph was going to manage a prizefighter, and he said to Alice, 'You know, I've always wanted to get into sports. But I was too short for basketball, too slow to be a runner, and too fat to be a jockey.'

"And Alice said, 'You're too fat to be a horse.' "

HOW A JACKIE GLEASON CHARACTER SKETCH COMES INTO BEING

Jackie ("Mr. Saturday Night") Gleason, whose "live" full-hour comedy-variety show is featured on CBS Television Saturday nights (8:00–9:00 PM, EST), has had numerous requests to explain how his various characterizations which have become so well known to millions of viewers, are created and what steps are taken toward this end.

Gleason and script supervisor Joe Bigelow, explain that the building of a Jackie Gleason characterization routine or sketch procedure is about as follows:

This being a variety show, the Gleason characters do a variety of things, thus there's a variety of approaches to the construction of the sketches themselves.

Ideally, the writers (there are six writers working in teams of three, plus a script editor) conceive an idea for a "Poor Soul" sketch, or a sketch involving one of the other Gleason characters—Reggie Van Gleason III, Fenwick Babbitt, *The Honeymooners,* Joe the Bartender, Mother Fletcher,

Rudy the Repairman and the others. They work out this idea in sufficient detail to be articulate in its telling. It is then described verbally to Gleason. Gleason then rejects the basic idea, or accepts the outline in whole or in part. If accepted, Gleason and the writers work out the idea in more detail, then the writers put a first draft on paper. There is another discussion with Gleason regarding further changes, and the writers complete the final draft.

This is the ideal procedure, but there are variations. Some times the idea originates with the writers. Sometimes with Gleason himself. For example, the "Poor Soul" sketch for the first show of the year was written in its entirety by Jackie himself.

Thus there is no set rule in the building of a sketch. The one rule followed is that set down by Gleason for all the characters, and that is that fundamentally all situations must be based on truth—on something that "could happen." The characters and their antics may seem fantastic at times, but the "story" must be legitimate. Another rule is that the characters must at all times remain in character. Ideas that take them out of character, no matter how good or funny they may be in themselves, are rejected. The "Poor Soul," for example, must at all times be precisely what the name implies. First this is a pantomime sketch, and neither the "Poor Soul" nor the other characters ever speak. The "Poor Soul" must have no job, no worldly possessions beyond the bare necessities, cannot indulge in luxuries, must never reject anything or anyone, but is always rejected himself. This limits the field for the writers in the conception of ideas, but it is this constant and vigilant insistence of Jackie's that all characters remain "in character" that has resulted in the Gleason characters having a life expectancy far beyond those of any other character creations on television.

Beyond the writing itself, there are two additional steps in the building of a sketch, with the writing of course the necessary first step. Then, and of equal importance, comes the rehearsal, when the sketch is put "on its feet" before the cameras. Here the flaws, if any, are found, and here too improvisations and additions will be found, and deletions made, and here Gleason builds it into a playable vehicle. Then, most important, comes the actual performance on the air, and here as well Jackie will add to its value not only in the playing of what has been written and rehearsed, but by the extension of one or more pieces of business, or an ad-lib, very often guided by the reaction of the audience as he goes along.

The Gleason writing staff, besides Gleason himself, consists of: Marvin Marx, Walter Stone, Syd Zelinka, Andy Russell, Herb Finn, Eli Basse, writers; Joe Bigelow, script editor.

Jack Philbin is executive producer of *The Jackie Gleason Show;* Jack Hurdle producer, Stanley Poss assistant producer and Frank Satenstein director. Jack Lescouli announces the show. Ray Bloch conducts a thirty-five piece orchestra. The entire production is supervised by Mr. Gleason.

This is a press release from the Columbia Broadcasting System, December 4, 1956.

THE WORDS AND MUSIC

*We've never worked with anyone who's more of a joy
to work with. Jackie knows what he wants;
that's 90 percent of the battle.*

LYN DUDDY AND JERRY BRESLER

When the Trip-to-Europe episodes of *The Honeymooners* have been rerun a few dozen times, people will be singing the words and music of Duddy and Bresler the way they now quote the show's dialogue.

When this happens, they will have been exposed to the songs about a few dozen hours longer than Jackie was when he first performed them. Of course, he approved the music in advance, frequently contributing to its composition. But on the subject of rehearsal, he was as casual as ever. Often he heard the words and music only once before show time; what he couldn't remember he got from Jerry between scenes in the wings while the show was in progress. This approach might have shaken other less seasoned professionals; this team never missed a beat.

Altogether, Lyn Duddy and Jerry Bresler wrote forty-four complete musicals for *The Honeymooners* in the late 1960s. They wrote to order, averaging five to six songs a week but sometimes racking up as many as fourteen for one *Honeymooners* show. Their "week" consisted of three days; by the fourth day they started rehearsing with a cast as big as that of a Broadway musical.

The flavor of the production numbers ranged widely. Whatever an episode's setting, the music would be in character with the surroundings—a paso doble in Spain, a tarantella in Italy, modal music in Ireland. When set in Brooklyn, the songs would celebrate rooftops, the Raccoon Lodge, and supermarkets. (In the supermarket number, the June Taylor Dancers did their kicks from grocery carts.)

Some of the duets and solos written for *The Honeymooners* are still being performed. And the song "There's Nothing I Haven't Sung About" became a Bing Crosby classic; it was created for Crosby for an episode which brought Ralph and Ed to Hollywood under the mistaken impression that they were born songwriters.

Jackie has said that Duddy and Bresler "captured things in a way more renowned songwriters couldn't have done because the whole trick for these TV shows is *getting* the audience on the first eight bars."

But the talented team, while accepting the compliment with justifiable pride, is generally more philosophical about its accomplishment. "Do you know what it means to write a musical comedy in three days?" asks Lyn Duddy. "It means taking a pad and pencil everywhere you go. And never letting a good idea slip by."

THEY CREATE A MUSICAL A WEEK

Most Broadway songwriting teams would be regarded as paragons of pro-ductivity, to be looked on with envy by their less industrious colleagues, if they turned out the music and lyrics of more than one show a year. But what would you say if I told you that there are two words-and-melody fellows who actually create the equivalent of a Broadway musical once a week?

You'd probably come back with, "Incredible!" or "Aw, you're puttin' me on!" But two such miracle workers really exist—Lyn Duddy and Jerry Bresler—and millions of Americans from coast to coast hear the results of their creativity on the Jackie Gleason Saturday night shows over CBS-TV.

It is they who produce the scores of Jackie's *The Honeymooners* on a weekly basis, to the amazement of some of the most famous songwriters of America.

"Difficult, yes," Lyn told me, "but it's an overwhelming thrill when we get a call or a note from such masters as Richard Rodgers, Irving Berlin, Johnny Mercer, Harry Warren, Arthur Schwartz or Jerry Herman. And we have heard from all of them."

And now, even more important, they have also heard from Jackie Gleason. He has come up with the greatest challenge of their careers.

"I'm going to give you a chance to show what you can do with a complete hour devoted to your songs," The Great One announced.

So on next Saturday night over CBS-TV, you'll see a special hour-long "Calendar Show," featuring no less than twelve Duddy-Bresler songs. And delivering these numbers will be such *Honeymooners* stars as Gleason him-self, Art Carney, Sheila MacRae, and Jane Kean, with special guest, Marilyn Maye.

This occasion will be a challenge not only to the two songwriters, but also to the producers of Broadway musicals. For when one considers their records of achievement, their versatility and the top-notch quality of the numbers they have created, it would seem that Duddy and Bresler are ready for the Big Street. As a matter of fact, the chances are good that soon they'll be hailed as among the top men of the musical theater.

"How do you feel about this assignment?" I asked.

"It's by far the most demanding we've ever had," said Jerry, "and remember we've had some tough ones."

"For examples?"

"Well, we've created nightclub and concert material for such stars as Robert Goulet, Gordon and Sheila MacRae, Steve Lawrence and Eydie Gorme, Kate Smith, Totie Fields, Connie Francis and many others."

"Tell me this: Is it true that some of the biggest names in the music world shy away from writing for television?"

"Yes; even the best songwriting teams, as a rule, try to avoid TV," Lyn said. "Some of them have taken occasional fliers in the medium, gambled their hard-earned reputations on specials, only to have their shows flop. And remember, when you flop on TV, it's a megathon bomb that echoes through millions of living rooms.

"But coming back to our special song show, here's a point that should be emphasized. We couldn't do it if we didn't have a star like Jackie," Lyn explained. "Gleason is a perfectionist; knows exactly what he wants; and that's a tremendous help. You have no idea how frustrating it is for writers who have to work with a star who has vague ideas about what he wants, but can't spell them out. With Gleason that's never a problem.

"Also we have another advantage. In addition to his collection of stars, which includes June Taylor who could stage the Russian Revolution, we work

The mutual admiration society accepts applause on stage. Jerry Bresler (left) and Lyn Duddy (right) appreciate Gleason's sense of showmanship. and Gleason likes the way the team turns out quality tunes under unbelievable pressure.

with Walter Stone, Rod Parker and Bob Hilliard, three of the funniest writers in TV.''

"Just how do you work with them on a show?" I wanted to know.

"They give us a rough outline of the following Saturday night's story. Then we try to come up with song ideas that will advance their plots.

"Quite often we don't hear their finished scripts and they don't hear our songs until the entire show is performed in a practice production presentation for Jackie and the rest of the cast. And surprisingly enough, it almost always works. So far this season we've had to cut only one song because it didn't fit the script.''

"How are you preparing for this January 3 show?"

"Intensely," Jerry confided. "We've gone three or four days at a stretch without sleep.''

"But we love it," Lyn added. "The anticipation . . . the excitement . . . it really peps you up. We're never without pads, pencils and manuscript paper—whether in restaurants, phone booths or planes.''

Life for them is a constant exchange of musical notes and lyric ideas. On one occasion when Lyn was working in New York and Jerry remained in Miami Beach, the former dictated his lyrics to the latter over the long distance phone. Then after about a half-hour, they discovered they had been cut off and Lyn had been talking into a dead phone. Since then they tape every lyric and melody to be worked on during the absence of one or the other.

But regardless of where they may be, they love working together. "We're like two teachers feeding each other ideas. We try to complement each other, never compete," Lyn said.

Lyn Duddy, who was born of a show business family in the Hell's Kitchen section of New York, was a child prodigy and became a writer and choral director of many of the most important shows of radio and TV, including the *Kate Smith Hour*. Jerry Bresler, a native of Chicago, also has had a distinguished career as conductor, arranger and composer on such programs as *The Arthur Godfrey Show*, the Ford, the Dinah Shore, Andy Williams and dozens of other specials.

"What are your plans for the immediate future?" I asked.

"We intend to write those *Honeymooner* songs just as long as Jackie enjoys doing them. They're such fun that we hope we never finish," Jerry answered.

"However, the Gleason schedules permit us to work also on other projects. And now we'd love to do something exciting for the theater," Lyn told me.

And this statement, if you ask me, should be a tip to some imaginative stage musical producer to dash—not saunter—immediately to a telephone. And then having reached Duddy and Bresler, to say: "How about you fellows doing something for the Broadway theater?"

This article by Ben Gross appeared in the *New York Daily News*, Dec. 28, 1969.

THE GLEASON STYLE

A FANTASY WHEREIN RALPH KRAMDEN MEETS REGINALD VAN GLEASON III, THE POOR SOUL, CHARLIE BRATTON, AND JOE THE BARTENDER

BY MICHAEL R. LAULETTA

The people in Ralph Kramden's life were many and varied, and quite a few of them—for obvious reasons—were unable to make an appearance at the Kramden apartment in Bensonhurst. However, they are worthy of mention in a compendium such as this. Ralph knew them and associated with them on a hit-and-miss basis for years.

The first was Reginald Van Gleason III, the spoiled son of a spoiled millionaire. He had a penchant for expensive whiskey and expensive women but was seldom able to handle either. Ralph first became aware of him in the offices of the Gotham Bus Company. For almost a week straight, on a daily basis, he was seen coming and going from the offices of Mr. Marshall and Mr. Harper. Rumors of the rotund gentleman in the white tie and tails spread quickly through the depot and it was later learned that Van Gleason's father was trying to buy the bus company for his son. It seems Van Gleason had gotten bored with his electric train set and wanted a bigger fleet of toys at his disposal. Why the sale was never finalized, no one could say.

"... Reggie Van Gleason III, the high-society rake. You'll notice he always combs his hair flat, because he has no time to fool around with it. He's always wearing formal clothes, because he associates them with his most enjoyable moments. He has an utter disregard for his parents, because he considers them only a means for booze money."—Jackie Gleason, *Liberty* magazine, February 1955

However, it wasn't long afterward, while working an infrequent weekend night, that Kramden again saw Van Gleason. With his top hat replaced by a driver's cap, Van Gleason got on the Madison Avenue bus—accompanied by the ever-present flask and ever-attentive blonde. At the very next red light, with all the pomp and ceremony of a strutting matador, Van Gleason removed his white gloves and flowing cape, ready to "take the controls."

Ralph refused the request, even after "a-hum, a-hum, a-humming" his way past an offer for a share of the flask's contents and the blonde's attention. Van Gleason, though, was just as adamant. Fortunately, three more red lights into the argument, a patrol car containing two policemen, Van Gleason's parents, and the mayor, caught up to the bus and escorted Reginald home.

Ralph still sees Van Gleason from time to time, usually on an early Sunday morning. He steps aboard, pays his fare with a fifty-dollar bill (explaining any change due him should go to the "Bus Drivers' Benevolent Fund") and orders Kramden to "get me to the Ritz and step on it." Ralph, depending on his mood, smiles or scowls and takes the millionaire into the depot with him. Once there, an exaggerated bow and sweep of his top hat, signals Van Gleason's appreciation and the two part company. Ralph often wonders if he will be mentioned in Van Gleason's will.

Another irregular on Ralph's Madison Avenue run is the Poor Soul. He is usually greeted by mixed emotions from the driver. The Poor Soul is the nicest man in the world, but trying to dig a few coins out of his pocket purse takes enough time to try the patience of a saint.

Once he's paid his fare and given Ralph that weak smile of his he takes the seat directly behind the driver. Ralph grits his teeth, wipes a meaty hand across his chin and lips, and waits. He has always hated people who sit right behind him and strike up conversations about everything from the latest political news to the state of their grandmother's cat. With the Poor Soul, though, it's ten times worse. Think of how trying it must be for short-tempered Ralph Kramden to drive a bus through rush-hour traffic while carrying on a conversation with a mute.

And the conversation is always the same—the Poor Soul's latest job. Over the years, Ralph has heard about his putting cherries on whipped cream cakes that travel down a conveyor belt at superhuman speed, putting shoes in boxes that move on a conveyor belt faster than they can be counted, and seemingly hundreds of other jobs—all connected with conveyor-belt work. Ralph once asked him why he always took the same kind of work and the Poor Soul mimed his way through an explanation that that was all he knew. Ralph just rolled his eyes and almost drove up on a curb.

Trying to ignore him was impossible. The Poor Soul used the rearview mirror to "talk," and he expected Ralph to "listen." If Ralph didn't keep his eyes on the mirror, a sharp tap on the shoulder and an index finger in the mirror got his attention again.

It was while carrying on one of these conversations that Ralph almost got into his first accident. Only quick reflexes at the last second avoided a pileup and a short time later Ralph received his award as the safest bus driver in the city.

He still sees the Poor Soul—on a daily basis when he's working and not at all while between jobs—but as aggravating as the Poor Soul is while on the bus, Ralph worries about him when he's out of work. Every once in a while, he'll hope against hope the Poor Soul has found a permanent job in another part of the city—accessible by subway. But he knows better.

"The Poor Soul is the most saint-like of my characters. He accepts the harshness of life without complaint, and never fights back. You'll observe he wears a sweater and a lot of buttons. These give him a sense of security. His many buttons suggest he can lock himself in, womb-like." —Jackie Gleason, *Liberty* magazine, February 1955.

Ralph Kramden doesn't like Charlie Bratton. "Loudmouth," as everyone calls him, thinks he knows everything. He certainly has an opinion about everything. Thank goodness he doesn't ride Ralph's bus!

Ralph usually sees him on those infrequent days when Alice doesn't fill his lunch pail, or on those more frequent days when his lunch pail just isn't filled enough. When Norton can't meet him at the Gotham Cafeteria, Ralph

"Joe the Bartender is a garrulous raconteur based on all the bartenders I used to know in Brooklyn."—Jackie Gleason, *Liberty* magazine, February 1955

stops in at a small diner near the depot. And it never fails—Loudmouth is always there, sitting next to a skinny little guy who orders things like watercress sandwiches and fishbone soup. Along with this, he gets a healthy helping of insults from Bratton. And while waiting for his own order, that ridiculous straw hat perched on his head, Bratton passes the time by banging the salt and pepper shakers on the counter while singing at the top of his lungs. The skinny guy seems impervious to all of Loudmouth's crudities, however, and it isn't long before Bratton goes looking for another dining partner. It's always Ralph and there's always an argument.

Ralph has tried everything—from counting to ten to quoting a rhyme that starts "pins and needles, needles and pins . . ." but nothing seems to work. An argument always ensues and nine times out of ten it's about bus drivers being inconsiderate and ill-mannered. Words like "bum" and "nut" and phrases such as "Oh, yeah" and "You're gone" fly back and forth the entire time.

Once it was rumored that Bratton was going to challenge Kramden to a fistfight, but then word spread around the place about Ralph knocking out a bully with one punch and helping to capture two killers that had threatened Alice and him. Since then, things have quieted down a bit but everyone expects Bratton to start up with him again at any time. Ralph had decided not to eat at that diner anymore, but how could he pass up the free chili every Tuesday, bought by the regulars for his heroics against the two killers?

Ralph does like Joe the Bartender. Even though he has a reputation as one of the world's worst drinkers, Ralph does enjoy stopping in to see Joe from time to time, just for a short beer or two.

After a hard day along Madison Avenue or a rough evening with his mother-in-law, walking through those swinging doors is like stepping into another world for him. Joe is always there with a "Hiya, Ralph" and later a "Hiya, Mr. Dennehy." Even Ed Norton drops in once in a while. He doesn't drink either, but he says he likes to sit at the bar and sniff the aromas from the Hong Kong Gardens next door.

Ralph always leaves Joe with a smile. After an hour of stories about Crazy Guggenheim and the rest of the gang, Ralph feels refreshed. He usually stops off on the way home for a pizza or wedge of Fattiamamata cheese for him and Alice. Maybe one of these days, he'll convince Joe the Bartender to join the Raccoons. He certainly has all the qualifications.

There were plenty of others Ralph knew, too (he even met Reginald Van Gleason's brother once), but he doesn't see them as often as Joe, Charlie Bratton, Van Gleason, or the Poor Soul. It's just too bad he can't invite them over for dinner one night. But Alice would never stand for it. Think of the scene in that tiny apartment!

Michael Lauletta is a writer of western and macho fiction who was born and grew up in Brooklyn within five miles of Jackie Gleason's old neighborhood.

HOW TO TELL A STORY
By Jackie Gleason

AUTHOR'S NOTE: *There is a hilarious* Honeymooners *episode, first broadcast on April 21, 1956, in which Ralph practices a shaggy dog story he is going to tell the Raccoon Lodge. Gleason's performance is brilliant—Ralph's is hopeless. Was this perfectly straightforward article in* Good Housekeeping *of March 1956 the inspiration for that classic scene?*

There must be an answer to the question of how to tell a funny story and be the life of the party, and someday I hope to find it out.

There are parties at which everybody is the life of the party. Take the one we threw in New York last year, a small ball to celebrate the opening of the new offices of jackie gleason enterprises. There are twenty-four floors of the Park Sheraton Hotel beneath our quarters, and complaints about the noise were recorded from every one of the floors; they tell me the switchboard resembled the control panel of a Univac machine. That party must have been a success: Nobody spoke to anybody else for weeks afterward.

Seriously, though, the reason the party was a success is that it was carefully planned, and the same thing is necessary when a partygoer wants a good response from his jokes and stories. I don't mean to say that you should actually rehearse your lines for a party, but a little forethought can make you a much more entertaining guest.

For one thing, all successful storytellers have a good sense of organization and an instinct for the surprise twist at the end, which is one of the most important elements of humor. Abe Burrows, who was a great comedy writer for radio before he found out that he was a great comedy writer (and director) for the legitimate stage, used to say that a funny line was a straight sentence with a curve at the end. For example, there is S. J. Perelman's famous comeback to the reporter who inquired if he'd ever been sick. "Why, yes," said Perelman, "I've had Bright's disease—and Bright's had mine."

Or there is Groucho Marx' famous "I'd horsewhip you—if I had a horse."

Of course, one of the most horrifying aspects of comedy is the basic fact that what is funny to one person or group is not equally amusing to others. The shoeshops of the world are now full of would-be comics who never learned that. It took me some time to realize that certain things that break me up leave many of my pals stony-faced. (I like to tell about the day Jimmy Ryan waltzed into my apartment with a little box of nutmeg in his hand. "Let's make some brandy milk punches," he lisped. This kills me—and when I tell it to some people, it makes them wish it really did.) But there are some raconteurs whose stories have never got a real laugh and never will—for example, the guy who begs you to stop him if you've heard his story before. He begins, and you have indeed heard it before—but try to stop him! Even if you nod pleasantly and attempt to wander away, he follows you. When you fail to laugh, he's indignant.

There's also the indefatigable laborer who wants to tell the story directly into you ear—but if he can't get that, any other part of your face will do. He usually has some success, because by the time he's three sentences into his jokes you're so numbed that almost any finish is acceptable.

The laugher is another offender. This man really enjoys a good story—so much so that he not only laughs constantly as he tells it but collapses at the end, thereby ruining it.

Possibly the worst offender is the fighting-uphill type. This chap has to untangle himself from a million roadblocks before he gets to his point. "My brother Tom," he begins, "he's in the umbrella business in Schenectady—wonderful town, Schenectady: I've spent a lot of time there since Tom moved up that way from Davenport, Iowa. And there's another wonderful spot; it was Bix Beiderbecke's birthplace, you know, and you know who Bix was. . . ." and on, and on, and on.

By the time this character gets to his point you've been on a cross-country tour by slow bus, and you've forgotten what he was trying to tell you in the first place. That's all right; so has he.

He has a kind of mirror-image in the slow-downhill type. This one begins a story pretty smoothly but keeps forgetting details as he goes along. Finally, when he gets to the punch line, a beatific smile crosses his kisser. You're hopeful that even though he's omitted some things, the ending's going to be worth the wait.

"You probably won't believe this," says he, "but I forgot how it comes out."

Because I am a character comic, or sketch comic, primarily, it's hard for me to set down any specific rules for success in party joke telling. I've yet to learn all the rules. But there are a few that can be listed without too much danger of wholesale complaints.

Here they are:

1. *Know your audience.* It's silly to try any story unless you're reasonably sure you're not going to be tossed out on your ear. A good joke has never been topped as an icebreaker, but even the best joke told under the wrong conditions can act as a freezer. It's a good idea to size up your audience as much as possible before taking the plunge, no matter how small the audience may be.

2. *Know your joke.* If necessary, review it in your own mind before you attempt to utter it aloud. There are few people more exasperating than those who bog down in the middle of anecdotes or leave out pertinent lines.

3. *Don't clutter your yarn.* Avoid back alleys, detours, and diversions. If you're reminded of something else in the middle of a story, save it. You may be able to get an extra laugh later on. Of course, if it's an appropriate reference, good for a small subsidiary laugh, throw it in.

4. *Don't tell your story too fast or too slow.* Let all details follow each other naturally and unhurriedly. Don't snap them out, and don't drag them. Watch your listener's face constantly to see how he's taking it.

5. *If you're losing your audience, quit.* Don't tug at sleeves and insist on being heard. There's nothing worse than being a compulsive storyteller.

6. *Pause ever so slightly before delivering the kicker.* Every joke is a minuscule drama. It ought to be told as though it were being done by actors.

7. *Don't attempt dialects you can't handle expertly.* Dialect, if done improperly or mockingly, can be almost unbearable—and rude as well.

8. *Don't laugh as you finish, thereby obscuring the whole point.* Once your final line is out, it's fine to laugh along with your listeners—as long as you don't laugh harder than they.

9. *If the joke falls flat, don't apologize.* The apologizer is almost worse than the inept storyteller. Even more boorish is the man who insults his listeners' intelligence by implying that the joke is over their heads. If they didn't understand the joke they'll tell you and you can make it clear. If they did understand it, but didn't think it funny, remember that it takes all kinds, etc., etc. And don't under any circumstances say that they *might* think it funny if only they knew the people involved. If you've laid a bomb, it isn't necessary to draw a gun and blow your brains out. All that's needed is a graceful shrug. That might even draw the laugh you didn't get in the first place.

10. *Don't press your luck.* After scoring with one funny story, don't let it go to your head—unless you're pretty sure the next one is just as good. In other words, quit while you're ahead.

Don't think for a minute that any of these rules can't be broken. There are exceptions to every one. If there were foolproof rules for successful party storytelling, my own business would be fiercely overpopulated.

I don't pretend I know the answers. As I mentioned in the beginning, I'm still trying to find out how to be the life of the party. There is one consolation. The research is most agreeable!

IV. THE HONEYMOONERS PLOT SYNOPSES

THE BASIC SITUATION

Ralph is a fat, jealous, conclusion-jumping, bigmouthed bus driver with an ego that is dwarfed only by his waistline. He has a wife who alternately battles and babies him; a friend who is a constant source of companionship, aggravation, and sewer jokes; and a walk-up tenement "castle" on Chauncey Street in Brooklyn of which he has persuaded himself that he is the "king" to offset his pawn/jester status in the outside world. In his leisure time, he bowls, plays pool, rails about male supremacy, and dresses up like a Raccoon. Because he is poor and has always been poor (and because his wife is forced to share his poverty) he tries too hard to get rich overnight. Ironically, his crazy hairbrained schemes, though doomed to failure, seem to assure him that he is edging ever closer to success.

Given any one of a number of situations, Ralph can be expected to make a fool of himself, and to involve himself and his cohorts in the consequences of his behavior. Whatever the situation, Alice and/or Ed will get in the way (as might an occasional in-law, or even Ralph's conscience); minor flare-ups or full-scale wars always result. Sometimes, anticipating fireworks, Ralph resorts to deception to avoid an actual encounter (as, on occasion, does Alice); but deceptions, like every other variety of scheme on *The Honeymooners*, always backfire. At the close of a given episode, Ralph is no better or worse off than before. It is this never-ending journey from square one to square one, this combination of clearly defined character and predictable situation, that makes *The Honeymooners* a structurally successful situation comedy series.

Departure from the basic pattern only reinforces it: if Ralph ends an episode certain to lose his job (because his boss has identified him as the author of a caustic letter, or because he's going to humiliate a bus company executive in a golf tournament), we know that he will somehow salvage himself by the beginning of the next show. If he wins a trip to Europe, in every country he visits he will still be the same fool he's always been, and he will return to the same humble apartment when his tour is over.

Over the past twenty-eight years, *The Honeymooners* has had a variety of formats, from sketch within a variety show to hour-long special. Some episodes, filmed on kinescopes that are now lost or destroyed, have only been seen once. Others have been filmed for syndication and rerun scores of times. Many of the late 1950s episodes that were never themselves rerun were "revived" in updated musical versions to be performed in the late 1960s.

In revisiting the Kramdens and Nortons, the following plot synopses are presented in two parts: those episodes now in syndication; and those episodes, never filmed for syndication, that have appeared only on CBS or ABC network TV. The date listed with each show title is its original air date.

THE SYNDICATED SHOWS
1955-1956

For one season only (September 1955–September 1956), *The Honeymooners*, starring Jackie Gleason, Art Carney, Audrey Meadows, and Joyce Randolph, was filmed with the Electronicam process for later syndication. Each of these episodes has been rerun over one hundred times, making them, in all probability, the best-known scripts in the history of television. Because they are so familiar to viewers, they are summarized in some detail below. Accompanying each entry is its original air date, its official title, and a notation of emphasized theme elements.

①
Title: "TV or Not TV"
Date: October 1, 1955
Themes: *Deception (Alice), Poverty, Scheme, Ralph vs. Alice*

Ralph is suspicious of Alice, and no wonder. She's calling him "sweetums" and "Ralphie," and even "sweetheart face." But what does she want? At last, it comes out: a TV set. In fourteen years of marriage, Alice wails, they have not changed one stick of furniture. She has had it with looking at the icebox, the stove, the sink, and four walls while Ralph is out enjoying himself with his pals. She wants to look at Liberace.

Ralph, complaining that they can't afford a TV, decides to split the cost of a set with Ed. It will be kept in the Kramdens' apartment, although both Kramdens and Nortons will use it. Yet, once the set is installed, Ralph and Ed cannot agree on what they want to watch. Ed prefers *Captain Video*, Ralph prefers old movies. The two quarrel, compromise, try to outsmart each other, and quarrel again, night after night.

One night, although barely able to stay awake, Ralph is up till 1:00 A.M. watching the Late Show. He goes out the wrong door on his way to the bedroom and falls down the stairs. No sooner does he find the bedroom than Norton sneaks into the apartment, turns on a murder mystery, and awakens Ralph with the sound of gunshots and a screaming woman. There's a three-way battle among Alice, Ralph, and Ed, until Alice retreats in futile annoyance and the boys agree to watch the rest of the movie.

They fall asleep in front of the set. Alice reappears to tuck them in, admitting out loud to her snoring spouse that for once he was right: they never should have gotten a TV.

②
Title: "Funny Money"
Date: October 8, 1955
Themes: *Conclusion-Jumping, Mother-in-law, Ralph vs. Alice, Ralph vs. the World, Poverty*

There's this cellar, see, and counterfeiters. In walks Ziggy with a tale of woe: he had a suitcase full of counterfeit bills, a total of 50 grand, that he had to leave on a Madison Avenue bus when a cop started following him. Since he can't risk going to the lost-and-found department of the Gotham Bus Company to reclaim his suitcase, he decides to wait the thirty days until the unclaimed suitcase becomes the property of the driver who found it—Ralph Kramden. Then he will follow Ralph home.

Ralph of course, suddenly $50,000 richer, doesn't stop to wonder why nobody showed up for the money. He starts buying tailored suits, new furniture, a car, even a telephone. He quits his job. Norton becomes his uniformed chauffeur. Even Ralph's mother-in-law, who usually can't stand the sight of him, starts treating him with fawning respect. Not until a neighborhood youngster is jailed for passing counterfeit money (money Ralph gave him to run an errand) does Ralph catch on. But it's too late. The crooks come to his apartment, pretending to be police detectives. They learn that Ralph threw the money in the stove to destroy the evidence. They blow their cover and come at Ralph.

In the nick of time, the real police arrive. (It seems Ralph also gave Officer Grogan a counterfeit bill.) Everyone is marched off to the station house for questioning.

A sadder but wiser Ralph returns home cleared of all charges, with the brief memory of extravagant wealth to tide him over the rocky road ahead . . . as he pays for the tailored suits he ordered, and returns humbled to the bus company to plead for his old job back.

3 **Title:** ''The Golfer''
Date: October 15, 1955
Themes: *Ralph's Big Mouth, Conclusion-Jumping, Ralph vs. Ed, Ralph vs. Alice, Scheme*

Ralph has started a rumor that he's going to be the new assistant traffic manager at the Gotham Bus Company, but it is totally unfounded and highly unlikely, since Mr. Harper, the traffic manager responsible for naming his new assistant, hardly knows Ralph is alive.

Determined to get on Harper's good side, Ralph pretends to be a great golfer. Harper, genuinely interested, sets up a golf date with Ralph, who actually thinks he can master the game in time. Then the date of the game is moved up.

Then, at home, Ralph learns that he has no aptitude whatever for golf. Just as he is lamenting his big mouth to Alice, word arrives that Harper can't play because he has chipped a bone in his ankle. Ralph, who can never be accused of learning a lesson, shoots off his big mouth once again, with the result that he is slated for a new partner in the forthcoming golf tournament: Mr. Douglas, a vice president of the bus company.

(A. J. Russell, one of the writers of this episode, recalls that this was the first to dress Ralph in an outlandish costume—his golfer's togs—and that the wild response to his appearance inspired such later episodes as ''The Man from Space.'')

④ Title: "A Woman's Work Is Never Done"
Date: October 22, 1955
Themes: *Ralph vs. Alice, Ralph vs. the World, Male Supremacy, Scheme*

Ralph lights into Alice for not having his bowling shirt ready for the big tournament. She tells him how sorry she is, and how busy she has been. He, of course, refuses to believe that a housewife can be busy, and decides to set up a system of demerits and penalties to keep Alice in line. She rebels, deciding that she will get a job to get out of the apartment; she will pay for a maid out of her salary.

At the employment agency, Ralph and Alice attempt to hire a maid and are offered jobs as domestics themselves. Ralph puts on his best windbag airs. For his troubles he is offered Thelma, a maid built like a brick oven who refuses to do heavy work because she's "sickly."

Needless to say, the arrangement doesn't work out. Ralph spends a good deal of his time at home, with Norton, ordering Thelma around and ringing for her with an idiotic bell. She quits; as do the three little maids who succeed her, all in a row.

Without a maid, Ralph is stuck doing the housework. Norton is willing to help him, but for a dollar an hour. Ralph comes up with a scheme to flatter Alice back to home and hearth. It doesn't work, and he is forced to admit to Alice that her job at home is at least as hard as driving a bus.

Who has won the battle of the sexes? Who wins the war? Who knows! Alice has won in the only way she wants to: she gives up her job, to keep house for a momentarily more appreciative Ralph.

And where is Ed through all this? He's out in the hall ringing for Thelma—his new maid.

⑤ Title: "A Matter of Life and Death"
Date: October 29, 1955
Themes: *Mother-in-Law, Poverty, Conclusion-Jumping, Deception (Alice, Ralph), Ralph vs. the World*

Alice is home, awaiting the vet's report on her mother's ailing collie, but she is being secretive so that Ralph won't find out about the $10 she paid for the examination. Ralph is also awaiting a doctor's report, since he's been under the weather of late. Naturally, the vet's report arrives while Alice is out and Ralph thinks that *he* has the collie's arterial monochromia—and only six months to live!

In order to have some money to leave Alice in his will, he decides to sell his story to a magazine. *American Weekly* offers him $5,000 for his week-by-week exclusive account that will end when he drops dead. He is happy to accept.

When Alice sees the first article in the series, she can't believe her eyes. Then, when Ralph tells her about the doctor's report, she is hysterical with laughter. She explains to Ralph, who is relieved until it dawns on him that the magazine could sue him for fraud.

Afraid to admit the truth to the *American Weekly,* he arranges for Norton to pose as a doctor who saw the article and rushed to his side to cure him. But the magazine accuses *Norton* of fraud when he reveals that the last school he attended was P.S. 31 in Oyster Bay.

Ralph is forced to confess. The magazine agrees to run the story with the new, happy ending, although of course Ralph will no longer get $5,000. Ralph goes home to Alice with his conscience clear and the episode ends with a good laugh.

6

Title: "The Sleepwalker"
Date: November 5, 1955
Themes: *Ralph vs. Ed, Ralph vs. the World*

Trixie awakens Ralph and Alice in the middle of the night. Norton is sleepwalking again, and Ralph has to go after him before he hurts himself. Norton, eating a banana as he sleepwalks across the roof, is safer than Ralph, who catches up with Norton just in time to slip on his banana peel.

Next night, Ralph is persuaded to swap beds with Trixie, but he sleeps so soundly that he doesn't hear Norton when his nightly somnambulism begins.

Ralph then sends for a psychiatrist who makes house calls, and who uses truth serum to get into Ed's subconscious.

In a trance, Ed reveals that he misses Lulu, the best dog he ever had. The psychiatrist wants to continue his tests on Ed, but Ralph concludes that all Norton needs is a new dog—and he throws the doctor out as abruptly as he would Norton.

By night number three, everyone including Ralph is congratulating Ralph for the "brainstorm" idea of getting Norton a little dog—until Ed enters, sleepwalking, holding the new Lulu in his arms.

7

Title: "Better Living Through TV"
Date: November 12, 1955
Themes: *Scheme, Ralph vs. Alice, Ralph is Fat, Ralph vs. the World*

Ralph knows how to make a fortune. For $200, he can buy 2,000 Handy Housewife Helpers (gadgets that include everything from corkscrew to wart remover). He wants to sell them for a dollar each by means of a live TV commercial in which he and Ed will star. That way, they can reach a wider audience than any door-to-door salesman, and in less time.

Ralph asks Alice to help him with the expenses of the commercial. She flatly refuses, reminding him of all the other surefire schemes he's lost money on in the past (wallpaper that glows in the dark that would do away with electric lights; a uranium field in Asbury Park; no-cal pizza). He threatens to walk out on her, and takes a parting shot at her sympathy: "You don't love me, you never loved me. . . . You married me because you were in love with my uniform."

The next time we see Ralph and Ed, they're wearing exaggerated chef's outfits and they're rehearsing their live TV spot. When the cameras roll, Ed remains calm but Ralph panics. Ed, as the Chef of the Past, complains to the TV audience that it takes far too many appliances to prepare a meal. He wishes, aloud, that someone would invent a device that could do the work of all the implements on the table. He keeps wishing out loud until Ralph, walking like a fat robot, is finally pushed into camera range by a stagehand. He can barely make his mouth work to deliver his lines. He identifies himself, haltingly, as the Chef of the Future. With his gadget of the future, the Handy Housewife Helper, he proceeds to cut an apple, then his hand, to ribbons. Bellowing in pain, he stumbles back into the scenery. As the set comes down around Ralph and another one of his schemes, Ed closes the commercial: "And now, back to Charlie Chan."

(8)

Title: "Pal O'Mine"
Date: November 19, 1955
Themes: *Conclusion-Jumping, Ralph is Fat, Ralph vs. Ed*

Ed and Trixie are about to have a party, to which about twenty guys from the sewer will be invited, to celebrate the promotion of Jim McKeever to foreman. Ed shows Alice the ring he is going to give McKeever to commemorate the occasion, and he leaves it with her to wrap.

Ralph comes home dead tired from working double shifts. ("You couldn't get me out of this house if you told me Jane Russell was running a party upstairs and couldn't get started till I arrived.") But he is not too tired to notice the ring, with its inscription "To a great pal, from Ed Norton." He slips it onto his fat finger. Since he can't get it off, Ed is forced to bring his party down to Ralph's to present Jim with the ring; Ralph throws everyone out, vowing that his friendship with Norton is finished forever.

The next night, Ralph has made plans to go bowling with Teddy Overman instead of Norton. Norton, with nowhere else to go, answers an emergency call from the sewer company. Overman arrives, demonstrates himself to be a total creep; he and Ralph join in bad-mouthing Ed until someone races into the apartment to tell Ralph that Ed has been injured in a sewer explosion.

Ralph rushes to the hospital, not knowing that Norton has already been discharged. He volunteers to give a transfusion to a patient whom he believes to be Norton. He sees Norton as he is being wheeled in for the transfusion. The friends reconcile and as Ralph is taken away, Ed calls after him and the attending physician, "While you got him in there, will you see what you can do about getting that ring off his finger?"

(9)

Title: "Brother Ralph"
Date: November 26, 1955
Themes: *Poverty, Male Supremacy, Jealousy, Deception, Ralph vs. Alice*

At Ralph's suggestion, the Gotham Bus Company has taken on a traffic expert to relieve some of the congestion on certain routes. The plan backfires on Ralph when he is one of the first drivers to be laid off indefinitely. Ralph makes another suggestion, this time at home, when he tells Alice to economize by cutting out

124

luxuries and high living. He accuses her of squandering. Now she is forced to make a suggestion: Ralph can stay home and do the housework, she'll get a job. Ralph hates the idea, but doesn't have any choice. What is worse, he finds out that Alice is only able to get a job by telling her employers that she is unmarried (and living with Ralph, her brother). The job she takes is in an all-male office!

When Mr. Amico, Alice's handsome boss, comes to the apartment so that he and Alice can work late, Ralph is barely able to control his jealous rage. Amico asks Ralph to fix him up with Alice. Ordinarily, Amico would be on the moon by now, but Ralph's hands are tied by his unemployment.

Then word comes that Ralph's layoff is over—and Amico is on his way to the moon at last! Yet Alice isn't angry at all. In fact, she's delighted that Ralph can still be so jealous after fifteen years of marriage. Ralph is delighted too, and tells her "Baby, you're the greatest."

Title: "Hello, Mom"
Date: December 3, 1955
Themes: *Mother-in-Law, Ralph vs. Alice, Ralph vs. Ed*

Ralph comes home in his usual foul temper, exploding for the usual non-reasons at Alice and Ed. A telegram arrives, from "mother," who will be arriving uninvited on Wednesday. Ralph explodes again, making it quite plain to Alice that her mother is not welcome in his home. She resists; he storms out to spend the night at the Nortons.

While there, he manages to set Trixie against Ed with a mother-in-law argument of their own. Trixie storms down to the Kramdens' apartment to spend the night with Alice, and Ralph, blaming Ed for the unpleasantness (and for treason), spends the night alone in the Nortons' bedroom. Where is Ed? Ralph makes him sleep in the kitchen.

The next day, Ralph happens to be in his own apartment to pick up his uniform when his unwelcome guest arrives. But it is not Alice's mother, it is Ralph's mother. Ralph apologizes sappily to Alice, who greets the woman with open arms.

Later, Alice hands him a letter she found—a moving tribute to mothers-in-law which Ralph wrote when he and Alice were on their honeymoon. They make up but, in a moment tailor-made for a "Baby, you're the greatest," the penitent Ralph goes out for a long, long walk.

Title: "The Deciding Vote"
Date: December 10, 1955
Themes: *Raccoons, Ralph vs. Alice, Ralph vs. Ed, Ralph's Big Mouth, Ralph vs. the World, Conclusion-Jumping*

Minutes before Ralph is about to return home for the occasion of his and Alice's fifteenth wedding anniversary, Ed has asked Alice if he can use Ralph's name as a credit reference. She cheerfully agrees. But her cheer turns to something else when Ralph comes home with a surprise for her: a second-hand, $4.95 vacuum cleaner with attachments for every kind of dirt imaginable. (Without carpets, drapes, or upholstered furniture, Alice has only one kind of dirt.) Besides that, Ralph fails in his attempt to prove the value of the machine with "the oatmeal test." Alice and Ralph quarrel. Then Ed tries to help Ralph fix the machine, and although he cannot succeed in fixing it, comes close to vacuuming Ralph's tongue out of his mouth. Now Ed and Ralph are fighting too. Ralph throws Ed out of the apartment.

Next thing, Joe Munsey shows up to congratulate Ralph on his sure-thing victory as the Raccoons' next convention manager. He explains that with only two guys running for the post, Ralph is sure to get the majority of the votes—provided, of course, that Ed votes for Ralph. Now Ralph has to patch things up with Norton. It won't be so easy, since Ed is out bowling with Ralph's opponent.

Ralph loses by one vote. He blames Norton, and, when the credit reference request arrives, he firmly establishes Norton's character: "The applicant is a bum."

No sooner is the letter mailed than Ralph learns that Norton *did* vote for him. It was Joe Munsey who turned on him because, on Ralph's recommendation, he bought a $4.95 vacuum cleaner for his wife and it failed the oatmeal test.

Norton forgives Ralph, even when he learns about the credit reference. After all, he wanted it to buy furniture for Ralph and Alice's anniversary.

Title: "Something Fishy"
Date: December 17, 1955
Themes: *Raccoons, Ralph's Big Mouth, Male Supremacy, Deception (Ralph, Alice), Ralph vs. Alice*

The scene opens at the Raccoon Lodge, where Norton is beating Ralph at ping-pong. From there, Ralph moves on to another defeat when he has to admit to the lodge brothers that the membership campaign of which he is chairman has been a total failure. Things don't brighten for Ralph until the Raccoons discuss their annual fishing trip. Now Ralph redeems his shaken self-esteem with a vigorous speech about husbands' rights. The brothers vote unanimously that the wives not be invited along, no matter what the pressure at home.

But on the day before the fishing trip, both Ralph and Ed are still afraid to tell their wives the news. When Alice comes out of the bedroom in her new fishing outfit, Ralph finally has to take his stand. They argue. Alice is determined to go.

Ralph and Ed decide that the only way to handle the situation is to sneak out at four in the morning. But when they actually try it, the car won't start. Alice and Trixie, who have been hiding in the back seat of the car, show them how to get it running with a hairpin. Ralph still won't give in and, after much bickering, succeeds in souring Alice on the trip. Alice and Trixie go back to the apartment—until the boys, reflecting on what they've done, call them down to the car again for a day of fishing with the Raccoons.

Title: " 'Twas the Night Before Christmas"
Date: December 24, 1955
Themes: *Ralph vs. Alice, Deception (Ralph, Alice), Poverty*

Ralph can't wait till Christmas to see the gift Alice has bought for him. She hides it. He resents being treated like a child; she tells him where it is. He dives for it, and gets a painful handful of mousetrap. Alice is forced to hide it again.

Confident that turnabout is fair play, he hides Alice's present. Then Ed arrives to exchange gifts with Ralph. Ralph wants to show Ed what he is going to give Alice. He reaches for the package, and gets another handful of mousetrap.

He has bought Alice a box, handmade in Japan from two thousand match-sticks glued together, which, to the best of his knowledge, formerly belonged to the Emperor. Ed is suitably impressed until a neighbor, Mrs. Stevens, drops in to exchange presents with Alice. She gives Alice an identical box, and apologizes for its tackiness. Ralph realizes he was hoodwinked into spending good money for a piece of junk. There is still time before the stores close, so he hocks his brand-new bowling ball to buy Alice something else.

Christmas day, they exchange presents. Ralph gives Alice an idiotic orange squeezer . . . and she gives him a bag for his brand-new bowling ball! When he tells her why he has no ball to put in his brand-new bag, they both warm up to the real meaning of Christmas. And he tells Alice that the best part of the holiday season is knowing that you're going home to someplace where someone is waiting whom "you really love, somebody you're nuts about."

Title: "The Man from Space"
Date: December 31, 1955
Themes: *Scheme, Ralph vs. Ed, Ralph vs. Alice, Raccoons*

Ralph meets Norton for lunch at Norton's office, a manhole. Norton emerges in full sewer regalia, terrifying Ralph, but not for long; Ralph wants to con Norton out of $10. The Raccoons are having a costume party and first prize is $50. Ralph wants to go as Henry VIII and needs the ten-spot to rent a costume. But Norton had also thought of renting a costume and so refuses Ralph the money. Ralph, being Ralph, accuses Ed of stealing not only the $10 that he considers rightfully his own, but also the idea of renting a costume (despite the fact that Ed already has *his* costume in his hands). Ralph declares total war on Ed, then approaches Alice for the money. When she refuses, he decides to make a costume out of furniture.

When next we see Ralph, he is wearing his pajama bottoms, a saucepan on his head, parts of the dresser, the sink, and a box on his chest. He has gone light-years beyond being Henry VIII; now he's "The Man from Space."

At the party, the judges come extremely close to awarding Ralph the prize—for his "brilliant impersonation of a pinball machine"—when Ed arrives from a sewer emergency in his sewer outfit and wins first place as "The Man from Space."

H #4
0143

- (15)

Title: "A Matter of Record"
Date: January 7, 1956
Themes: *Ralph vs. Alice, Ralph vs. Norton, Mother-in-law, Poverty, Ralph's Big Mouth*

Ralph arrives home with the best possible news. He can finally keep a promise he made to Alice on August 5, 1942. He has tickets to take her to a real Broadway play. His boss couldn't use two tickets to *Murder Strikes Out* and has passed them on to Ralph. But Alice can't go. Her mother is coming to visit. Ralph is displeased. He knows what to expect. He bets Alice that even if he doesn't say a word, Mrs. Gibson will start on him within three minutes after she gets there.

She arrives, rude and ornery. Within three minutes, she has insulted Ralph in every possible way, including spilling the surprise ending of the play. Ralph throws her out of the apartment; Alice storms out after her mother.

To get Alice back, Ralph records an apology on Norton's record-making machine. His first attempt is a disaster because he gets carried away, calling Mrs. Gibson a blabbermouth who can't help herself because she was born mean. His second attempt is very moving, but so what? Ed sends Alice the first record. It looks like the end for Ralph. Luckily, Ed has the sense to play peacemaker. He takes Alice the right record, and she is ready to return home.

But again, for a while at least, so what? Ed has caught the measles from his stickball team and Ralph has caught them from Ed. The Department of Health quarantines Ralph and Norton, who have to remain in the Kramden apartment until they are no longer infectious. Alice throws Ralph a bag of steak and heads back for her mother's. And Ralph makes it clear to Norton that measles will be the least of his worries in the weeks to come.

Title: "Oh My Aching Back"
Date: January, 14, 1956
Themes: *Ralph vs. mother-in-law, Ralph vs. World, Ralph vs. Alice, Deception (Ralph), Raccoons*

HONEYMOONERS
#1 0000

NOT GIVEN
QUALITY AS
TOP

BAD TAPE

H #4
0271

Alice is preparing to visit her mother. Ralph refuses to go with her because he has his annual bus company physical exam scheduled for the following morning. At first, Alice doesn't believe him, but when Ralph shows her the appointment card, she apologizes and leaves without him.

When she returns unexpectedly a few minutes later, she discovers Ralph and Ed in their bowling clothes, ready to leave for the Raccoons' championship tournament. Although she is angry with Ralph for lying to her, she does not insist that he visit her mother, so long as he doesn't go bowling and risk ruining his back the night before his company physical. But no sooner does she leave than Norton again persuades Ralph to go bowling.

When next we see Ralph, he can barely straighten his back. Actually, he has two problems: doing something about his back before morning, and making sure that Alice never learns that he went bowling after all. He devises a plan to deceive her: when Alice gets home, Norton will pretend to be sleepwalking, and Ralph will have to go upstairs to keep him out of harm's way. Once in Norton's apartment, Ralph can use a heating pad on his back and his worries will be over.

The plan works like a charm until the following evening, when a few of Ralph's lodge brothers stop by with the Player-of-the-Year bowling trophy he won in the tournament. Then Alice knows all—and lets Ralph know she knows all—when she offers him a tasty dish of bowling trophy for dinner.

Title: "The Baby-sitter"

Date: January 21, 1956

Themes: *Deception (Alice, Ralph), Poverty, Jealousy, Conclusion-Jumping, Ralph vs. Alice*

Alice has a phone installed on the sly, and hides it, hoping Ralph will be in a good mood by the time she has to tell him about it. He comes home in a great mood because, by not having a phone, he has just escaped another call to work overtime. The phone rings, Alice tries to ignore it, but finally has to answer it. It's a wrong number. An argument ensues.

Next scene finds Ralph in a barbershop, getting spiffed up so he can apologize to Alice. He overhears and misunderstands a conversation between two men. They are actually discussing Alice's availability for baby-sitting, but he thinks they are discussing her general availability.

Ralph plans to trap her red-handed. He goes home. She tries to rush him through dinner. He resists. She says she wants to go to a movie. He says he'll give up his lodge night to go with her. She says he shouldn't bother, it's a love story, and "I know you have no interest in love stories."

Poor, pathetic Ralph finally allows Alice to leave, but only because he intends to follow her, accuse her, and walk out of her life forever.

The situation he encounters is compromising in appearance, but it is not what Ralph thinks. Alice confides that she has been baby-sitting behind his back to pay for the phone. Friends again, they clinch for the finale: "Baby, you're the greatest."

(This episode has the longest history of rescheduling of any *Honeymooners*. It was originally titled "BEnsonhurst 3-7741" and slated, in succession, for October 15, December 17, and December 31, 1955. When the episode finally aired it was retitled "The Baby-sitter.")

Title: "The $99,000 Answer"

Date: January 28, 1956

Themes: *Ralph vs. the World, Ralph vs. Ed, Ralph vs. Alice, Scheme, Poverty, Conclusion-Jumping*

Ralph is the tongue-tied contestant on *The $99,000 Answer*, a TV game show modeled after *The $64,000 Question*. He is hardly eloquent ("I brive a dus . . . uh . . . dus a brive"). He picks his category, popular songs, in a dither;

but before he can answer his first question, the show runs out of time and he is invited to return the following week.

All of a sudden, Ralph is Mr. Confidence. He invests every cent of his savings in renting a piano and buying sheet music. He has everyone in the building practicing song titles with him. He has Norton working with him at the piano until the wee hours of every night. Of course, Norton threatens his sanity by warming up for every song with a few bars of ''Swanee River,'' but Ralph's sanity is a small price to pay for fame and fortune.

Alice wants Ralph to take it easy. Ralph wants Alice to think big for a change. ''You have no idea how great this furniture will look in a Park Avenue apartment.''

By the time Ralph is on the show again, he is a qualified expert on popular songs. He is even a confident qualified expert. He announces grandly on the air that he will go straight for the $99,000 jackpot, with as little delay as possible.

But then, how could he guess that the first song would delay him permanently? It is ''Swanee River.'' He guesses feebly that the composer is Ed Norton . . . and a girl in a short flouncy skirt escorts him off the stage.

(19)
Title: ''Ralph Kramden, Inc.''
Date: February 4, 1956
Themes: *Scheme, Conclusion-Jumping, Ralph vs. Ed, Ralph vs. the World*

Ralph cons Ed into buying into Kramden, Inc.; for $20, Ed can purchase 20 percent of all monies made by Ralph over and above his regular salary. Ed refuses until Ralph offers him the vice presidency.

A week later, Ed threatens Ralph that he will withdraw his funds unless some profit accrues pretty fast; Ralph persuades him to leave his funds with the corporation by increasing his percentage to 35 percent.

No sooner does Ed agree than a lawyer knocks at the door, telling Ralph that the kind old lady he used to help on and off his bus has died, mentioning Ralph in the will of her $40 million estate.

Now Ralph tries to con Ed out of his percentage, but Ed clings like glue. He follows Ralph to the woman's mansion and the reading of the will. Ralph, who has been overbearing, obnoxious, and convinced right along that he will inherit the entire fortune, does indeed inherit Mary Monahan's Fortune—her beloved parrot, Fortune. Ralph and Ed respond to their disappointing windfall the only way they know how: by passing out on the floor.

(20)
Title: ''Young at Heart''
Date: February 11, 1956
Themes: *Ralph vs. Alice, Ralph vs. World, Ralph is Fat*

Ralph comes home to an Alice who has just been chatting with some neighborhood teenagers. She wants Ralph to take her out doing all the things they used to do when they were young. He ridicules her. She becomes defensive and nasty. By the next evening, Ralph feels sufficiently guilty to want to learn all the new dances from Ed. Alice comes home to find Ralph tossing his weight around to the music of "The Hucklebuck." Ralph invites her to go roller-skating with him.

At the skating rink, it is one disaster after another for Ralph, who can't skate. He tries to get coffee for Alice and Trixie, but only manages to spill it on them. Next he spills himself, crashing his full weight onto the floor and bringing Alice, Trixie, and Ed down with him.

Back home and broken in body and spirit, all four concern themselves with Ralph's bruises and bad temper, until they see how foolish they've been and burst into laughter. Then Ralph, turning philosophical, concludes that "Acting young isn't what keeps you young, but if you've got some memories, some good memories, of when you were young, that's what keeps you young."

And Alice, charmed as always by Ralph's boyish sincerity and affection, comes to see that she doesn't even mind growing old, as long as she and Ralph grow old together. What can Ralph say? "Baby, you're the greatest."

Title: "A Dog's Life"
Date: February 18, 1956
Themes: *Scheme, Deception (Alice), Ralph vs. the World, Ralph vs. his Conscience*

Alice is baby-sitting a dog, but Ralph mustn't know. So he has no way of knowing that the bowl of food Ed finds in the icebox is dog food. Ed digs in, raves about it; Ralph digs in, echoes Norton's raves. Then Ralph decides it's so good he shouldn't keep it to himself. That, in fact, it's so good it belongs in cans. This idea is going to make him millions, he concludes, and he's going to approach his boss, Mr. Marshall, for financing.

Before he sees Marshall at the bus company, he and Norton have to come up with a name for the product. Norton wisely suggests they incorporate Marshall's name in the brand name—"Kramden's Delicious Marshall" maybe? Ralph comes up with "KramMar's Delicious Mystery Appetizer," and, as he and Norton toast their imminent success, proclaims, "Just goes to prove what I always said: Every dog has his day."

The following morning, Ralph manages to make more than the usual fool of himself when he sees Marshall in his office—he laughs too hard at his boss' jokes. Finally he gets the man to taste the appetizer and Marshall calls in a few associates for their opinions. One of them immediately recognizes the mystery appetizer as dog food, and Ralph faints dead away.

One thing is certain when he gets home: that dog is going back to the pound. But, at the pound, when he realizes that the pooch will be put to sleep, he decides to keep it and take home a few more besides.

Title: "Here Comes the Bride"
Date: February 25, 1956
Themes: *Raccoons, Ralph's Big Mouth, Male Supremacy, Ralph vs. Alice, Deception (Ralph), Scheme*

Stanley Saxon, a lodge brother of Ralph's, is being feted by the Raccoon Lodge because he is about to be married. His bride, not entirely by coincidence, is Alice's sister (hence, Ralph's sister-in-law) Agnes. Stanley reveals himself to be mild-mannered and agreeable to Agnes' plans for the future. Ralph changes all that with a lecture about man being the king of the castle.

So, right after the wedding, Agnes shows up at the Kramdens' in tears because Stanley has become a beast. So far no one knows that Ralph is to blame, and he tries to keep it that way. On the other hand, he doesn't want Agnes moving into his apartment, so he and Norton and their wives concoct a scheme. They will invite Stanley to dinner while Agnes is there, and then demonstrate by example that all men order their wives around and all wives humbly obey. Alice reluctantly agrees to the plan. Stanley arrives and instantly makes up with Agnes. He complains that he never should have listened to Ralph. Alice is understandably annoyed that Ralph nearly ruined their marriage with his interference.

When Ralph once again starts giving orders, Alice tells him to go blow away. He can't deny that she's right this time. Young people, he agrees, should be allowed to solve their own problems, the way he and Alice always do. That, he concludes, is the secret of all good marriages—his, for instance.

Title: "Mama Loves Mambo"
Date: March 3, 1956
Themes: *Jealousy, Ralph vs. Alice, Ralph vs. the World, Male Supremacy*

Carlos Sanchez has just moved into Fogarty's old flat next door to the Kramdens'. From Alice's description of him, he sounds to Ralph like a kindly, lonely old bachelor. Then Ralph meets him; Sanchez turns out to be a handsome Latin lover type who works nights as a dancer, and hence is home all day when the wives are alone. What's worse, he is suave and courteous, and the wives are complaining to their husbands that Carlos is more fun to be around than they are.

The husbands, rather than mending their ways, declare war on Carlos— especially when Ralph comes home one evening to find that dinner hasn't been started because all the ladies in the building are learning the mambo from Carlos instead of doing their chores. He explodes, first at Carlos, then at Alice, who lectures *him* on the proper appreciation of women.

Ralph and the other husbands in the building get together with Carlos, prepared to tell him off, but Carlos persuades them instead to be more attentive to their wives. He even teaches them to dance. In the next few days, the husbands nearly kill their wives with kindness and the mambo—until Alice and Trixie beg them to go back to being their old selfish selves. And they do. Bedlam reigns again.

132

(24)

Title: "Please Leave the Premises"
Date: March 10, 1956
Themes: *Ralph vs. the World, Poverty, Ralph vs. Alice, Ralph vs. Ed, (variation on a) Scheme*

Mr. Johnson, the landlord, visits the Kramdens to inform them of a $5 rent increase. Ralph throws him out, announcing to both Ed and Alice that they are barricading themselves inside their respective apartments until Johnson changes his mind. Johnson threatens to evict them; Ralph is sure he's only bluffing.

Next scene, Johnson has cut off the gas, electricity, heat, and water. Norton makes his way through the Kramdens' blockade to announce that he has capitulated. Ralph, unable for once to throw him out, locks him in for the duration of the blockade.

Since the food supply is now down to celery, it appears that the duration can't last much longer. Ralph knots some sheets together and lowers himself out the back window to avoid the sheriff's deputies who are watching his door and his front window. He expects to return with food. Instead, the sheets give way and he lands in front of another of the sheriff's deputies.

Alice and Ralph are evicted, and now Ralph's plan is to stay outside on the street with his furniture until Johnson is shamed into relenting. When it starts snowing, Ralph agrees to pay the rent increase, but only because, he says, it would be just like Alice to get a virus from living in the snow.

(25)

Title: "Pardon My Glove"
Date: March 17, 1956
Themes: *Deception (Alice, Ralph), Jealousy*

The scene opens with Alice and Trixie discussing a surprise birthday party planned for Ralph. They hide the guest and shopping lists before Ralph comes home, but, no sooner have they left than he comes in and finds the lists. However, Ralph is determined not to ruin the party. He has, in fact, decided to come home with his eyes bulging out and surprise written all over his face.

But fate has something else in store for Ralph. Alice wins the free services of an interior decorator, who offers to redo the apartment while Ralph is at work; this will mean that the party has to be postponed, but it will also mean a much better surprise for Ralph's birthday.

Ralph, knowing nothing about the new surprise—and all rehearsed for the old one, comes home to disappointment when there is no surprise, and no party at all. Worse still, Alice seems too anxious to want to get Ralph out of the apartment for the evening. Ralph becomes suspicious, then jealous when he finds a glove the decorator has inadvertently left behind. He pretends to leave the apartment with Ed, but actually hides on the fire escape to spy on Alice and her "date."

When the decorator arrives to discuss his plans with Alice, Ralph thinks he overhears some very compromising dialogue: "I usually try to get the husband's approval." "But Ralph has such old-fashioned ideas, he'd just make things difficult." Ralph comes through the window like a fat kangaroo, confronts Alice, and drives the decorator away.

Within minutes, Alice has explained things to Ralph and seems more upset with him than she's ever been—until he tells her he's only jealous because he loves her so much. She gives him his birthday present and they end in a clinch, not just any clinch but a special birthday "baby, you're the greatest."

Title: "Young Man with a Horn"
Date: March 24, 1956
Themes: *Ralph vs. the World, Poverty, (variation on a) Scheme*

The civil service exams are coming up. Ed is going to try for sewer inspector, and Ralph is toying with the possibility of becoming a senior clerk for the transit authority.

When Alice finds a cornet Ralph used to play as a young man, he sees it as a symbol of his wasted years and worthless aspirations. In life, as in music, he has never been able to hit the high note—which he demonstrates by nearly popping his eyes out of his head midway through a cornet solo.

Shortly afterward, an aging millionaire appears at the Kramdens' door with his wife for a nostalgic visit to their first flat. The millionaire shares with Ralph the secret of his success—make a list of your strengths and weaknesses, stress your assets and correct your faults, and don't let anything stand in your way.

In the next few weeks, Ralph knocks himself out doing good deeds and concentrating on his virtues, convinced that success is just around the corner and that the senior clerk position is as good as his.

In the end, neither Kramden nor Norton win their civil service promotions; but Alice will not allow Ralph to feel sorry for himself after the personal progress he had made. He takes another crack at the cornet, and hits the high note. Then he realizes, and tells Alice, that he hit the high note once before—when he married her.

Title: "Head of the House"
Date: March 31, 1956
Themes: *Ralph vs. the World, Ralph's Big Mouth, Deception (Ralph), Ralph vs. Alice, Male Supremacy, Scheme*

Ralph and Ed are stopped by "Your Questioning Photographer" from a local newspaper, who asks each of them who is boss in his household. Ed asserts his prime position as head of the household until he learns that his answer will be printed in the paper along with his name and picture, then he backs down. Big mouth Ralph, by way of picking on Ed for being afraid of Trixie, says too much, with the result that his deathless words and stunned countenance make the evening edition.

At home Ralph tries to keep Alice from seeing the paper, without luck. When she reads the column, she is willing to forgive and forget, but Ralph makes

134

an issue of it and insists that he is the only head of their household.

Next morning, at the bus depot, Joe Fensterblau, who saw the column but doesn't believe a word of it, bets Ralph and Ed ten dollars each that Ralph cannot order Alice to prepare a special supper on command. Ralph accepts the bet, calls Alice with his orders, and she hangs up on him. He tries to save face (and win the bet) by cooking the meal himself. Instead, he ruins the food—and the kitchen. Joe arrives on schedule, sees that there will be no supper, taunts Ralph, and starts to collect his bet when Alice appears, apologizes for ruining dinner, and offers Joe a rain check. Amazed, Joe is willing to make good on the bet; Ralph tells him to forget it. When Joe leaves, Ralph realizes how lucky he is to have a wife like Alice, and tells her so: "Baby, you're the greatest."

Title: "The Worry Wart"
Date: April 7, 1956
Themes: *Ralph vs. the World, Ralph vs. his Conscience*

The show opens with much of the typical nonsense: Ed inviting the Kramdens to an antique show (perhaps they'll discover that their furniture is all antique); Ed inviting himself to dinner even though he's just eaten ("Let's face it, Dizzy Dean warms up in the bull pen before the game, but he still pitches."); Ralph revealing that his gas bill is ninety-three cents (breaking the all-time low record set by the Collier brothers in 1931). Then Ralph opens his mail, and finds that he is being called down to the IRS office to answer for an irregularity in his income tax.

As Ralph and Ed reexamine Ralph's tax return, they remember item after item of unreported income: winnings from pool and card games, a company bonus (a skinny chicken), a ceramic horse with a clock in its stomach (first prize in a pinball competition at Salvatore's Pizzeria). Norton tells Ralph to prepare himself for the worst, but, if the worst happens, to stand on the 18th Amendment: "Tell them you were drunk when you filled out your report."

Next morning at the tax office, Ralph finds that his only irregularity was failure to sign his return. He signs it grandly and makes ready to leave without confessing his undeclared income, but then, honest urchin that he is, he comes clean (as does Ed). They are given forms on which they can correct their oversights, and Ralph departs, his confidence back and his conscience clear, saying, "I want you to know that Ralph Kramden will never be accused of not putting a horse down with a clock in its stomach."

Title: "Trapped"
Date: April 14, 1956
Themes: *Ralph vs. Ed, Ralph vs. the World, Ralph . . . wins??*

Ralph, enraged with Norton after a typical quarrel, storms out of the pool hall. Shots are heard from off stage, and Ralph returns with a bullet hole in his hat. He has just seen a holdup and murder. He decides not to tell the police, since that would mean identifying himself in the papers as the killers' only eyewitness.

Once home, he is so jumpy that he cannot keep anything from Alice. They are just about to go down to the police department, at Alice's insistence, when Danny and Bibbo (brains and brawn, respectively) arrive at their door. Then Norton appears and, despite Ralph's every effort, pushes his way in. Ralph produces a gun, getting the drop on the thugs, until little Tommy, another neighbor, lets it be known that it's only a water pistol.

Now it looks like the crooks will be spending the night. When Bibbo gets too rough with Alice, Ralph stands up to him. Bibbo takes him into the bedroom to work him over. A wild brawl ensues, from which, much to everyone's surprise, Ralph emerges victorious with Bibbo's real gun. He gets the drop on Danny, whom Ed marches, with Bibbo, down to the waiting police. Moments later, Ralph dashes after him—to make sure Ed doesn't grab the credit.

Title: "The Loudspeaker"
Date: April 21, 1956
Themes: *Ralph vs. the World, Raccoons. Ralph vs. Ed, Conclusion-Jumping*

The Raccoons' annual award dinner is coming up, and Ralph has been asked by the Grand High Exalted Mystic Ruler, "the Emperor of all Raccoondom," to prepare a speech for the occasion. Ralph draws what he believes to be the only possible conclusion: he is to be named Raccoon of the Year. To Ralph, this is the best thing that ever happened to him; to Alice, it is totally unimpressive, even though the honor would automatically entitle her to free burial in the Raccoon National Cemetery in Bismarck, North Dakota.

Ralph goes to the greatest possible lengths to prepare a speech, develops the hiccups, loses his temper at Ed, and practices on Alice the shaggiest shaggy dog story ever told. When Alice doesn't laugh at his rotten jokes, he becomes furious with her. He storms out of the apartment. Moments later, the Grand High Exalted Mystic Ruler himself, Morris Fink, arrives at the Kramdens' door and leaves with Alice the speech that Ralph is to deliver—announcing Norton as Raccoon of the Year. When Ralph returns, Alice tells him the news. At first, he is shattered, but then takes pleasure in his pal's good fortune and heads upstairs to offer Ed the use of his shaggy dog story.

Title: "On Stage"
Date: April 28, 1956
Themes: *Raccoons, Conclusion-Jumping, Ralph vs. Ed, Ralph vs. the World*

The Ladies' Auxiliary of the Raccoons wants to raise money by putting on a play. Mr. Faversham, who is organizing the performance, flatters and cajoles Ralph until he takes the lead.

Alice, who is to play opposite Ralph, takes everything in stride. And Ed, who has no part at all, remains his old cheerful self, but Ralph lets stardom go to his head. When Joe Hannegan develops the flu and can't go on, Ed is called in to replace him. Ralph, who is nervous already, panics; he knows that Norton will drive him crazy. Norton rehearses: "I don't possess a mansion, a villa in France, a yakt, or a string of poloponies." Ralph was right. (What Norton meant to say was "a string of polo ponies") but it is too late. Ralph goes crazy.

Although Norton has given him the hiccups and a hard time, it evidently doesn't upset Ralph's performance (except that he reads the line about his "string of poloponies," on stage!). The show is a complete sellout, and afterward. Mr. Faversham stops by Ralph's dressing room with Mr. Whiteside, a Hollywood producer. Ralph, without hesitation, agrees to quit the bus company to become a star. Then he is informed that it is not him, but Alice, they want for the movies. Alice, however, turns them down. The only love scenes she wants to do are with Ralph, who obliges with an instant love scene: "Baby you're the greatest."

(32)

Title: "Opportunity Knocks But"
Date: May 5, 1956
Themes: *Ralph vs. the World, Ralph vs. Ed. (Variation on a) Scheme*

Ralph's boss, Mr. Marshall, has just acquired a pool table for his Park Avenue apartment. Since he doesn't know how to play the game, he invites Ralph and Norton over to give him a few lessons. To Ralph, this can mean only one thing—a big promotion—so long as he does everything in his power to score with the boss. But, as it happens, it's Ed who manages to say all the right things. Marshall is so impressed that he offers Norton the job Ralph has his eye on, bus driver's supervisor. Ralph's reaction is to declare total war on Norton. Ed's reaction is to unintentionally lord it over Ralph, making matters even worse.

After Ed leaves the Kramdens' apartment that evening, Ralph admits to Alice that his greatest annoyance is with himself for being hopelessly inadequate and a failure at life. Then Norton returns, because it suddenly dawned on him that all the good ideas he used to impress Marshall had originally come from Ralph; and he promises, first thing in the morning, to tell Marshall the whole story. And Alice, who has had ample faith in Ralph all along, receives ample reward: "Baby, you're the greatest."

(33)

Title: "Unconventional Behavior"
Date: May 12, 1956
Themes: *Raccoons, Ralph vs. Alice, Ralph vs. Ed, Scheme, Poverty*

The annual Raccoon convention is coming up in Minneapolis. Ralph wants to go, but he's sure Alice will not simply give him the money to cover his expenses. So he comes up, reluctantly, with a surefire scheme to get it: he will invite Alice to go with him. Meanwhile, Alice has already decided to give him the money without a fight. No sooner does he invite her along than he learns that he didn't have to, and he accuses Alice of high-handed tactics.

Ralph's next mistake occurs when he and Norton board the train to Minneapolis and can't find Alice and Trixie. As the train leaves the station, they are delighted to be rid of their wives, if only for a night.

They start kidding around, playing with the novelties they've bought for the convention, and Ed attaches himself to Ralph with trick handcuffs that can only be opened by the right snap of the wrists as someone says "boompf." Ralph doesn't think this is funny, particularly when Ed can't find the key. ("There ain't no key. You gotta 'boompf' your way out.") Eventually, Ralph and Ed have to spend the night handcuffed together; therefore, they have to sleep in their Raccoon uniforms in the same pullman bunk. In no time at all, they are at each other's throats. And as the conductor comes to investigate the commotion, they learn that they're on the wrong train. They're going in the opposite direction from Minneapolis; the train is headed for Norfolk, Virginia.

(34)

Title: "The Safety Award"
Date: May 19, 1956
Themes: *Ralph vs. the World, Ralph vs. Ed.*

It is the biggest day of Ralph's life. His story will appear in *Universal* magazine. He has won an award as the safest bus driver in the city. Ed arrives on the scene as the voice of doom, predicting Ralph will have an accident before he is presented with the award.

As the Kramdens and Nortons meet to drive to the award ceremony, Alice and Trixie discover that they're wearing identical dresses. Since neither is willing to change, they argue and refuse to go anywhere. Eventually, Norton and Kramden talk sense into their wives, only to discover that *they* have planned to wear identical sport jackets.

By the time they manage to iron out their difficulties, they barely have time to rush to City Hall for the main event. On the way, Ralph is in a minor auto collision. At City Hall, the man who presents Ralph's award is none other than the man responsible for his accident, Judge Lawrence Norton Hurdle. Hurdle is also a traffic court judge notorious for his stiff fines and even stiffer lectures. But Judge Hurdle surprises everyone by taking full blame for the accident (and fining himself $50) to keep the record straight. And Ralph, with a clear conscience and confidence to spare, is invited upstairs to shake hands with the mayor.

(35)

Title: "Mind Your Own Business"
Date: May 26, 1956
Themes: *Ralph's Big Mouth, Scheme, Poverty, Ralph vs. Ed, Deception (Ed and Trixie)*

On Ralph's advice, Norton has threatened to leave his job unless he gets a promotion. The next evening, Ed tells Alice that "after what Jim McKeever told me, I find it impossible to work one more day for him in the sewer." Alice asks, "What did he tell you?" Norton answers, "You're fired." He doesn't know how to break the news to Trixie. He considers telling her the sewer went bankrupt.

After two weeks without a job, he gets one as a door-to-door salesman for the Spiffy Iron Company selling steam irons. As he returns from his first day on the job, he confides to Trixie that out of 137 prospects, he only sold one iron, and that was to his mother. The future looks bleak, because, as Ed observes, "The day after tomorrow, we run out of mothers."

However, not to distress Ralph and Alice, they decide to pretend that business has been terrific. Unfortunately, Ed makes it sound too good ($40 a day in commissions), and Ralph wants to quit his job and work at Spiffy with Ed. Ed naturally refuses to get him the job, infuriating Ralph. Then Ralph tells Alice that he's going to use a little of his own advice, and threaten to quit the bus company to work for Spiffy if they don't give him a raise.

At program's end, Ed has been called to return to work *with* his promotion; Ralph has tried "the old squeeze play" and failed, but managed to keep his job anyhow; and Ralph presents Alice with a Spiffy iron which immediately explodes when he tries to demonstrate it.

36

Title: "Alice and The Blonde"
Date: June 2, 1956
Themes: *Raccoons, Scheme, Ralph vs. Alice, Deception (Ralph)*

Alice catches Ralph sneaking home at 2:00 A.M. in his Raccoon uniform. He pretends that he just got up for a snack, but his outfit is a dead giveaway. Norton arrives, then Trixie, and the four of them quarrel about how much time Ralph and Norton spend away from home. So Ralph, hoping to kill two birds with one stone, invites Alice and the Nortons to join him at the home of newlyweds Bert and Rita Wedemeyer. Bert is the new general manager at the Gotham Bus Company; Ralph hopes to score points with him by making a fuss over his new wife. Alice and Trixie have their own plan: to make themselves glamorous for the evening, thereby restoring the dwindling flame of their marriages.

Rita is vain and self-centered and Bert is a dope, but Ralph and Ed go out of their way to compliment them both. Alice and Trixie are ignored, even when Alice "develops a headache" and wants to go home. When Ralph returns home the next evening, Alice is dressed to kill and Ralph is fit to be tied. Has she lost her mind? Hit the bottle? Nibbled too much of the old rum candy? No, she's only modeling herself after Rita, who is evidently the sort of woman Ralph admires. Then Ralph, admitting that he's been an unappreciative lummox, sets the record straight: "*You're* the greatest."

Reruns began June 9, 1956, with a repeat showing of "The Golfer" in the regular *Honeymooners* time slot. Three new episodes were shown September 8, 15, and 22; no new episodes of *The Honeymooners* were filmed after that until the Gleason troupe made the move to Miami in the 1960s.

Live, not-on-tape, programming for *The Honeymooners* was resumed December 8, 1956.

Title: "The Bensonhurst Bomber"
Date: September 8, 1956
Themes: *Ralph's Big Mouth, Scheme*

At the local poolroom, Ralph is demonstrating "the glorious results of a misspent youth" and Norton is unnerving him with his misspent, energetic idiocy. George, a little guy, comes along wanting their pool table, since he and his pal Harvey reserved it earlier. Ralph won't budge. Next thing you know, George returns with a gigantic person named Harvey. Ralph tries to back down, but Ed manages to twist his words around until Ralph, big mouth and all, is challenging Harvey to a fight at Kelsey's Gym.

At home, it takes Ralph no time at all to realize that there is no honest way that he can defend himself in the ring. He and Ed come up with a scheme: they will stage a fight in front of Harvey. A friend of Ed's from the sewer, someone even bigger than Harvey, will take a dive for Ralph. Harvey will back down.

That night at Kelsy's it's a great success. Ralph decks another big bully and Harvey flees in fear. Then Ed arrives to tell Ralph that his friend won't be able to make it. Ralph, confident now that he must have muscles he never knew existed, calls Harvey back and takes a confident wack at a punching bag. He recoils in pain. Poor Ralph—even his silver linings have their clouds.

Title: "Dial J for Janitor"
Date: September 15, 1956
Themes: *Scheme, Ralph is Fat, Ralph vs. the World, Ralph vs. Alice*

Ralph comes home with a terrible headache, but building noises only make it worse. He complains to Alice, who tells him she has been after the janitor to fix everything, to no avail. Mr. Johnson, the landlord, arrives, and Norton and Kramden start on him for the bad service in the building. He, however, is just as angry at them, and he blames his inability to keep janitors on the way Norton and Kramden abuse them. He threatens to evict his malcontent tenants when Ralph gets an idea—why not take the janitor's job (at $150 a month plus free rent and whatever tips might come his way) and thereby have two salaries? Johnson agrees. Alice sees where this will end, but Ralph won't listen.

He installs a "house phone" as part of his new "efficiency system." This, he explains, will enable tenants to contact him without hollering out the window or down the hall.

Eventually we find Ralph in the cellar trying to correct Norton's water pressure from the main pipes, in which Ralph becomes immovably lodged. Norton comes down, tries to help him, only to get him jammed in even tighter. Then he goes into the furnace room to turn off the steam, managing to turn it up full blast. The Fire Department has to be called to rescue Ralph.

That night, Ralph calls Mr. Johnson up to his apartment to resign, only to find that Johnson has already hired another janitor behind his back—Norton!

Title: "A Man's Pride"
Date: September 22, 1956
Themes: *Ralph vs. the World, Ralph's Big Mouth, Deception (Ralph), Jealousy*

Upon leaving the fights with Ed, Ralph runs into Bill Davis, an old school chum who used to date Alice when she was still Alice Gibson. The last thing Ralph wants to hear is that Alice would have been better off marrying someone like Bill, but Bill is even more successful, and more obnoxious to Ralph, than Ralph feared. To save face, he tells Bill that he "runs things" for the Gotham Bus Company. Next thing you know, Bill has trapped Ralph into inviting him over to the Gotham offices after work some time.

The evening Bill is to appear, Ralph's boss is working late. In the few moments the boss is out of his office, Ralph zips Bill in and out for a fast look, pulling off that deception but making a fool of himself when his boss returns.

When Ralph gets home, he learns that Bill and Millie Davis have just invited the Kramdens to dinner at the expensive Colonnade Room. Ralph's objections ("Name one truck driver that eats there") are overruled by Alice, and there is no avoiding dinner with the Davises.

Ralph expects Bill to pick up the check, Bill expects that Ralph will. At dinner, Ralph gets stuck for the check by shooting off his big mouth. He has to admit that he's only a lowly bus driver; Bill has to admit that he's a mere assistant plumber. Confession being good for the soul, everyone has a hearty laugh over their deceptions and they all chip in to pay the check together.

THE TRIP-TO-EUROPE SEASON

1966–1967

Although new *Honeymooners* episodes continued to be produced at varying intervals through the late 1950s and early 1960s, it was not until the 1966–67 season that a series of *Honeymooners* shows again became available for syndication. These starred Jackie Gleason, Art Carney, Sheila MacRae, and Jane Kean. Of the more than forty *Honeymooners* shows that featured this team, only the Trip-to-Europe series has been released for syndication. Detailed plot synopses follow.

Title: "In Twenty-Five Words Or Less"
Date: September 17, 1966
Themes: *Ralph vs. the World, In-laws, Poverty, Scheme, Deception (Ralph)*

Ralph has been left out for the last time. When his brother-in-law wins a trip to Europe, he tries to win one too. He buys out the local grocery store to get all kinds of box tops for contest entries. Norton helps him write slogans and he wins two contests. First, he is awarded a monstrous dog which he tries to foist off on

Norton. Then, he wins a $40,000 ranch house from Flakey Wakey diet breakfast cereal.

To win the house, he had faked before- and-after pictures (Norton his usual thin self, and Norton padded with pillows to look fat) to accompany the slogan "Flakey Wakeys add to the taste/But take away from your fat little waist." Unfortunately for Ralph and Norton, the Flakey Wakey people catch on to the ruse. But because Flakey Wakey wants the slogan, Ralph is awarded the second prize: a trip to Europe for four.

Title: "Ship of Fools"
Date: October 1, 1966
Themes: *Ralph vs. the World, Ralph vs. Ed*

A Flakey Wakey representative meets the Nortons and the Kramdens at the pier to start them on their way to Europe. Trixie is the last to arrive, because she's hauling most of the suitcases. Pictures are taken, and Norton and Ralph vie to dominate the foreground.

During the voyage, Ralph and Ed reveal their true selves by trying too hard to act like swells. They play hopscotch on the shuffleboard squares, become seasick from the hors d'oeuvres, and set themselves adrift on the ocean in a lifeboat. They reminisce, declare their friendship, and abandon all hope. (Art Carney even manages to work in a Crazy Guggenheim impersonation.) They are rescued by the liner and finally land in France, where Ralph falls off the deck while posing for more Flakey Wakey publicity photos.

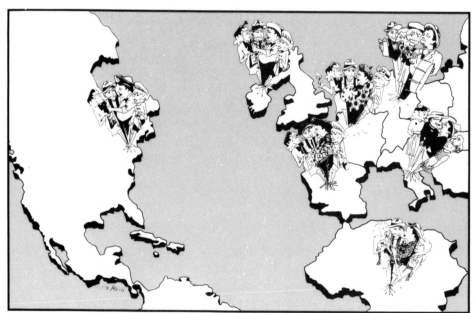

The itinerary of the Kramden–Norton Trip-to-Europe.

Title: "The Poor People of Paris"
Date: October 8, 1966
Themes: *Ralph vs. the World, Poverty, Scheme*

Ralph and Norton get into trouble as soon as they reach Paris, when a bellboy persuades them to exchange their dollars for francs through friends of his rather than through the bank. Feeling rich because they have saved a fortune on the rate of exchange, they shower Alice and Trixie with money for a shopping spree. Then they go off for a spree of their own. But their spree lands them in jail for passing counterfeit money. Soon their wives meet the same unhappy fate.

They are released with the help of the American Embassy, but later, when they spot the counterfeiters and identify them to the police, they are arrested again. Because the gendarme speaks no English, he allows the crooks to convince him that Ralph and Ed are the counterfeiters.

Title: "Confusion Italian Style"
Date: October 15, 1966
Themes: *Ralph vs. the World, Jealousy, Conclusion-Jumping, Scheme, Deception (Ralph, Alice), Ralph is Fat*

Our fearless foursome is in Rome and the episode opens with Ralph barely able to squeeze himself out of a foreign car. This puts Ralph in a foul temper, and Alice and Trixie are left to manage for themselves. Alice meets up with a local waif, Tony, who offers to be her guide because she's beautiful and he loves her.

When the girls return to the hotel, Ralph overhears Alice talking on the phone to Tony, finds flowers and a note that Tony has sent. He immediately concludes that Alice has a lover. And, because he overheard only a small bit of the conversation, he is convinced the wife-stealing so-and-so is named Harry Verderchi.

Ralph and Norton dress up in ludicrous Italian costumes and phony faces, hoping to catch Alice and her mystery man at a local Festa l'Uva. Alice and Trixie recognize their husbands immediately but don't let on. They flirt wildly with Angelo (Ed) and Luigi (Ralph) and leave the poor slobs more upset than ever.

Back in the hotel, Ralph confronts Alice with her perfidy. Then little Tony appears, Ralph is made to see the error of his ways, and the time-honored reconciliation takes a foreign (if ungrammatical) twist: "Bambino, you're the greatest."

Title: "The Curse of the Kramdens"
Date: October 29, 1966
Themes: *Ralph vs. The World, In-laws, Deception, Ralph's Big Mouth*

A special welcome awaits Ralph in Dunellin, Ireland, because he is a descendent of Patrick Kramden who ran off to America with Shamus O'Toole's daughter in 1827. In a rage, Shamus placed a curse on the village. The crops were blighted and Dunellin's famed beer was ruined.

The curse can only be broken if a Kramden stays the night in the ancestral Kramden castle haunted by the ghost of Shamus O'Toole. At last, Ralph has found a castle he has no desire to be king of, but the mayor flatters him until he changes his mind. Alice and Trixie remind him of his duties to the Kramden name and honor, but refuse to participate themselves. Ralph leaves Norton no choice in the matter.

As they begin their accursed vigil, Ralph and Norton are presented with ample evidence that the castle is indeed haunted. Eventually, they stumble across the "ghosts" who are haunting it—counterfeiters (of sweepstakes tickets) who are using the castle as their headquarters. They manage to capture the crooks and return to the village as heroes.

Title: "The Honeymooners in England"
Date: November 12, 1966
Themes: *Ralph vs. the World, Ralph's Big Mouth, Ralph vs. Ed, Ralph vs. Alice*

Ralph is invited to appear on London television in a Flakey Wakey commercial. He offers to write, direct, and produce it American-style.

It is a stilted and self-conscious commercial staged around the breakfast table of Lord and Lady Chumly Farthing-Gay, titled nobility of Rathbone. Ralph thinks it is a masterpiece. As he rehearses with Alice and the Nortons in his hotel room, his cast complains about the size of their nonexistent parts (Ed is a mere butler, Trixie is a maid; Alice is Lady Penelope but her part is still terrible).

By the time the commercial goes on the air on the *Gaylor Farquard Show*, styled after the *Jackie Gleason Show* (even to the point of having Sammy Spear conducting a familiar theme song from the orchestra pit), Ralph is a nervous incompetent.

The commercial is a disaster. Ed overturns a piano. Ralph makes a fool of himself. The only thing that saves the Flakey Wakey name is a Flakey Wakey jingle, created by Ed, which everyone but Ralph sings in uncomfortable harmony. The Kramdens and Nortons attempt to flee London in shame, only to be informed that their commercial was a big hit and they are wanted back to do another one.

Title: "You're In the Picture"
Date: November 19, 1966
Themes: *Ralph vs. the World, Deception (Ralph), Jealousy (Alice!)*

Ralph is taking home movies in Madrid when Miguel, a Spanish photographer, and his girlfriend Rosita ("a Spanish kindergarten teacher") spot him for a sucker and manage to snap a faked shot of him embracing Rosita.

Ralph suspects nothing until Miguel and Rosita threaten to blackmail him with the picture. Not one to be bullied, Ralph tries to tell Alice the truth but panics and changes his mind. Unable to level with Alice, Ralph tries to do the next best thing: trick her out of money to pay the blackmailers. In the process, he accidentally hides Rosita in a closet with Alice.

Alice demands an explanation; Rosita shows her the picture. Alice will not believe the truth no matter how much Ralph pleads—until police arrive to arrest Rosita for her illegal activities. This episode, based on Alice's jealousy, has been something of a reversal all along. And now it is Alice who must ask forgiveness for being a jealous fool.

Title: "We Spy"
Date: December 3, 1966
Themes: *Ralph vs. the World, Deception (Ralph)*

In Germany, Ralph is tired of being a tourist and wants to see the countryside the way the natives do. While Alice and Trixie go shopping, Ralph and Ed go picnicking in the woods. They come to rest on a Russian firing range, where they are arrested and taken for interrogation.

In attempting an escape, they masquerade as Russian commissars and end up as guests of honor at a Russian banquet. Norton is prodded into giving a speech, before he and Ralph dance the kazotsky, as a means of getting away. Having introduced Thanksgiving as a national holiday to the Russians, they make it back to the Berlin station just in time to depart with Alice and Trixie.

Title: "Petticoat Jungle"
Date: December 10, 1966
Themes: *Ralph vs. the World, Deception (Ralph), Scheme, Ralph vs. Alice*

Ralph wants to go on a safari before ending his fabulous tour. The wives would prefer to go to the Riviera, but Ralph and Norton talk them out of it.

Alice and Trixie are having no fun at all. They are doing the work and taking the criticism; the husbands are playing hunter. Ralph bags a rabbit, Norton gets an elephant. Alice is told to get into the spirit of things by bagging an elephant; she deflates Ralph's spirit by reminding him that she already has, by marrying one. Alice schemes to get the boys to give up the hunt, but Ralph refuses to admit defeat. After more than his share of disasters, Ralph is ready to go home, but he wants Alice to think he's doing it on her account.

He talks Norton into wearing a gorilla suit to scare the girls. The scheme backfires when a "real" gorilla appears and scares them all.

In the final scene, Ralph and Alice patch up their difficulties aboard ship as they head back for Brooklyn, U.S.A.

Title: "King of the Castle"
Date: January 7, 1967
Themes: *Ralph vs. Alice, Ralph vs. Ed, Male Supremacy, Deception (Ralph), Scheme, In-laws*

This episode, which takes place a few weeks after the Kramdens and Nortons return from Europe, is included in "The Honeymooners Trip To Europe" syndication package as a fitting end to Ralph's un-Kramdenlike windfall.

It begins with Ralph and Ed enjoying a night out, bowling. Trixie phones Ed to come home because her mother is visiting. Ralph tells Ed that he's crazy to give up his leisure time when he can easily assert himself as king of the castle. Ed follows Ralph's advice and Trixie walks out on him. She moves in with the Kramdens. When Alice discovers that Ralph is behind the Nortons' domestic spat, she and Trixie move upstairs, forcing Ed to move in with Ralph downstairs.

After a week, Ralph and Ed are hungry and the apartment is a mess. They try some typical schemes to get the wives back, but nothing works until Trixie and Alice themselves get to feeling lonely and invite their husbands for turkey dinner and a reconciliation. The dinner goes beautifully, only to end abruptly with Ralph and Ed leaving early to go bowling.

ABC: THE HONEYMOONERS SPECIALS
1976 — 1977

Title: "The Second Honeymoon"
Date: February 2, 1976
Themes: *Deception (Ralph, Alice), Ralph vs. the World, Raccoons, Conclusion-Jumping, Ralph's Mother-in-Law*

More charming than even the plot of *The Honeymooners'* twenty-fifth anniversary show are its intentional echoes of past moments from the lives of the Kramdens and Nortons: Ralph and Ed getting smashed on punch that they falsely believe to be spiked, Ed warming up to play the piano with a few bars of "Swanee River," and the Grand High Exalted Mystic Ruler of the Raccoon Lodge in his three-tailed coonskin cap.

The story itself concerns the Kramdens' intention to celebrate their silver wedding anniversary with a second ceremony—at the Raccoon Lodge (the Grand High Exalted Mystic Ruler himself will perform the honors). Along the way, Ralph jumps to the conclusion that Alice is pregnant—she even confesses that another member of the family is on the way.

At episode's end, Ralph learns that Alice is indeed expecting . . . her mother! And he has to spend the big night of his twenty-fifth anniversary sleeping in the kitchen, because Mrs. Gibson is going to be sleeping in the bedroom with Alice.

Title: "*The Honeymooners* Christmas Special"
Date: November 26, 1977
Themes: *Ralph's Big Mouth, Ralph vs. the World, Deception (Ralph), Ralph vs. Alice*

In the locker room of the Gotham Bus Company, Ralph is noisy and excited about the vacation he and Alice are going to take to Miami. But along comes his boss with a script for *A Christmas Carol;* he needs someone to direct the show for the benefit of his wife's charity (finding homes for stray cats). Although it means giving up his trip, Ralph volunteers himself for the positions of director, writer, and star. Alice, disappointed over the change in plans, makes Ralph sleep on an unopenable, inoperable cot in the kitchen.

The play itself features Ralph, Alice, Trixie, and Ed. Ed, as both Scrooge and Tiny Tim, occasionally gets the mannerisms and wigs for the two roles confused . . . and ties them both neatly together with a Walter Brennan-Frankenstein sort of limp.

For the grand finale of the play-within-a-play, the cornflakes that Alice and Trixie spray-painted white to look like snowflakes descend on the cast in one incredible thud. However, the boss is so impressed that he gives Ralph a reward for his efforts: a pregnant cat. And yes, at long last, Ralph gets his promotion to the position of traffic manager.

Title: "*The Honeymooners* Valentine Special"
Date: February 13, 1978
Themes: *Deception (Ralph, Alice), Jealousy, Conclusion-Jumping, Ralph vs. the World, Ralph vs. Alice*

With another anniversary coming up, Ralph and Alice are planning to buy absolutely wonderful surprise presents for each other. Ralph is going to buy an all-electric kitchen, a color TV, and a stereo system on the installment plan; Alice is going to buy Ralph a custom-tailored suit with money she earns working, behind his back, for an answering service. When Ralph comes across a list of answering-service calls that Alice has hidden, he jumps to the conclusion that she is seeing another man and plotting to do away with the one she already has. Why? Because there are messages about druggists and cemeteries, and because there are an abundance of calls for one man, Armand (who is a professional escort).

Ralph and Ed, to expose Alice's infidelity, dress up as women and invite Armand to the apartment. Alice, meanwhile, is trying to measure Ralph for his expensive new suit without his knowing it. Unfortunately, he knows it, and thinks he's being measured for a coffin.

When Armand arrives, he develops a crush on Ed; then Alice arrives and explains everything. Ed is disappointed: Armand doesn't want to take him to the movies now. And Ralph is about to be disappointed: his surprise electric kitchen has overloaded the circuits—it will explode (live, on stage) the first time he tries to demonstrate it.

THE LOST SHOWS

Fewer than fifty episodes of *The Honeymooners* have been rerun in syndication. The remaining episodes, representing over a quarter-century of TV history, are unavailable for syndication. For much of the early material, film has been lost entirely. Many of the later episodes, while on usable film, do not fit either a one-hour or a half-hour format (since Gleason has always enjoyed varying the length of *Honeymooners* sketches within his variety shows) and therefore would be difficult to syndicate as a series.

Note that many air dates are not represented at all in the following brief plot synopses, since all Jackie Gleason shows did not include *Honeymooners* episodes. Furthermore, some CBS and all DuMont episodes cannot be represented due to the inadequacy of available information after nearly three decades.

The strong similarity between some of these story lines and stories of the early and late 1950s is no mere coincidence. Since any episodes not on film are lost forever, the *Honeymooners* team updated and expanded several "vintage" scripts, and, with the added features of color and music, made them available once again to a whole new generation of viewers.

The date listed with each entry is its original air date.

CBS: Before Electronicam

The episodes performed live from 1952 to 1955 are lost; no filmed record of them exists. What follows are plot summaries of the few of those episodes that can be verified.

February 13, 1954: Robert Q. Lewis and Art Carney do a takeoff on Edward R. Murrow's at-home interview show *Person to Person*, giving TV audiences their first view of Ed Norton's apartment.

April 10, 1954: Ralph Kramden decides to supplement his bus driver's income by becoming a prizefighter in his spare time.

June 5, 1954: Alice's aunt comes to live with the Kramdens. Ralph, who has to sleep on a cot for the duration, tries to get rid of her by marrying her off to the neighborhood butcher. Instead, the butcher, who has been living at the YMCA, comes to live with the Kramdens.

November 20, 1954: Ralph and Alice appear on Bud Collyer's TV game show *Beat the Clock*. Since the show runs out of time before they are able to finish their stunt, they are invited back to try again the following week. But Alice can't make the return engagement, and Ed goes on in her place.

November 27, 1954: Pat Harrington, playing Ralph Kramden's fast-talking brother-in-law, talks him into investing money in a hotel deal.

December 11, 1954: Kramden and Norton form a song-writing team, with Norton at the piano and Kramden belting out lyrics.

December 18, 1954: Ralph refuses to pay a rent increase and the landlord evicts him.

January 15, 1955: Ralph invites Alice and the Nortons out to the movies to celebrate Ed's birthday. Ed's ticket wins a television set which Ralph tries to claim since his money paid for the winning ticket. The two quarrel, and, since they refuse to fraternize with each other, have to start playing pool and other "men's games" with their wives—at least, until they come to their senses.

January 22, 1955: Ralph is promoted to assistant company cashier of the Gotham Bus Company. One night he accidentally locks the vault from the outside with the money still in his hand. He has to take it home with him, intending to return it early the next morning, but he becomes an overnight embezzler when he comes down with the flu and can't return to work for days.

January 29, 1955: The only way Ralph can get money from Alice and go to the Raccoon's annual convention in Chicago is by having her hypnotized.

February 5, 1955: Ralph, trying to find the right wife for a bachelor friend of his, interviews candidates who get the wrong idea.

February 12, 1955: Ralph's temper is so bad that his boss sends him to see a psychiatrist.

February 19, 1955: Ralph befriends a fatherless neighborhood boy and becomes his honorary father.

February 26, 1955: Ralph gets in trouble with Alice when he takes up a collection at the bus company to buy the boss' daughter a wedding present.

March 5, 1955: Trixie awakens the Kramdens in the middle of the night because Norton has left home after an enormous argument. Ralph not only has to find Norton and reconcile him with Trixie, he also has to fight off the urge to kill Norton by the end of the episode.

March 26, 1955: Ralph and Alice, wanting to adopt a baby, fib about their finances and allow the adoption agency to believe that the Nortons' fully equipped apartment is really the Kramdens'.

April 2, 1955: Ed gets Ralph interested in astrology and it affects every aspect of their behavior.

April 9, 1955: The Kramdens and the Nortons share the same apartment to save money.

April 16, 1955: Ralph can have a new, important job if he loses enough weight to meet the company's physical requirements. This endangers Ralph's job with the Gotham Bus Company, but he throws caution to the winds . . . until his new job offer looks like it will fall through.

April 23, 1955: Alice and Trixie, who feel that their husbands spend too much time bowling, playing pool, and meeting with the Raccoons, come up with a plan to get Ralph and Ed right where they want them.

April 30, 1955: Ralph refuses to pay his rent when the landlord refuses to make necessary repairs on the Kramden apartment. Instead, he applies the rent money to making the repairs himself, unprepared for the landlord's infuriating retaliation.

May 14, 1955: When their wives enter a neighborhood amateur show, Ralph and Ed try to get into the act.

May 21, 1955: When Ralph hears that he is going to be fired, he writes a biting letter to the bus company. Then he learns that, far from being fired, he is going to be promoted—that is, if he can retrieve his letter before the damage is done.

June 4, 1955: Gleason plays a double role in this episode, both as Ralph Kramden and as a look-alike mob boss. When a total stranger offers Ralph a posh job and a posher apartment, it never occurs to Ralph to be suspicious. Only later does he learn that he has been set up for a mob killing . . . while the man who looks just like him gets far, far away.

CBS: The Final New York Season

December 8, 1956: Live (not on tape) programming resumes with Ralph and Ed trying to buy a candy store that they hope to resell to a big chain. To finance their operation, they hit upon a risky plan that gets them into trouble at the Automat.

December 15, 1956: It's double roles for Gleason, Carney, Meadows, and Randolph when Kramden and Norton try to get big-name TV stars to attend the Raccoons' annual dance.

February 2, 1957: The first Lyn Duddy-Jerry Bresler musical *Honeymooners,* in which the Kramdens and Nortons win a trip to Europe when they coin a catchy slogan for Flakey Wakey cereal.

February 9, 1957: The Kramdens and Nortons are jailed in Paris for black market entanglements.

February 16, 1957: Ralph and Ed, in Germany, wander off from a picnic and cross into East Berlin, where they are arrested as international spies.

February 23, 1957: In Italy, Ralph becomes suspicious of an unknown rival who is introducing Alice to the wonders of Rome. The rival turns out to be a shoeshine boy, and Ralph, as usual, turns out to be a jealous dope.

March 2, 1957: In Ireland, the Kramdens and Nortons visit Ralph's ancestral castle. There is a curse on it now, which can only be broken by a Kramden spending the night within its walls. Ralph agrees to break the curse, unaware that a band of counterfeiters are determined to spook him out.

March 9, 1957: The Kramdens and Nortons appear on BBC-TV in England, performing a Flakey Wakey commercial written, directed, and sabotaged by Ralph.

April 13, 1957: Ralph and Ed persuade their wives to go on an African safari before returning home from Europe.

CBS: The Honeymooners in Miami

In the years that Art Carney was not on Jackie Gleason's show, there were no new *Honeymooners*. When Art returned briefly for a few guest appearances, Jackie revived the episodes within the format of *The American Scene Magazine*. In these, Sue Ane Langdon played Alice and Patricia Wilson played Trixie.

September 29, 1962: Ralph and Ed become interested in civil defense and spend their vacations in the cellar.

October 20, 1962: Ralph and Ed try to watch a Saturday football game on Ralph's new television set.

December 17, 1966: Ralph doesn't know that Alice has taken in knitting to pay for his Christmas present, so when he discovers baby things around the apartment, he assumes he's going to be a father. He takes a job as a sidewalk Santa, with Norton as his helper. For his efforts, he and Norton are jailed as operatives in a bookmaking operation. As the inmates sing "They're Springing Santa for Christmas," Ralph and Norton are released to help trap the real bookies. Then Ralph returns home, if not to an expectant mother, at least, to an expensive present.

January 14, 1967: Ralph takes himself, Alice, and the Nortons to the movies for Ed's birthday. Norton's ticket wins the door prize, a color TV; but since Ralph bought the ticket, Ralph wants the set. Ralph declares war on Ed, and is forced to spend his nights-out with Alice. Eventually, Ralph and Ed take their case to court, and, when they hear Alice's testimony, reconcile.

February 4, 1967: Ralph's unlikable brother-in-law Stanley tries to interest Ralph in a hotel which is strategically located along the route of a proposed state highway. Ralph likes the idea, but he doesn't like Stanley, so he and Norton buy the hotel, hiring themselves and their wives as staff. Then they learn that the highway will by-pass the hotel, taking business away from them but giving it to Stanley—who has a job with the construction team.

February 11, 1967: Alice and Trixie and Ralph and Ed enter a talent contest (as also does Robert Goulet, who, in the role of a neighborhood nobody, sings "If Ever I Would Leave You" . . . and gets "the hook"). Alice and Trixie win first place, and Alice uses her winnings to buy Ralph the expensive fishing gear he has had his eyes on.

March 4, 1967: Ralph, with his heart set on the traffic manager's job at the Gotham Bus Company, schemes to score points with the boss by collecting money from the drivers at the depot and buying the boss' daughter an elegant watch as a wedding present. He is thwarted when Alice and her mother (played by Pert Kelton) discover the watch and, since it is Alice's birthday, jump to the wrong conclusion. Ralph is forced to stage a phony holdup to get the watch back—and is thwarted again when a real crook overhears his scheme.

March 18, 1967: Ralph, as chairman of the Raccoons' annual dance, is asked to invite his celebrity friend he always brags about, Jackie Gleason. Ralph and Ed, in desperation, go to the hotel where Gleason and Carney are staying. Ralph does get to talk to Art Carney, and Norton does get to talk to Gleason (and Sheila MacRae and Jane Kean appear as themselves), but in the confusion, no one is invited to the dance. In the end, Jackie does appear at the dance . . . thanks to Alice's promise to give him the recipe for her anchovy pizza.

April 11, 1967: The Kramdens and Nortons, unable to make ends meet around tax time, decide to move to a large two-bedroom apartment in Flushing and split all expenses. The plan fails when Ralph complains of a dwindling food supply and insufficient time in the bathroom, so they all pack up and return home to Chauncey Street.

April 22, 1967: At Coney Island, Ralph learns from the fortune teller Madame Zelda that he is going to commit a murder within the week. For her own protection, Ralph wants Alice to stay with her mother until the week is up. She refuses and so Ralph moves in with Norton. Then Ralph gets so exasperated with Norton that he nearly kills him. In the end, Ralph manages to get himself arrested, and safely "on ice," by assaulting a police officer.

September 9, 1967: Rather than pay a $5 rent increase, Ralph buys a duplex in the country and takes the Nortons as his tenants. He forces them to sign a 99-year lease. But he is a negligent superintendent, and the Nortons attempt to break the lease with a 3:00 A.M. party and a firecracker in Ralph's fireplace.

September 16, 1967: For $500, Ralph and Norton buy a phony hair-restoration formula from a sharp promoter in Central Park. Over Alice and Trixie's objections, they mix up their first batch and try it on Ralph's boss. Using the formula he loses all his hair.

September 23, 1967: Ralph becomes a hero for recognizing "Knuckles" Grogan from his newspaper picture and aiding in his arrest. Then Knuckles escapes, and Ralph has to be the bait so the police can recapture him. Local politicians ask

Ralph, on the strength of his heroism, to run for state assembly; he agrees, and campaigns vigorously, until he realizes that his sponsors are dishonest. And, at the big pre-election rally, he tells the voters the whole story.

October 7, 1967: Ralph, as treasurer of the Raccoon Lodge, has been entrusted with $200 in cash, which he loses at Dennehy's Bar. He plays a long shot at the tracks to replace the money, and his horse wins but he doesn't, because he tore up his ticket at the beginning of the race when it looked like he was going to lose. Fortunately, the money turns up right where Ralph left it—in the pocket of the Raccoons' Grand High Exalted Mystic Ruler.

October 21, 1967: Alice's Aunt Ethel moves in with the Kramdens. Ralph, who has to sleep on a cot in the kitchen, plays Cupid for her and Krausmeyer, the butcher. His plan succeeds, Ethel and Krausmeyer elope, and they return to the Kramdens' for a place to live until they can find a home. And Ralph moves to the YMCA.

November 4, 1967: Ralph is sent to the company psychiatrist when he loses his temper once too often on the job. He is advised to give up his friendship with Norton. Norton mistakes his farewell note for a suicide note, and shadows Ralph to keep him out of trouble. Ralph, seeing Norton everywhere he looks, thinks he's losing his mind . . . until the truth comes out and the psychiatrist decides that Norton and Kramden belong together.

November 18, 1967: Ralph is set up as an "insurance executive" by mobsters because he is a dead ringer for their boss (also played by Gleason). Their real boss is fleeing the country with his moll; Ralph, as his stand-in, is due to be exterminated momentarily. Only the intervention of Norton, Alice, and Trixie saves Ralph's life.

December 2, 1967: Boxer "Dynamite" Moran is living with the Kramdens and Ralph is his new promoter. His first knockout, strictly unofficial and off the record, is staged for the benefit of the manager of heavyweight contender "Killer" Cuoco. The scheme works until Norton accidentally decks Dynamite. Undaunted, Ralph vows to stay in the fight game. Only this time, he will train Norton for the ring.

December 16, 1967: Ralph, told to turn in his bus driver's uniform, dashes off a scathing letter to his boss, only to realize he was not being fired but promoted to traffic manager. He retrieves the letter, then mails it again by mistake. His boss receives the letter, but has no one to blame, since it is unsigned. Then Norton stops by the boss' office to plead for another chance for his pal . . . and Ralph's professional aspirations take another nose dive.

September 28, 1968: Ralph meets a hypnotist, the Great Fatchoomara, at the Raccoon Lodge, and persuades him to put Alice in a trance. That way, she will have to show Ralph where she hides her emergency cash. Unfortunately for

Ralph, Alice overhears his scheme and substitutes a got-you-this-time note for the money. He doesn't realize until too late, on a train to the Miami Beach Raccoons' Annual Convention, that Alice was wise to him all along.

October 12, 1968: Alice, planning a surprise birthday party for Ralph, borrows a cookbook recipe from Trixie. Ralph, discovering the cookbook, finds in it an old love letter written by Ed. He concludes that Ed and Alice are lovers and takes the appropriate actions: following them and telling Trixie. But Trixie just laughs at Ralph, then she tells him the truth.

October 26, 1968: When the wives complain that their husbands don't fuss over them anymore, Ralph and Ed come up with a compromise: one night a week will be "boys' night out," the other nights they will spend with Alice and Trixie. But this is just another scheme that backfires on Ralph, who is planning to wear out the wives on the first night, but overcomes himself with exhaustion instead.

December 7, 1968: This year Alice is determined to receive a birthday gift from chronically forgetful Ralph even if she has to buy it herself, which she does. But she's not home when the present is delivered and Ralph, who signs for it, is sure she has a mysterious suitor.

January 4, 1969: Against Alice's advice, Ralph, who has broken his leg in a bus accident, is suing the Gotham Bus Company for $75,000. The lawyer thinks he has a good case until he learns that Ralph was driving the bus when the accident occurred.

April 5, 1969: Norton moves in with the Kramdens because his apartment smells of paint . . . until Ralph, who is going crazy from sharing a cot with Norton, throws paint all over his own place to drive Norton out.

TIMELINE

GLEASON AND THE WORLD OF TV

1907 The word *television* used in *Scientific American*.

1916 (Feb. 26) Herbert John ("Jackie") Gleason born to Mae and Herbert Gleason.

1931 Jackie Gleason wins amateur night at Halsey Theater.

1940 Gleason's first big break on the New York nightclub scene—at Club 18.

1941 Jackie Gleason goes to Hollywood to make pictures for Warner Brothers.

1945 Gleason's first major Broadway success, *Follow the Girls*.

President Harry Truman makes his first network telecast at Navy Day celebration in Central Park.

1947 First telecast of *The Howdy Doody Show*.

ABC joins CBS, NBC, and DuMont as a major TV network.

1948 AT&T's first intercity coaxial cable television.

Martin & Lewis TV debut on Ed Sullivan's *Toast of the Town*.

Arthur Godfrey TV debut with *Talent Scouts*.

Ted Mack brings *The Original Amateur Hour* from radio to television.

1949 Gleason's first TV series, *The Life of Riley*.

Sid Caesar appears on *Admiral Broadway Revue* (later titled *Your Show of Shows*).

1950 Gleason returns to television as guest emcee on *Cavalcade of Stars* on the DuMont network. Within weeks, he is the regular host of the show, and has introduced most of his popular sketches and characterizations, including *The Honeymooners*. Pert Kelton, Art Carney, and Joyce Randolph join cast.

Burns and Allen Show TV debut.

CBS institutes loyalty oath as part of its regular policy.

1951 Harry Truman addresses the Japanese peace treaty convention in San Francisco on the first coast-to-coast telecast.

Amos 'n' Andy TV debut.

155

I Love Lucy TV debut.

1952 Jackie Gleason moves his variety show to CBS. *The Honeymooners* goes with him, minus Pert Kelton. Audrey Meadows becomes the new Alice Kramden.

1953 Jackie Gleason and Art Carney star on *Studio One* in *The Laugh Maker*, an original television play written by A. J. Russell. Gleason is so impressed with Russell's feeling for character and situation that he invites him to write for *The Honeymooners* and other Gleason sketches.

Tommy and Jimmy Dorsey join the *Jackie Gleason Show*, reuniting their famous bands for the first time in years.

Tawny, Jackie's tone poem/ballet in four parts, presented for the first time on *The Jackie Gleason Show*.

Lucille Ball gives birth to the real "Little Ricky" (January 19). Newspapers the following day give Desi Arnaz, Jr. and President Eisenhower's Inauguration equal coverage.

1954 Gleason's CBS cast in person at the Paramount Theatre, performing live variety show numbers and sketches including *The Honeymooners*. They share the bill with the movie *Drum Beat*.

Jackie Gleason breaks leg, live and on stage.

DuMont network covers Senate Army-McCarthy hearings.

Jimmy Durante's series, *The Texaco Star Theatre*, debuts.

Steve Allen makes debut as the TV host of *The Tonight Show*.

1955 Electronicam process introduced by DuMont.

Gleason launches, then drops, plans for a series of one-hour "nightclub" television programs. *Cafe Mardi Gras*, as originally conceived, would feature Marlene Dietrich, Sammy Davis, Jr., Kate Smith, Hildegarde, and others. Trappings are so elaborate that part of a theater wall must be torn down to make room for a huge hydraulic lift.

The Honeymooners, starring Jackie Gleason, Art Carney, Audrey Meadows, and Joyce Randolph, is filmed for one season with Electronicam. It is presented in conjunction with the live variety program, *Stage Show*, to fill out a one-hour time slot. Only thirty-nine episodes are filmed, to be rebroadcast later as half-hour situation comedy reruns.

DuMont network folds.

Disneyland and Davy Crockett take America by storm. Davy Crockett cards, coonskin caps, and canvas "buckskins" sell like mad, everyone wants to go to California to see Disneyland, and Disney is richer than ever.

Mickey Mouse Club debuts.

Gunsmoke comes from radio to TV. William Conrad, the Matt Dillon of radio, is replaced by James Arness.

Ronnie Burns joins his parents in a regular role on *The Burns and Allen Show*.

Poet Louis Untermeyer predicts that television "will eventually boost the quality and reduce the quantity of fiction written in the U.S."

1956 *The Honeymooners* goes back to all-live broadcasting, as a sketch of varying lengths within the one-hour *Jackie Gleason Show*.

1957 Art Carney leaves the program to pursue other aspects of his acting career. There will be no new episodes of *The Honeymooners* until his return.

Jack Paar takes over as host of *The Tonight Show*.

Nikita Khrushchev on *Face the Nation*.

1958 Buddy Hackett joins *The Jackie Gleason Show*.

1959 The quiz show scandals.

1960 The Nixon-Kennedy TV debates.

1961 Jackie Gleason's TV game show *You're in the Picture* debuts.

Jackie Gleason stars in the movies *Gigot* and *The Hustler*.

The Dick Van Dyke Show debuts.

1962 Gleason nominated for Academy Award (Best Supporting Actor) for his role as Minnesota Fats in *The Hustler*.

Gleason stars in the movie *Requiem for a Heavyweight*.

"The Great Gleason Express" makes the ten-day cross-country journey to Miami as Gleason relocates to Florida and plans for a new TV variety show.

Johnny Carson takes over as *The Tonight Show* host.

1962–66 *The Jackie Gleason Show: The American Scene Magazine* is a comedy/satire variety show. Frank Fontaine is introduced in the role of Crazy Guggenheim. *The Honeymooners* is revived briefly when Art Carney appears as a guest star; Sue Ane Langdon plays Alice and Patricia Wilson plays Trixie.

1963 Gleason stars in the movie *Papa's Delicate Condition*.

1964 "The Great Gleason Express" is back, this time taking Gleason's crew from New York to Miami.

1965 "The Great Gleason Express" rides again, New York to Miami.

Get Smart, created by former *Honeymooners* writer Leonard Stern, debuts.

1966 Last black-and-white episode of *The Honeymooners*, reuniting Art Carney, Audrey Meadows, and Jackie Gleason in a one-hour special entitled "The Adoption," wherein Ralph and Alice try to adopt a child.

1966–1970 *The Jackie Gleason Show* has a new cast. Art Carney returns on a regular basis. *The Honeymooners* is revived, with Sheila MacRae as Alice and Jane Kean as Trixie.

1967 Pert Kelton, the first Alice Kramden, appears February 18 as Alice's mother, Mrs. Gibson.

1969 Moon landing televised.

Sesame Street debuts.

1970 CBS cancels *The Jackie Gleason Show*.

CBS cancels *Gunsmoke* (after fifteen years) and *The Red Skelton Show*, signs *All in the Family*.

1971 *All in the Family* debuts.

The Ed Sullivan Show goes off the air after twenty-three years.

1972 Last year of Jackie Gleason's exclusive contract with CBS, which pays him $100,000 a year even if he does not work for CBS—provided that he does not work for any other network either.

Maude, produced by former *Honeymooners* writer Rod Parker, debuts.

The Waltons debuts.

1973 Watergate hearings televised.

1974 *Happy Days* debuts.

1975 Art Carney wins Academy Award (Best Male Performance in Starring Role) for his performance in *Harry and Tonto.*

Saturday Night Live debuts.

1976 *The Honeymooners* twenty-fifth anniversary special on ABC, with Jackie Gleason, Art Carney, Audrey Meadows, and Jane Kean in the leads.

1977 *The Honeymooners* Christmas Special on ABC.

Roots, the TV–mini-series, draws largest TV audience in history.

1978 *The Honeymooners* Valentine Special on ABC.

CBS marks its fiftieth anniversary with a five-day special that is almost a mini-series in itself.

ABC's four-hour-long silver anniversary celebration special.

Twenty-fifth anniversary of American public television marked by retrospective program, *The Great American Dream Machine Revisited.*

Kraft marks its seventy-fifth anniversary on radio and television with a television special.

V. THE HONEYMOONERS HIGHLIGHTS

The 1955 Jackie Gleason Bus,
made of tin, measured
a little over a foot long.

Jackie Gleason
comic books were
on the stands from 1956 to 1958.

In 1955, the Jackie Gleason
Story Stage game sold for $2.98.

THE PHILOSOPHY OF RALPH KRAMDEN

"I am the king in my castle."
   "Better Living Through TV"

To Alice:
"A man's home is just like a ship. And on this ship, I am the captain. . . . You are nothing but a lowly third-class seaman."
   "The Baby-sitter"

To Stanley, his brother-in-law-to-be: "You are the king, because a man's home is his castle, and in that castle you're the king. . . . Tomorrow afternoon when Agnes says 'I do,' that is the last decision you allow her to make."
   "Here Comes the Bride"

"Every time you get into the habit of saying yes to your wife, you're getting into the habit of saying no to your independence."
   "Something Fishy"

On the subject of philosophy, Ralph does seem to have a one-track mind. But there are other times when he mellows.

"Acting young isn't what keeps you young, but if you've got some memories, some good memories, of when you were young, that's what keeps you young."
   "Young at Heart"

"Boy what a pleasure it is to think that you've got someplace to go to. And the place that you're going to, there's somebody in it that you really love. Somebody you're nuts about."
   "Twas the Night Before Christmas"

FAVORITE FAT JOKES

"Some kids are small, some kids are tall, Fatso Kramden is the only kid who walks down the hall wall to wall."
—Bill Davis, writing in Ralph Kramden's school yearbook *"A Man's Pride"*

"I'm not losing a daughter, I'm gaining a ton."
—Alice's mother at Alice and Ralph's wedding *"Hello, Mom"*

RALPH: "You ain't talking me out of it, Alice. I'm going for that pot of gold!"

ALICE: "Just go for the gold—you've already got the pot."
"The $99,000 Answer"

RALPH: "Six hundred bucks is peanuts! Peanuts! What am I going to do with peanuts?"
ALICE: (although the line was originally written for Garrity, the neighbor, to holler from upstairs): "Eat them—like any other elephant!"
"The $99,000 Answer"

RALPH (accusing Alice of being too gullible): "You're the type that would bend way over and pick up a pocketbook on April Fool's Day. I wouldn't."

ALICE: "You couldn't."
"The Deciding Vote"

RALPH: "You're the only man who turns my stomach upside down."

ED: "There ain't a man in New York City that's strong enough to turn your stomach upside down."
"Trapped"

BRUCE GREENE

RALPH: "I promise you this, Norton. I'm gonna learn. I'm gonna learn from here on in how to swallow my pride."
ED: "That ought not to be too hard. You've learned how to swallow everything else."
"A Man's Pride"

RALPH (declaring another total war on Norton): "If you see me coming down the street, get on the other side."
ED: "When you come down the street, there ain't no other side."
"The Man from Space"

RALPH (refusing to join Alice and the Nortons for dinner): "They can eat now. I'll wait. It won't hurt me to wait a couple of hours to eat."
ED: "No, it won't hurt you, but it'll be tough on the farmers."
"The Man from Space"

ED (after Ralph tells Ed that Alice used to call him her "Little Buttercup" before they were married): "You were a cup of butter and now you're a whole tub of lard."
"A Woman's Work Is Never Done"

RALPH (vowing to Alice that he will get Norton's job back): "There's nothing in this world gonna stop me going down to the sewer tomorrow morning."
ALICE: "Oh no? There isn't a manhole in New York you could fit through."
"Mind Your Own Business"

ED (finding Ralph passed out and thinking he's passed on to the Pearly Gates) "At this time, they're probably tearing down part of the fence to let him in."
"A Matter of Life and Death"

ED (when Ralph considers selling his body to science so he will have some money to leave Alice when he dies). :"If they pay by the pound, Alice'll be a millionaire."
"A Matter of Life and Death"

ED: "Boy oh boy, how could anyone so round be so square?"
"Young At Heart"

RALPH (boasting about another sure-fire scheme): "This is probably the biggest thing I ever got into."
ALICE: "The biggest thing you ever got into was your pants."
"Better Living Through TV"

RALPH (afraid that, if Alice gets a phone, she will start cutting down on his food to save money): "Then you know what I'll look like?"
ALICE: "Yeah. A human being."
"The Baby-sitter"

SELECTED SEWER JOKES

"**L**ike we say in the sewer, time and tide wait for no man."
—Ed Norton *"Ralph Kramden, Inc."*

"As we say in the sewer, here's mud in your eye."
—Ed Norton *"Head of the House"*

"When the tides of life turn against you
And the current upsets your boat
Don't waste those tears on what might have been;
Just lay on your back and float."
—Ed Norton *"The Safety Award"*

"If pizzas were manhole covers, the sewer would be a paradise."
—Ed Norton *"Pardon My Glove"*

"You can take the man out of the sewer, but you can't take the sewer out of the man."
—Trixie Norton *"Mind Your Own Business"*

"A sewer worker is like a brain surgeon. We're both specialists."
—Ed Norton *"Mind Your Own Business"*

"As we say in the sewer, if you're not prepared to go all the way, don't put your boots on in the first place."
—Ed Norton *"Confusion Italian Style"*

RALPH: "It's rush hour. "We'll never be able to get across town in this traffic."

ED: "Trust me, we'll go by sewer."
"Beat the Clock"

RALPH (annoyed with Norton for helping himself to the barber's after-shave lotion): "How would you like him to come down to the sewer where you work and help himself to anything down there?"

ED: "Help himself to what?"
"The Baby-sitter"

RALPH (sarcastically explaining to Norton why his water pipes don't work): "I hope that you realize that water always seeks its level."

ED: "Yes, we've heard rumors to that effect down in the sewer."
  "Dial J for Janitor"

RALPH: "What do *you* know about golf?"

ED: "I've been working in the sewer for ten years. If that don't qualify me as an expert on holes, I give up."
  "The Golfer"

RALPH: "I've always followed that old adage: Be kind to the people you meet on the way up, because you're going to meet the same people on the way down."

ED: "Happens to me every day in the sewer."
  "On Stage"

HONEYMOONERS SONGS

Two *Honeymooners* songs by Lyn Duddy and Jerry Bresler. "There's Nothing That I Haven't Sung About," written for Bing Crosby to sing to Kramden and Norton, subsequently became Bing's unofficial theme song, which he performed frequently and later recorded.

THERE'S NOTHING THAT I HAVEN'T SUNG ABOUT

I've sung about the bird and the bees,
The daffodils, the shady trees;
I've covered Mother Nature inside out.
There's the Old Ox Road, the Old Mill Stream,
And Pennies from Heaven and Darn That Dream;
There's nothing that I haven't sung about.

I've sung some songs of sacrifice,
And some that offered good advice;
I've covered all emotions, there's no doubt.
There's A Fine Romance and Learn to Croon,
And Sing You Sinners and Love in Bloom;
There's nothing that I haven't sung about.

There's many a chorus,
I sang Dolores.
Remember Marquita
And Sweet Rio Rita.
There's Mary and Sally,
And Rose, Mexicali;
From Evaline to Clementine,
They all got equal time.

Yes, music'lly I've been around,
I've covered almost ev'ry town.
I've always been a vocal gadabout,
From the Swanee River to Galway Bay,
The Atchison Topeka and the Santa Fe;
There's nothing that I haven't sung about.

I Found a Million-Dollar Baby in the Ten-Cent Store,
A Pocketful of Dreams and plenty more,
Since Anything Goes, I picked Sweet Sue,
I suppose it's the natural thing to do.

We began the Beguine, I could feel it start,
I said, Please Be Careful, It's My Heart.
In the Cool of the Ev'ning, 'neath the Autumn Leaves,
We called for Music Maestro, Please.

There was such Temptation as we cuddled near,
And I whispered, I Surrender Dear.
The Bells of Saint Mary's rang in the steeple,
For all the Dear Hearts and Gentle People.

I said, Babe, I've Got You Under My Skin,
And, It Hadda Be You, 'cause Love Walked In.
From Here On In, You'll Be Going My Way,
'Til the Blue of the Night Meets the Gold of the Day.

I've crooned about Dolly.
I've tuned up a trolley.
I've sung of Chicago,
and Doctor Zhivago;
The ol' Mississippi,
and Tin, Tippi-Tippi.
The Winter, Summer, Spring, and Fall,
I've covered one and all.

Yes, these are just a very few,
A few of which I've shared with you.
The rondelays I couldn't do without,
From the land of vaudeville and video;
To the movies, records, and radio.
With the possible exception of the gout,
There is nothing,
Almost nothing,
That I haven't sung about!

Jerry Bresler (left) and Lyn Duddy (right), who wrote lyrics and music for a musical comedy a week for *The Honeymooners*. "It's a chore that might, conceivably, faze Cole Porter or Giacomo Puccini. But not Lyn Duddy and Jerry Bresler. They're thriving. And preparing to write a Broadway show during Mr. Gleason's summer layoff." —Harriet Van Horne, *New York World Telegram and Sun*, 1957.

RACCOON ALMA MATER

ALL
From the hallowed streets of Greenpernt,
To the shores of Sheepshead Bay,
From the Verrazano Narrows,
To Canarsie across the way . . .
We have come together, one and all,
In fellowship to commune,
And to glorify the Grand Exalted
Brotherhood of Raccoons. [*Howl*]

THEME SONGS

You're My Greatest Love

Theme Of "The Honeymooners"

Lyric by
BILL TEMPLETON

Music by
JACKIE GLEASON

Slowly and broadly

YOU'RE MY GREAT-EST LOVE, You're heav-en-ly, you're stars from a - bove, You set my heart a-

fire with de - sire con - stant - ly. _____ You're

my great - est dream, to hold you close is my great - est scheme, The vis-ion of your

You're My etc.-2

TRAFFIC MANAGER'S TEST (TRIVIA QUESTIONS FOR THE EXCEPTIONALLY GIFTED)

Q: What is the answer to the most often-asked question regarding *The Honeymooners?*
A: They only filmed 39.

Q: What is the question?
A: How come people remember *Honeymooners* shows from the 1950s that are never rerun on TV?

Q: What are the entrance requirements for the Raccoon Lodge?
A: Applicant must have a public school diploma, must have been a U.S. resident for the last six months, and must pay a $1.50 initiation fee.

Q: What's in it for the Raccoon of the Year?
A: He wears platinum braid on his uniform. He can run for Grand High Exalted Mystic Ruler. He opens the first clam at the annual clambake, steers from the bridge on the Raccoon boat ride up the Hudson River as they pass Raccoon Point, and he enjoys, with his wife, free burial in the Raccoon National Cemetery in Bismarck, North Dakota.

Q: Who makes more money, Ralph or Ed?
A: They both make the same: $62 a week.

Q: What is the room number of *American Weekly?* Of the hospital room where Ed stayed when a sewer explosion on Himrod Street landed him in Bushwick Hospital?
A: Room 1623; Room 317.

Q: What is Ralph's social security number?
A: 105-36-22.

Q: What happened to the rest of the digits?

A: That's what makes it funny.

Q: What does the Pullman berth that Ralph and Ed share to Norfolk, Virginia, have in common with the alley on which they bowl?

A: They're both Number 3.

Q: Calculating distances by the rate at which the aroma of Egg Foo Yung travels upward, how high off the ground does Ralph live, and how high is the ceiling of his apartment?

A: If Ed is correct in stating that the aroma travels at 320 feet per second, and that it reaches Ralph's window 116 seconds after it leaves the ground, Ralph lives 37,120 feet off the ground. If the same aroma, as is alleged, reaches Norton's window (directly over Ralph's) 4 seconds later, then Ralph's ceiling is an exceptional 1,280 feet high. (And this was in a walk-up apartment!)

Gleason and Carney in one of the later (Miami) episodes.

"Together they have performed a resurrection, almost as rare on television as it is in a graveyard. They brought 'The Honeymooners' out of the boneyard and, in a season of ailing comedies, prompted some reviewers to greet them as the greatest comedy team of their time."—Ted Crail, *TV Guide*, January 14, 1967

Scoring: Score 10 points for each correct answer, and rate yourself as follows: 0–10 points. Drip pan under Kramdens' icebox; 20 points, Moax; 30 points, Chef of the Future; 40 points, Chef of the Past; 50 points, Honorary Raccoon; 60 points, King of the Castle; 70 points, Raccoon Convention Manager; 80 points, Raccoon of the Year; 90 points, Grand High Exalted Mystic Ruler; 100 points, Traffic Manager.

CYCLE OF LIFE GAME

by Jim Fairbrother

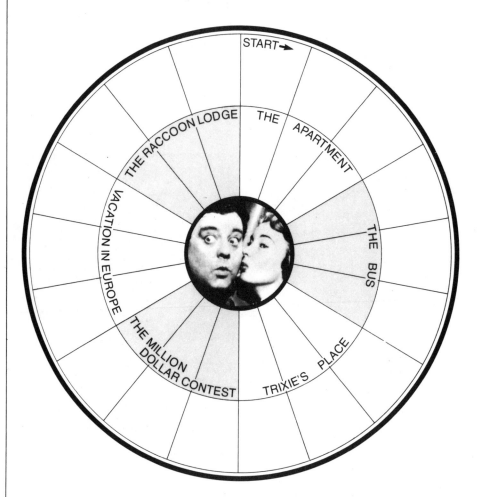

START→

THE RACCOON LODGE

THE APARTMENT

VACATION IN EUROPE

THE BUS

THE MILLION DOLLAR CONTEST

TRIXIE'S PLACE

INSTRUCTIONS

The game is for two players. The one who is pretty and blonde plays Alice. The one who cannot see his feet plays Ralph.

Roll dice to see who goes first. If Alice gets the higher roll, she goes first. If Ralph gets the higher roll, Alice goes first anyway.

Each player moves the number of spaces rolled on two dice according to the instructions. (Separate instructions for Alice and for Ralph.)

Players move around the Cycle of Life according to their instructions, trying not to land on the same space as the opposing player.

In order to avoid landing on Ralph, Alice may detour through the lighter area in which she is most "at home"—the Apartment, the Vacation in Europe, or Trixie's Place. Each space of the inner area corresponds to one space of the Cycle.

In order to avoid running into Alice, Ralph may detour through the shaded areas—the Raccoon Lodge, the Million-Dollar Contest, or the Bus.

When both players land on the same space, Ralph says, "Baby, you're the greatest," kisses Alice, and the game is over.

The game will last half an hour (an hour when it is played in Europe).

There are no winners, but there are no losers either.

RALPH'S MOVES

2: Ralph could be the *big* winner on a TV contest, but he can't remember the name of Norton's favorite tune—"Swanee River." *Move back 1 space.*

3: "I gotta Biiiggg Mouth!!!" Ralph challenges boss to a golf match. *Move back 3 spaces.*

4: Norton—not Ralph—wins the "Raccoon of the Year" Award. *Move back 3 spaces.*

5: "Humunah Hum Hum . . ." *Lose one turn for stalling.*

6: Ralph boasts that he is king of his household—Alice crowns him. *Move back 4 spaces.*

7: Ralph challenges a big man to a big fight down at the gym . . . then loses his nerve. *Lose 1 turn.*

8: Ralph discovers that KramMar, his new taste sensation, is dog food. *Move back 2 spaces.*

9: Ralph inherits a millionaire's fortune—a parrot named Fortune. *Move back 3 spaces.*

10: In a suitcase left on his bus, Ralph finds a million dollars—counterfeit bills, of course. *Move back 4 spaces.*

11: Ralph gets the fatal disease Arterial Monochromia, sells his story to a magazine, then doesn't die. *Move back 1 space.*

12: Ralph and Norton decide to get drunk—on grape juice. *Lose 1 turn.*

ALICE'S MOVES

2: Alice's mother visits. *Move ahead 2 spaces.*

3: Alice—instead of Ralph—is offered a part in a Hollywood production. *Move ahead 4 spaces.*

4: Finally! Alice wins free interior decoration. *Move ahead 1 space.*

5: Alice takes mambo lessons from the new, dashingly handsome neighbor. *Move ahead 3 spaces.*

6: Alice lands a job. *Move ahead 1 space.*

7: Alice gets a maid. *Move ahead 2 spaces.*

8: Alice is allowed to go on the Raccoon Lodge fishing trip. *Move ahead 6 spaces.*

9: Alice gets a phone. *Move ahead 1 space.*

10: Ralph takes Alice roller skating. *Move ahead 3 spaces.*

11: Ralph rescues Alice from holdup men. *Move ahead 1 space.*

12: Pow! Go directly to the moon. *Return to Start on next turn.*

Jim Fairbrother still owns a black-and-white television set.

FAN MAIL

The Great One with (left to right) Polly Bergen, Jayne Meadows, Joyce Randolph, Audrey Meadows, and Jayne Mansfield.

"The story of Jackie Gleason, his friends will tell you, is the story of a man violently in love with life; relishing today, yet always a little bit afraid of tomorrow."—*TV Revue*, August 1954

Call it "star quality" or "chemistry" or nothing at all. When something is right, you don't have to know why, you just have to sit back and enjoy it.

But if it helps you to enjoy *The Honeymooners* more, here is what some prominent fans think about the show:

STEVE ALLEN Not many viewers can watch the finish of one of his [Gleason's] *Honeymooners* scenes without feeling an unexpected lump in the throat and a tug at the heart strings. At its best a husband-and-wife playlet between Sid Caesar and Nanette Fabray is funnier, but the same sort of scene enacted by Gleason and Audrey Meadows has more emotional impact. Indeed, it is Jackie's ability to engender *sympathy* that is one of his most powerful assets.

IMOGENE COCA I was, and am, an ardent fan of *The Honeymooners*. To me the four people were all basically fine actors, who were comedic because of the basic truth they brought to their characters, and the situations. They worked so beautifully together; and one felt the overall pull to give the situations, and their relationships, the *very* best they were capable of giving.

I wish I were capable of really telling you how much I've enjoyed their shows, and why I have. Unfortunately, I am not a writer—but what I've written is most sincerely how I feel.

BOB CUMMINGS About 1954 there emerged on the networks, first NBC then CBS then ABC, a resounding hit, *The Bob Cummings Show*. It became No. 1 on the networks, both NBC and CBS, but the star of that show was really an ardent fan of another piece of highly rated entertainment, *The Honeymooners*, starring a brilliant actor and a brilliant cast. Audrey Meadows was a friend of mine and so was Rosemary DeCamp. Rosemary played my sister on *The B. C. Show* for some five years so I became an expert on the talents of Jackie Gleason. She can go on by the hour about the beauty, majesty, magnetism, resourcefulness, and electrifying presence of this great man, and it was an education in showmanship to hear her. Both Audrey and Rosemary had played his wife, Rosemary in a seldom-mentioned TV show, *The Life of Riley*, and of course Audrey in *The Honeymooners*.

Both women displayed unlimited respect for "The Great One," "The Genius" Jackie Gleason. They also said he was one of the most eccentric men on earth, but *all man* and a yard wide. I unfortunately only met him once very briefly. I'm still an ardent fan of his, and *The Honeymooners*.

BOB HOPE I naturally have always been interested in *The Honeymooners* because it involved a lot of my friends—people whose talents I admire, and I watch the show every chance I get. I don't think I have to give them a good notice as far as the quality of the entertainment is concerned because millions of people give them their approval from all around the world. Jackie Gleason of course holds a special spot in my heart because he is not only a man with talent but also a wonderful friend.

NORMAN LEAR *The Honeymooners* represents one of the great creative collaborations in television history. Seldom has there been a better marriage between writing and performing. Happily, it also caught Jackie Gleason and Art Carney as their genius was just beginning to flower. Despite the relatively few episodes made, it has stood the test of time because it is a true classic. It will run forever with each new generation, I am sure, for that very reason.

SAM LEVENSON *The Honeymooners* are symbolic of all young marrieds' hope for a happy forever-after. Its success lies in its truthful depiction of the successes and failures of the dream. We rejoice with them and lament with them. They are us.

JOHN O'HARA Jackie Gleason is an artist of the first rank. An artist puts his own personal stamp on all of his mature work, making his handling of his material uniquely his own. Millions of people who don't give a damn about art have been quick to recognize a creation. Ralph Kramden is a character that we might be getting from Mr. Dickens if he were writing for TV.

JOAN RIVERS *The Honeymooners* is probably the best consecutively written series of sketches ever done on television. Every one totally proves what I believe about comedy: what is said and how it is said are what count and make something funny, not the trappings and background.

BETTY ROLLIN Hope springs eternal has never seemed like a particularly funny idea. But the apoplectic fervor with which Kramden pursues an idea, the way Norton dogs along—his face graver than a brain surgeon's, arms flailing the air like a deranged orchestra conductor's—this is hope at its most hilarious. It's the kind of hope that, in life, may be tragic. In the hands of *The Honeymooners*, it's a kelly-green fandango.

LEO ROSTEN Gleason brings shudders to the shoulders of the carriage trade, which he finds just peachy; he is aiming for the bleachers. He is the Brooklyn Bum of comedy, and inspires the same kind of loony affection. With the exception of one gentle character he portrays, the Poor Soul, his approach to the risible makes Sid Caesar look like Noel Coward.

THE SATURDAY NIGHT LIVE HONEYMOONERS

Music: The Honeymooners Theme
Set: In the Kramden kitchen. Jane, as Trixie, and Gilda, as Alice, are drinking coffee at the table. Gilda is knitting.

JANE: . . . and Ed's first lover was a fly, Alice.

GILDA: Gee, Trixie, I can't see Ed with a fly. They're so uptight, so closed.

JANE: Well, Ed's fly was open. (Looks at watch and gets up.) I better get going and fix Ed's dinner.

GILDA: Thanks. I'm gonna lie down. I'm feeling a little nauseous. Bye, Trixie.

(Jane exits. Gilda leaves knitting and knitting needles on chair and goes into bedroom. John, as Ralph, enters.)

Cue: Applause.

(John puts lunch pail down, removes cap, and sighs.)

JOHN: Alice, I'm home.

GILDA: (offstage) Hi Ralph. I'll be right out.

(John seats himself on chair with knitting needles, jumps up screaming in pain, with two knitting needles poking out of his seat. Gilda rushes in from bedroom.)

GILDA: Ralph! What's wrong? What's gotten into you?

JOHN: Your knitting needles, Alice, that's what's gotten into me. Get 'em out. I can't go to my lodge meeting like this. What'll the Raccoons think?

RAIN WORTHINGTON

John Belushi and Gilda Radner appeared in the parody of *The Honeymooners* on *Saturday Night Live*.

GILDA: That you swallowed a porcupine.

JOHN: Har de har har. You're a real riot, Alice. You're going places, Alice.

GILDA: Where am I going, Ralph?

JOHN: To the moon! Bang zoom! Now pull these needles out!

GILDA: I can't. I'm feeling sick, Ralph. (Walking towards bedroom.) Get Norton to help you.

(Gilda exits into bedroom. John crosses over to window and leans out. Danny enters as Ed Norton.)

Cue: Applause.

JOHN: Norton! Norton!

(Danny approaches him from the rear and taps him.)

DANNY: Hey, Ralphie boy!

JOHN: Norton! Get these things out of me!

(Danny stands there, examining them from a few angles.)

DANNY: Ya know, Ralph, with those knitting needles poking out of you, from a certain angle you look like a geisha school bus. Heh heh heh.

JOHN: (Pointing to the door screaming.) Out! Out! (Danny goes to leave.) No, wait, get them out first.

(Danny does hand shtick as if he is preparing to pull them out. John turns around and reacts.)

JOHN: Cut that out!

(Danny pulls the needles out, using one to pick his teeth.)

JOHN: Gimme those. (He throws them down, and starts pacing.) Ya know, I don't understand what's going on around here, Norton. First Alice is knitting, then suddenly she's nauseous . . . .

DANNY: Wait, Ralph, you say she's knitting and nauseous . . . ya know what that means!? A little drone. A queen perhaps. Hey hey hey hey Ralphie boy, congratulations. Quite frankly I didn't think you had it in ya. (He hands John a cigar.)

JOHN: (Instantly humbled and deeply moved.) My Alice . . . pregnant . . . with a little Ralph. (Danny takes a fast take on "little Ralph.") Thank you pal o' mine, you're a real buddy.

DANNY: That's okay, Ralph. (Starting to cry with emotion.) Congratulations. (He exits.)

JOHN: (Calling out in a lovey dovey voice) Alice! Oh Alice sweetie. . . . (Gilda enters.)

JOHN: Why didn't you tell me we were going to have a baby?

GILDA: Because, Ralph, it's not yours. It's Ed Norton's baby.

JOHN: (Grabbing her in an embrace.) Baby, you're the greatest!

(John and Gilda kiss.)

Cue: Applause.

VI. THE HONEYMOONERS BIOGRAPHIES

RALPH KRAMDEN

JACKIE GLEASON

He is real. He is regular. He is sincere. He is possibly one of the great theatrical talents of this century.

JIM BISHOP, *THE GOLDEN HAM*

Born Herbert John Gleason (his mother always called him "Jackie") in Brooklyn in the neighborhood he has immortalized on *The Honeymooners*, Jackie Gleason never stopped to ponder over what he would be when he grew up. He was a born showman.

He won the amateur-night contest at Brooklyn's Halsey Theater at the age of fifteen, and was hired that same night, by the manager, to work as emcee for three dollars a week. Next he worked at Brooklyn's Folly Theater. Before long, he was emceeing for small theaters all over New York's five boroughs. When he wasn't doing stage shows, he worked as a carnival barker, a radio disc jockey, a daredevil driver, and an exhibition diver in the water follies.

When he began to work in more famous nightclubs, he acquired a reputation for brash humor and fast ad libs. It was during his engagement at Club 18 in New York that he was discovered by Jack Warner and signed for the movies. He made five films in Hollywood, then returned to New York for Broadway musicals including *Hellzapoppin* and *Along Fifth Avenue*.

He made his television debut on Ed Sullivan's *Toast of the Town*. After that, in 1949, he played Chester A. Riley in the series *The Life of Riley*. From there, he returned to stage shows and nightclubs until, in 1950, a brief engagement on DuMont's *Cavalcade of Stars* made him an overnight TV sensation. He remained on *Cavalcade of Stars* for two years, creating most of his famous characterizations (Ralph Kramden, Joe the Bartender, Charlie Bratton, The Poor Soul, and Reggie Van Gleason III. He left *Cavalcade* and the DuMont network in 1952 to sign one big contract after another with CBS, and later, with NBC and ABC.

He returned to Broadway to star in *Take Me Along* in 1959, and to Hollywood to star in such pictures as *Gigot* (1961), *The Hustler,* for which he received an Academy Award nomination (1962), *Papa's Delicate Condition* (1963), *How To Commit Marriage* (1969), and *Don't Drink the Water* (1969).

He has achieved success in the field of popular music with his immensely popular records, such as *Music for Lovers Only,* and as composer of the theme songs for *The Honeymooners* ("You're My Greatest Love") and *The Jackie Gleason Show* ("Melancholy Serenade") and the tone poem/ballet *Tawny* (1953).

As early as 1954 he had the idea of freezing special dieters' TV dinners with the exact number of calories printed on the label. He maintains an absorbing interest in occult phenomena and parapsychology. In the early 1970's, with the Haft-Gaines Company, he launched the richest seventy-two-hole golf tournament in the United States, the Jackie Gleason Inverrary Classic.

He has been called "the Great One," and the "Noel Coward of Toots Shor's," yet for all his achievements over the past half-century, he is doubtless best known for 20.5 hours of syndicated situation comedy—thirty-nine filmed-on-Electronicam episodes of *The Honeymooners*.

ED NORTON

ART CARNEY

He brings to comedy the deftness, imagination and pathos of yesterday's most eloquent loser, Charlie Chaplin.

LOOK

Born in Mt. Vernon, New York, Art Carney won an Oscar in 1975 for his first starring movie role—in *Harry and Tonto*—although he never had an acting lesson. (He had made his debut, in the 1930s, as an entertainer at the local Elks Club, and performed locally as an impressionist and tap dancer.)

After graduation from high school he traveled for three years with Horace Heidt, who had a very popular orchestra and radio quiz show in the late 1930s. While with Heidt's group, he landed a bit part in his first movie, *Pot o' Gold,* which starred James Stewart and Paulette Goddard.

He became active in radio in the 1940s, on daytime serials, mysteries, spot recordings, and children's shows, essentially in character and dialect parts. He did a serious political program called *Report to the Nation*, for which he did the voices of prominent figures of the day, among them Churchill and Roosevelt. He worked with Morey Amsterdam on a radio show that turned into a television show, and thereby, Art Carney entered television.

Although he was particularly well known from the early 1950s on as Ed Norton, he was also much in demand as a serious actor, appearing on *Suspense, Studio One, Kraft Theatre, Playhouse 90, Climax!,* and *Best of Broadway.*

By the 1960s, he was appearing only infrequently on television, as Broadway (*The Odd Couple, The Rope Dancers,* and *Take Her, She's Mine*) and the movies (*A Guide for the Married Man, W.W. and the Dixie Dance Kings, Harry and Tonto,* and *The Late Show*) brought new facets of Art Carney to an ever-enthralled public.

He first became interested in *The Honeymooners* at the suggestion of writers Arne Rosen and Coleman Jacoby, who were then writing for Jackie Gleason on DuMont's *Cavalcade of Stars.* He joined the show in 1950 and continued with it until it left New York. He rejoined *The Honeymooners* for guest spots on *The American Scene Magazine* in 1962, for several seasons beginning in 1966, and for the three ABC specials in 1976, 1977, and 1978.

ALICE KRAMDEN

PERT KELTON

The special prettiness that femininity always gives.

CLIVE BARNES, *THE NEW YORK TIMES*

Born on a cattle ranch near Great Falls, Montana, and named ''Pert'' after the role her show business aunt was playing when she was born, Pert Kelton grew up in the world of vaudeville. Her parents, Ed and Susan Kelton, used her in their act, and by the age of twelve, she had an act of her own.

She appeared in both the Broadway and movie versions of *Sunny,* with Marilyn Miller and, toward the end of her career, in both the Broadway and movie versions of *The Music Man* with Robert Preston. In addition to her many successful Broadway roles (*The Bad Seed, The Threepenny Opera, Greenwillow*), she was extremely active in radio and early television. She did the voices for the five women on the Milton Berle radio show, and was a featured comedienne on the TV shows of Milton Berle, Phil Silvers, and Danny Thomas.

In 1950, the McCarthy-era booklet *Red Channels* listed her as a possible Communist sympathizer. Although she continued to appear with Jackie Gleason, she was, in effect, blacklisted in the industry for the next few years.

Pert Kelton was the first Alice Kramden, from the first *Honeymooners* episode in 1950 until mid-1952, when a heart condition prevented her from following Gleason to the CBS network. Kelton died October 30, 1968.

AUDREY MEADOWS

Probably the best deadpan comedienne in television

TV FORECAST

Born in Wu Chang, China, to Episcopal missionary parents, Audrey Meadows spoke nothing but Chinese until she came to the United States with her family. She was going to study for a career in journalism until her sister Jayne persuaded her to try show business. She made her debut as a coloratura soprano at Carnegie Hall when she was sixteen, toured in light opera and musical comedy (including *Top Banana* with Phil Silvers), and came to TV on *The Bob and Ray Show* (it was a cast of three).

Later television work included, in addition to *The Honeymooners,* guest appearances with Sid Caesar, Red Skelton, Jack Benny, George Gobel, and Carol Burnett, as well as straight dramatic acting in every major television playhouse production. She was named "TV's Most Promising Star of 1953" by the editors of *Television* magazine; she was awarded an Emmy in 1954 for Best Supporting Actress. Her motion picture work includes features with Doris Day, James Stewart, Rosalind Russell, and Cary Grant.

Today, except for appearances on the *Honeymooners* specials, she has left show business behind; she serves as the first woman director of the First National Bank of Denver, and as honorary vice president of sales for Continental Airlines (she created the interior styling of the first-class section of Continental's DC-10s, from rug design to ceiling decor).

Audrey Meadows joined *The Honeymooners* when the show left the Du-Mont network for CBS in 1952, after persuading Jackie Gleason that, with effort, she could look frumpy and bone-tired. She remained with the show until it left New York, returning once in 1966 for the last black-and-white *Honeymooners* ("The Adoption," broadcast from Miami), and for the three ABC specials.

SUE ANE LANGDON

When Jackie launched her she turned out to be the most talented new song-and-dance girl of the fledgling television season.

LIFE

Born in Paterson, New Jersey, Sue Ane Langdon made her theatrical debut at the age of five as Tinker Bell in a production of *Peter Pan* directed by her mother, former opera singer Grace Lookhoff.

Langdon continued to perform in local and college productions whenever possible, then headed for New York and Broadway. In her first New York job she sang in the Radio City Music Hall Chorus. Soon after, she was winning praise for her road and stock appearances in such shows as *Kiss Me Kate*, *Guys and Dolls*, and *Oklahoma*, and for her Broadway success with Alan Alda and Hal Linden in *The Apple Tree*.

In Hollywood, she became involved in both television (*Bachelor Father*, *Bonanza*, *The Dick Van Dyke Show*, game and talk shows) and the movies (*The Great Impostor*, *A Fine Madness*, *A Guide For The Married Man*, *The Cheyenne Social Club*). She is probably best known as the co-star of *Arnie*, for which she won the Golden Globe Aard for Best Supporting Actress in a television series.

Sue Ane Langdon became the third Alice Kramden when, in 1962, she joined Jackie Gleason for a few *Honeymooners* episodes on *The American Scene Magazine*. When she left the show, she ran a gag notice in the papers saying that Ralph Kramden of 518 W. 57th (then the CBS address), having left her bed and board, would no longer be responsible for any of his wife Alice's debts.

SHEILA MACRAE

Miss MacRae is one of the best satirical comediennes of our time.

VARIETY

Sheila MacRae was born Sheila Margot Stephens in England, and raised in Canada and New Orleans. Although her earliest ambitions were to be a writer, she turned to theater in her late teens. She married singer and actor Gordon MacRae when she was seventeen and he twenty, and, for a while, devoted herself full-time to raising a family.

She wrote nightclub material even when she wasn't performing it, but in 1957, at the urging of her friend Lucille Ball, she joined husband Gordon's nightclub act and together they became one of the hottest teams in show business. Her impressions of Carol Channing, Zsa Zsa Gabor, Lena Horne, Dinah Shore, Lucille Ball, and Jackie Kennedy were familiar to most TV viewers.

She has starred at The Sands, the Desert Inn, the Fontainebleau, the Waldorf, and most major clubs in the country, and appeared in the New York City Center's production of *Guys and Dolls* (with Alan King) as well as national companies of *Luv* and *Damn Yankees.*

Sheila MacRae joined *The Honeymooners* in Miami in 1966, playing Alice Kramden in more than forty hour-long musical episodes, including the now-syndicated Trip-to-Europe series.

TRIXIE NORTON

ELAINE STRITCH

La Stritch is the gal who can give a sardonic line a lethal wallop.

NEW YORK MIRROR

Born in Detroit, Michigan, Elaine Stritch attended drama classes in Greenwich Village with Marlon Brando and made her stage debut as a tiger and a cow in the show *Babino* at the New School, New York, at the age of eighteen.

She then appeared regularly, on the stage, in serious as well as musical comedy roles. Her performance as Martha in *Who's Afraid of Virginia Woolf?* was a resounding success, and her work in William Inge's *Bus Stop* won her the vote of the New York drama critics, as polled in *Variety*, for the season's best performance. Her musical credits include the coast-to-coast tour of *Call Me Madam* (in the role created on Broadway by Ethel Merman), *On Your Toes*, *Pal Joey*, *Company*, *Mame*, and on Broadway and in London, the Noel Coward comedy *Sail Away!*

She first appeared on television in the 1949 series *The Growing Paynes*, and, soon after, on *The Ed Sullivan Show*, *The Milton Berle Show*, *Studio One*, *Climax*, *The Alcoa Hour*, and two Art Carney shows, *Full Moon Over Brooklyn* and *Red Peppers*. She co-starred in the series *My Sister Eileen*. Her movie credits include *A Farewell to Arms* and *Three Violent People*.

Elaine Stritch created the role of Trixie Norton on *Cavalcade of Stars*, in 1950.

JOYCE RANDOLPH

*Among the nation's sewer workers, she has a
rating comparable with Garbo's.*

CUE

Joyce Randolph was born Joyce Sirola in Detroit, Michigan. She was only nineteen when she joined a road company of *Stage Door*. From there she went to New York and a revival of *Abie's Irish Rose,* and later, a Broadway run of *A Goose for the Gander* with Gloria Swanson.

Although she continued to appear in Broadway musicals through the 1940s and into the 1950s, she became increasingly active in early TV, appearing with such superstars as Eddie Cantor, Dean Martin and Jerry Lewis, Danny Thomas, and Fred Allen.

From appearances on General Electric's early experimental television programs, she went on to roles on *Four Star Revue* and *Colgate Comedy Hour*.

Even before *The Honeymooners,* Joyce Randolph worked with Audrey Meadows in a summer-stock production of *No, No, Nanette*. She first worked with Jackie Gleason on *Cavalcade of Stars* in a serious role, and was later called back to play Trixie Norton—a role which she continued to play until *The Honeymooners* left New York.

PATRICIA WILSON

*There are almost as many millions of Wilsons as there are Joneses,
and long-legged, Ohio-born Pat Wilson. . . is definitely one for you
to keep your contact lenses focused on.*

EARL WILSON

Proud of the fact that she was, in true show biz fashion, "born in a trunk,"
Patricia Wilson made her stage debut at the tender age of three as part of her
mother's act.

She made her Broadway debut in *Fiorello!* in 1959, playing opposite Tom
Bosley (now of TV's *Happy Days*), who was also making his Broadway de-
but—he as Fiorello LaGuardia, she as the mayor's wife. The play won a Pulitzer
Prize for drama; for her role as Marie LaGuardia, Pat Wilson was nominated
Best Actress of the Season by the Critics' Circle.

She then co-starred with Gene Kelly in a national production of *Take Me
Along,* in which Kelly filled the role created by Jackie Gleason on Broadway.

Her television credits include roles in *Happy Days, Starsky and Hutch, The
Mary Tyler Moore Show, The Waltons, Police Story, Ellery Queen,* and the
made-for-television movie *The President's Mistress.* She has also been seen in
the movies *The Sting* and *Demon Seed,* and in top night clubs across the country.

Patricia Wilson became the third Trixie Norton in 1962, when she joined
Jackie Gleason, Art Carney, and Sue Ane Langdon for a short series of *Honeymooners* episodes on *The American Scene Magazine.*

JANE KEAN

Excruciatingly funny.

BILLBOARD

Jane Kean, born in Hartford, Connecticut, was known for many years as one-half of the riotously funny Betty and Jane Kean sister act. When Betty married, Jane continued in the theater and went on to score some of her greatest triumphs.

In 1943, when only a teenager, she was an overnight success in her first Broadway musical comedy, *Early to Bed*. Subsequently she starred on Broadway in *Call Me Mister* (in which she replaced Betty Garrett, currently of TV's *Laverne & Shirley*) and *Will Success Spoil Rock Hunter?* (in which she replaced Jayne Mansfield), in New York City Center revivals of *The Pajama Game* and *Show Boat*, and in a Las Vegas production of *Last Of The Red Hot Lovers* (a virtuoso performance in which she had two roles). Recently she appeared with Helen Reddy and Mickey Rooney in the Walt Disney movie *Pete's Dragon*.

She was no stranger to Jackie Gleason when she joined *The Honeymooners* to play Trixie Norton in 1966; they had appeared together on Broadway in *Along Fifth Avenue*, in summer stock in *The Show-Off*, and even on Gleason's first TV variety show, *Cavalcade of Stars*.

VII. THE CHAUNCEY STREET IRREGULARS GLOSSARY

THE CHAUNCEY STREET IRREGULARS GLOSSARY

Star Trek has its Trekkies, Sherlock Holmes has his Baker Street Irregulars, Ralph Kramden has his Honeymoonies (a.k.a. the Chauncey Street Irregulars). They are all fanatics, but they have their reasons.

Simply stated, they have learned to take infinite delight in an extremely finite body of lore. They have learned to substitute intensive for extensive appreciation, even at the risk of being labeled "trivia freaks." They need all the help they can get.

Yet, of the three groups, only the Honeymoonies have been entirely on their own. They know that the specials, even the Trip-to-Europe reruns, are few and far between. So, glued to their television sets, they watch the thirty-nine "core" episodes over and over, until they can recite each one by heart. They memorize

names and dates, then seek out fellow followers of the Kramden saga to get more names and dates. They have done what they can with the available lore; they can do no more.

It is, therefore, time that Honeymoonies had a concordance with which to extend their enjoyment of what have become the most familiar scripts in television history. It is time they had access to some of the unavailable lore.

Over twenty-eight years, *Honeymooners* scripts have been remarkably consistent with regard to details. The effect is one of realism, as the Kramden roster of friends and associates fleshes out, and as the streets and families of Kramden's neighborhood reveal themselves to be those of Gleason's own boyhood.

Along with Gleason's contributions of names and places are those of the writers. Marvin Marx and Walter Stone's accountant, Mr. Puder, becomes Mr. Puder of the IRS when Ralph has his taxes audited. Bill Davis, personal friend of Syd Zelinka, becomes Bill Davis, friend of Alice and Ralph.

Some names are out of the headlines; Ralph is, after all, a citizen of twentieth-century Brooklyn, U.S.A. Some names are pure invention, yet they ring true. Says writer A. J. Russell, "Names can be funny without being farce. (Liver is funnier than steak.) A name like Wedemeyer fits. . . . He's the guy you went to school with."

For decades, the Chauncey Street Irregulars have shown real ingenuity in their stalwart pursuit and mastery of Kramdeniana and Gleasonology. The following references (and cross references in small capital letters) can only be expected to whet their appetites, not to satiate them. Readers with additional references are invited to submit them to:

THE HONEYMOONERS' COMPANION
Workman Publishing Company
1 West 39 Street
New York, New York 10018

A dedicated team of Honeymoonies will see that they are duly recorded.

A. Ralph Kramden's blood type.

Aberdeen Proving Grounds. *See* PROVING GROUNDS, ABERDEEN.

address. Ralph's and Gleason's during his early years, was CHAUNCEY STREET. Also, what Norton suggests you do to a golf ball by telling it "hello."

Adelphi Theater. Theater on Manhattan's West Fifty-fourth Street where the ELECTRONICAM episodes of *The Honeymooners* were rehearsed and filmed. *See also* STUDIO 50.

Adventureland. *See* DISNEYLAND.

Akron. The Ohio city where Bill DAVIS allegedly has his (nonexistent) manufacturing plants.

alley number 3. "Our alley" to Ralph and Ed when they go bowling.

America. *See* COLUMBUS, CHRISTOPHER.

American Weekly. One week, they ran the article "I Was a Mambo Dancer for the FBI." But more famous, perhaps, is the series they almost run about Ralph Kramden dying of ARTERIAL MONOCHROMIA. They are going to run a color spread when his tongue turns blue. When it is learned that not Ralph Kramden, but his mother-in-law's dog GINGER, has the disease, the series is canceled.

Amico, Tony. *See* TONY.

Anchovy. *See* PIZZA.

Andre. When Morgan's Department Store offers to redecorate the Kramdens' apartment for free, Andre is the interior decorator they send over. Unfortunately, Ralph draws the wrong conclusions about Andre, and throws him out in a fit of jealous rage.

Andrews. Member of the RACCOON LODGE who works in a brewery.

Angelo. Ed's ridiculous disguise at the FESTA L'UVA.

anniversary. Good news and bad news for the Kramdens. The bad news is what happens on their anniversarys: the dining room set they don't get from the Nortons; the second-hand exploding vacuum cleaner that Ralph gets Alice; the night of their twenty-fifth anniversary when Alice's mother comes to sleep over. The good news is that, despite the bad news, they're still very much in love.

antiques. Ed has been an antiques aficionado ever since he answered a newspaper ad for a dog and sent away for a "genuine four-legged Chippendale." Sometimes he goes to the antique show at MADISON SQUARE GARDEN. He has even appraised the Kramdens' icebox as "early Ma and Pa Kettle" (any excuse to help himself to a turkey leg . . .).

Antony, Mark. *See* RILEY.

A&P. The Great Atlantic and Pacific Tea Company goes back to the earliest days of chain grocery marketing. As the A&P, its familiar signs still dot the nation. One of Ralph's first jobs was delivering groceries for the A&P.

appetite. Ed's is probably bigger than Ralph's. (You never hear of Ralph brown-bagging three corned beef sandwiches to eat on the way to lunch.) It's just that Ed doesn't express his appetite around his waistline. (Or is that he only expresses it around Ralph?) Ed, for as long as he can remember, has weighed 165 pounds. Ralph can barely remember *pictures* of when *he* weighed 165. And when he asks Ed if he ever saw them, the answer he gets is, "No Ralph, I never did see your baby pictures."

appliance. Be it a SPIFFY IRON, a HANDY HOUSEWIFE HELPER, a second-hand VACUUM CLEANER, or a kitchenful of new major appliances, if Ralph buys it, it is bound to cost him money and not work.

Armand. He runs an escort service. Alice is his answering service. When Ralph finds out, he jumps to the wrong conclusions.

arterial monochromia. A rare disease that usually affects boxers. The symptoms are hair loss, irritability, a bluish tongue, chills, fatigue, and a strong desire to waste away by the warmth of the stove. Ralph thinks he has it—but it's a disease that dogs get when they scratch for fleas.

Arthur, King. *See* SHAGGY-DOG STORY.

Asbury Park. Seaside resort town in New Jersey, and site of Kramden's failed uranium field.

Astoria. Neighborhood in Queens, New York (bounded on the south by Long Island City, on the east by Jackson Heights, on the north by the Berrian's Island Con Edison facility, and on the west by the Hell Gate Channel and eventually Manhattan), where Alice's mother sometimes lives. *See also* KOSCIUSKO STREET.

Baby Snooks. The Fanny Brice character featured on the radio programs *Good News* (originally *Good News of 1938*) and *Maxwell House Coffee Time*. It was for the *Maxwell House* version that Snooks acquired parents, and it is their domestic scraps that are said to have inspired later husband-wife sitcoms like *The Bickersons* and *The Honeymooners*.

badurndurn. Term introduced into Brooklynese by JOE THE BARTENDER. Originally coined by Teddy GILANZA, whose name and person turn up in the Joe the Bartender sketches, it connotes a ferndyke, a gizmo, a whuzzit, as in: "I think I broke my badurndurn," or "Is that a new badurndurn, or have you done something with the old one?"

Baker, Kenny. Movie and radio crooner of the 1940s. Ralph says he appeared in *Rhythm on Ice.* (Could he have meant *Silver Skates* of 1943?) Or was just a hint of Stanley R. SOGG creeping into *The Honeymooners?*

Barnes, Chester. One of Alice's first boyfriends, who was (and remains) slim, handsome, and the man Mrs. GIBSON would most like Alice to leave Ralph for.

Bascom, Herbert. Butler to MARY MONAHAN who inherits $50,000 from her.

Bayonne. The town in France where bayonets are said to have originated. Also, the town in New Jersey where Mrs. STEVENS' sister lives and home of the bowling team that Ralph's team has to play for the RACCOON LODGE championship the night his back goes out.

Beat the Clock. Bud Collyer's 1950s daytime *and* nighttime game show that ran for years. Contestants were asked to perform complex feats of coordination while racing against The Clock. Ralph and Alice appear on the show and, when Alice cannot return to complete the stunt, Norton goes on in her place.

Bellevue. New York City hospital well known for its extensive mental-health facilities. Often referred to, as in the following exchanges. Alice: "I call you killer because you slay me." Ralph: "I'm calling Bellevue cause you're nuts." And, Ralph: "This thing is the key to my future, the key to my future." Alice: "Don't tell me they have an attachment on here (the HANDY HOUSEWIFE HELPER,) for opening the door at Bellevue."

Bennett, Johnny. Captain of the COUGARS stickball team, of which Norton is coach.

Bensonhurst. A Brooklyn neighborhood made popular by *The Honeymooners*. Actually, the streets such as HIMROD and CHAUNCEY which Kramden mentions are not in Bensonhurst but in Bushwick (which the writers felt would be a less recognizable name to most viewers). Bensonhurst is also a popular *Honeymooners* telephone exchange.

"Bensonhurst Bunny Club." A 1960s *Honeymooners* episode that was scrapped by Gleason, despite the fact that Lyn Duddy and Jerry Bresler had already written all the words and music and the script was finished. It concerned another of Ralph's get-rich-quick schemes: raising rabbits for fur coats that would be marketed as minks. When Gleason thought about what animal lovers would think about Ralph and Ed skinning little bunnies, he thought twice and decided to kill the episode.

Bibbo. *See* DANNY.

The Bickersons. Don Ameche and Frances Langford were John and Blanche Bickerson, first on *The Charlie McCarthy Show*, and, by 1946, on their own radio program. They fought about everything, and are said to be the inspiration for many of the later husband-wife domestic situation comedies. Some historians say that The Bickersons were influenced by BABY SNOOKS.

Big Apple. Mid-'30s jitterbug-type dance. Performed in a circle until the words "the big apple" come up in the song, then everyone dances toward the center of the circle. Clever, huh? (Actually, so many people thought so that there was even Big Apple fabric on the market.) One of the "new dances" Ralph is going to learn when Alice tells him he's forgotten how to be young.

Big Broadcast of 1933. *See* "PLEASE."

Billy the Kid. The five-dollar costume Ralph is going to rent to enter the Raccoon's annual costume party. When Alice refuses him the five dollars, she suggests he go as Billy the Goat instead, but Ralph surprises her by wearing furniture and going as The MAN FROM SPACE.

Birnbaum, Nat. Works with Ed in the sewer and, unlike the bug in Ed's crossword puzzle, does not spell his name with a *g*.

Bismarck, North Dakota. Site of the RACCOON National Cemetery, where the RACCOON OF THE YEAR is entitled to be buried with his wife.

Bloomgardens. Where Alice and Trixie buy identical dresses for the Safest Bus Driver Award ceremony. Though Bloomgardens is not the name of an actual store, it is derived from the real-life Bloomingdale's.

Bogart, Humphrey. *See* DEAD MEN TELL NO TALES.

boompf. What you say to get out of magic handcuffs. But don't bother. It doesn't work on moving trains.

bop contest. A dance contest in the 1950s. *See* WALLACE.

boxer. *See* ROSENBLOOM, MAXIE; ARTERIAL MONOCHROMIA.

Bradley, Robert Hilliard. Mary Monahan's ne'er-do-well gambling nephew, who inherits one dollar when she dies. But a greater indignity is Ralph's condescending attitude toward him at the reading of Mary Monahan's will.

Brady, Frank. When he was named RACCOON OF THE YEAR, he got so egotistical he quit the Raccoons to join the Elks.

brain surgeon. *See* SEWER WORKER.

Bratton, Charlie. The loudmouth character made famous by Jackie Gleason would meet mild-mannered Clem Finch (Art Carney) at the lunch counter, despite Clem's every effort to get through his meal before Charlie's arrival. Invariably, he would announce his presence loudly, immediately ruin Clem's appetite with, "What's that slop you're eating?" (a line that became famous throughout the country, and frequently turned up on the lips of innocent little children at family dinner parties). He would gleefully describe Clem's order in the worst possible way (comparing it, say, with things that float in the GOWANUS CANAL), then rope Clem into some scheme that always backfired—on Clem! Clem ended each episode with the frustrated, "I'm gonna kill that man!" But he never did.

Brigid. Trixie's role as the maid in Kramden's made-for-British-TV FLAKEY WAKEY commercial.

Briosky, Pierre Francois de la. Did he design and build—or condemn—the sewers of Paris? Only Ed Norton knows for sure.

Brutus. Ralph's (bad) example of history repeating itself. Claims Kramden, jumping to his usual wrong conclusions about his buddy Ed, "Brutus had his Caesar, Kramden's got his Norton," confusing his sentiments but coming closer to the truth than he realizes.

Buckingham Palace. Which Trixie Norton proclaims on her trip to London to be even bigger than KLEIN'S ON FOURTEENTH STREET.

Bugsy Malone. *See* MALONE, BUGSY.

Bunny. Ralph's pet name for Alice when they were first married.

Bushwick. The section of Brooklyn where Gleason was born and lived his early years. Also, the setting for *The Honeymooners*. *See also* BENSONHURST.

Bushwick Hospital. Where Ed goes after a manhole cover lands on his head, although, as it happens, he doesn't need treatment.

buying on time. The way the Nortons finance everything they own, from water softeners to the dining room set they almost buy Alice and Ralph Kramden for their fifteenth wedding anniversary. *See also* ICEBOX.

Caesar. *See* BRUTUS; RILEY.

cake. Chocolate is Ralph's favorite, hence Alice's decision to serve coconut cake at his surprise party. Otherwise his birthday belt won't fit . . . and it's the largest size there is.

Callahan the Plumber. Ralph's idea of a great doctor is the doctor who kept Callahan alive until his wife could catch up on the insurance payments.

Canarsie. Section of Brooklyn northeast of Bensonhurst. Where Freddy the Raccoon's seventy-three-year-old mother lives. *See also* MAMBO.

Carson, Mr. Mary MONAHAN's attorney.

Cassidy, Joe. One of the guys at the Gotham bus depot.

Cassidy. Might even be Joe Cassidy. This Cassidy is the Raccoon who goes to the Raccoons' annual costume party, year after year, wearing his wife's cut-down dress and calling himself TUGBOAT ANNIE.

Central Park. Bagels, apples, nutbread, noshes, ices, nectarines, and galoshes. At one time or another (sometimes all at once), Norton has probably brown-bagged them to Central Park to meet Ralph for lunch. The galoshes permit him to go straight to work after eating. It's there one afternoon that Ralph and Ed meet the con men who sell them a get-rich-quick scheme—a hair-restoration formula.

Chan, Charlie. Created by E. D. Biggers in *The House Without a Key* (1925), the famous Chinese-American detective has appeared in novels, in comic strips, on television, in a TV cartoon show, and on the screen; but probably never, despite what Ralph says when he and Ed jointly purchase a TV, in *Galloping Ghost of Mystery Gulch* (See SOGG, STANLEY R.) It is during a commercial break of an unnamed Charlie Chan movie that Ralph and Ed make their famous TV appearance to sell HANDY HOUSEWIFE HELPERS.

Charleston. The favorite dance of the 1920s, first introduced in the little-known revue *Runnin' Wild* in 1923. It is the dance Ralph contends that he gave up his architectural studies to learn.

Chauncey Street. A real street in the Bushwick area of Brooklyn; it is the street on which the real Jackie Gleason lived while he was growing up. Kramden's address is 328 Chauncey Street most of the time, although an occasional live-TV slip has been known to alter it.

Chef of the Future. *See* HANDY HOUSEWIFE HELPER.

Chef of the Past. *See* HANDY HOUSEWIFE HELPER.

Chicago. Where Bill DAVIS allegedly has his main office, and where the RACCOONS have held more than one annual convention.

Chicken Chow Mein. *See* WEDNESDAY NIGHT, POTATO PANCAKES, CHINESE CUISINE.

Chinese Cuisine. *See* CHINESE RESTAURANT, MOO GOO GAI PAN, EGG FOO YUNG, MONEY MATTERS.

Chinese restaurant. Usually the HONG KONG GARDENS on special occasions. There is one Chinese restaurant outside Ralph's front window, another outside his back window. Norton, who can see the same Chinese restaurants from his windows, sets his Mickey Mouse watch by the one out the front. It opens at 5:00 P.M. every day. At 5:26, they put on the Egg Foo Yung; its aroma reaches Ralph's apartment by 5:27 and 56 seconds and Ed's by 5:28. Since Ed knows the aroma to travel at a speed of 320 feet per second, he is able to keep his timepiece accurate. At 5:37, the Moo Goo Gai Pan begins. . . .

chocolate cake. *See* CAKE.

Churchill, Winston. When Ralph finds Alice dressing up and behaving suspiciously, he immediately concludes that she's seeing another man. When he discovers that the caller (actually, only ANDRE,) left behind an expensive glove and a good cigar, it is Ed who jumps to conclusions . . . when he reasons that Winston Churchill must have come for tea.

clam suit. Gleason's term for not just any ill-fitting suit, but the slouchiest MOAX suit known to man or beast, and hence, the most appropriate attire for Ralph's forays into the outside world.

coconut cake. *See* CAKE.

Collier brothers. Wealthy real-life eccentrics who horded vast mountains of refuse in their home, then constructed (and booby trapped) mazes through the rubbish to discourage thieves. *See also* MONEY MATTERS.

Collyer, Bud. *See* BEAT THE CLOCK.

Colonna, Jerry. American comedian of movies and TV (beginning in the mid-'30s) with bulging eyes and a walrus moustache. See RHYTHM ON ICE.

Colonnade Room. Reputed to be the most expensive restaurant in New York—or, according to Ralph, in the world, although he's sure the food can't be very good because no truck drivers eat there. *See also* DAVIS, BILL.

Columbus, Christopher. Says Ralph, there wouldn't be any America if it weren't for him. Says Alice, there wouldn't be any him if it weren't for his mother. You can see why Ralph rarely wins his debates with Alice on the subject of MALE SUPREMACY.

Columbus, Mrs. *See* COLUMBUS, CHRISTOPHER.

Coney Island. Amusement park area due south of Bensonhurst, where Norton lost Lulu, his first great love (and favorite dog) in the Tunnel of Love, and where the fortune teller Madame Zelda warns Ralph that he is going to commit murder within a week.

Continental. One of the "new dances" Ralph is going to learn when he wants to be young again. "You kiss while you're dancing," say the lyrics of the Magidson-Conrad tune which was the first movie song ever to win an Academy Award. Introduced by Fred Astaire and Ginger Rogers in *The Gay Divorcee* (1934), the Continental was in all probability too fancy for any but the most expert dancers.

Cooper, Gary. (Frank J. Cooper) Has been compared to Ralph Kramden's finger in the remark, "That's like King Farouk trying to get into Gary Cooper's bathing suit," spoken by Ed when Ralph gets his finger stuck in Jim MCKEEVER's ring.

Cougars. Stickball team coached by Norton, of which Johnny BENNETT is captain, on which the MANICOTTI boy and the GARRITY boy play, and through which the measles have been transmitted to both Norton and Kramden.

Cramden. Not to be confused with KRAMDEN, which is the correct spelling, although it has been in numberless news releases and magazine articles. Spelling Kramden with a *C* is like spelling fatso with a *ph*. No style.

Crazy Guggenheim. *See* GUGGENHEIM, CRAZY.

Crockett, Davy. Was born on a mountaintop in Tennessee (a.k.a. the greenest state in the land of the free) and wore a coonskin cap, causing Harvey WOLHSTETTER Jr. to remark, on seeing Ralph Kramden in his RACCOON UNIFORM, "Gee, I never knew Davy Crockett was so fat." Also, when *American Weekly* is making plans to give Ralph's blue tongue a color spread, an editor exclaims with ghoulish glee, "We'll make this guy a national hero. He'll be another Davy Crockett." The Davy Crockett boom was a $30 million media-plus-merchandising phenomenon of 1955, and the man behind the millions was Walt DISNEY with his movie and TV versions of *Davy Crockett, King of the Wild Frontier,* starring Fess Parker. There were spin-off Davy Crockett products ranging from coonskin caps to bubble gum cards.

Crosby, Bing. *See* "PLEASE"; "THERE'S NOTHING I HAVEN'T SUNG ABOUT."

Cunningham, Zamah. Regular "GLEASON PLAYER" who doubled as Mrs. MANICOTTI and Mrs. VAN GLEASON.

curtains. The Kramdens manage to do without them, although, on at least one occasion, when Alice is shopping for curtains at MORGAN'S DEPARTMENT STORE, she wins an opportunity to have her whole apartment redecorated. And many real-life viewers of *The Honeymooners* sent curtains to the network to make the Kramdens' life a little brighter.

Custer, General George Armstrong. Ralph's efforts to separate Ed from his money to finance the HANDY HOUSEWIFE HELPER venture meet resistance from Ed, who calls Ralph's pitch "the biggest understatement since General Custer said, 'Over that hill, I think they're friendly Indians.' "

Danny. One night Ralph witnesses a holdup and murder. The thugs follow him home, holding him, Alice, and Norton hostage in his apartment. Danny is the brains of the outfit. Bibbo is the one Ralph beats up.

Darro, Frankie. Child and teenage star of the 1930s, who Ralph claims appeared in RHYTHM ON ICE.

Davis, Bill and Millie. Bill and Ralph went to school together, courted Alice at about the same time. It was Bill who wrote in Ralph's autograph book, "Some kids are small, some kids are tall, but Fatso Kramden is the only kid who walks down the hall wall to wall." It is Bill Davis whom Ralph is trying to impress when he says he "runs things" at the GOTHAM BUS COMPANY, and when he gets stuck for the check at the COLONNADE ROOM. A real-life Bill Davis was a personal friend of writer Syd Zelinka, but the real Mrs. Davis wasn't named Millie.

Dead Men Tell No Tales. In another manifestation of the Stanley R. SOGG effect, Norton tells Ralph to forget about the men who want to kill him and just go home and see a movie. The movie he has in mind is Humphrey Bogart in *Dead Men Tell No Tales.* Bogart made *Dead End, Dead Reckoning,* and *Deadline-U.S.A.* But no *Dead Men Tell No Tales.* Ralph doesn't get to see the movie anyhow because DANNY and Bibbo follow him home that night to try to kill him.

Dean, Dizzy. Norton's excuse for eating two suppers in a row, as in, "Let's face it: Dizzy Dean warms up in the bull pen before the game, but he still pitches."

DeKalb Avenue. Real-life street in Bushwick. *See* DOWSERS.

Dennehy. Gleason's closest friends in the old neighborhood were the Dennehys. He grew up in a Chauncey Street apartment owned by the Dennehys, "Dennehy's Flats," and moved in with the Dennehy family when his mother died. His first girlfriend was Julie Dennehy (now Julie MARSHALL) and it is the unseen Mr. Dennehy to whom JOE THE BARTENDER always speaks.

Dennehy's Bar. Where Ralph loses $200 in Raccoon funds (by misplacing it in the pocket of the Grand High Exalted Mystic Ruler) the night he is named treasurer of the RACCOONS.

Dennehy's Flats. The real-life railroad flats on which the Kramdens' Chauncey Street apartment is based. *See* DENNEHY.

Desert Hawk. 1950 Arabian Nights–type movie starring Richard Greene and Yvonne DeCarlo, with Jackie Gleason in the minor role of Aladdin the camel driver. It is *Desert Hawk* that the Kramdens and Nortons are off to see the night that Norton wins a free black-and-white television set with a ticket purchased for him by Ralph as a birthday present.

deus ex machina ("god from a machine"). Theatrical device by which action is resolved somewhat unnaturally, usually when natural means are exhausted. In ancient Greek and Roman drama, a god was lowered onstage mechanically to announce some dramatic reversal of events. In contemporary situation comedy, it can take the form of an unexpected eleventh-hour phone call or, on *The Honeymooners,* a well-timed knock at the Kramdens' door. However, since Kramden never leaves well enough alone, it is a rare deus ex machina that isn't neutralized by the effect of his big mouth. *See also* TELEPHONE.

Dewey, Admiral. *See* RACCOON UNIFORM.

Dicurtis, Ernesto. *See* "TAKE ME BACK TO SORRENTO."

Disney, Walt. Creater of DAVY CROCKETT, KING OF THE WILD FRONTIER, DISNEYLAND, and Norton's watch (*See* CHINESE RESTAURANT).

Disneyland. Like Davy CROCKETT, a super-Disney phenomenon of 1955. It is also Alice's description of her apartment: The view is Fantasyland, the sink is Adventureland, the stove and icebox are Frontierland. All she's missing is the "world of tomorrow" (Tomorrowland), but Ralph offers to fix that by sending her to the moon.

dogs. In some, but not all episodes, Norton is allergic to them. *See also* LULU, KRAMMAR, GINGER, and ANTIQUES.

"Don't Fence Me In." Written by Cole Porter, from the picture *Hollywood Canteen* produced by Warner Brothers in 1944. One of the songs Ralph identifies correctly while rehearsing to win big on THE $99,000 ANSWER.

double role. A *coup de theatre* in which Gleason revels. He has played both the good and bad brothers Van Gleason in the Reggie VAN GLEASON III sketches, and in more than one *Honeymooners* episode, he has played both Ralph Kramden the bus driver and Jackie Gleason the star.

Douglas, Mr. Vice President of the GOTHAM BUS COMPANY who invites Ralph to play tournament golf with him when Mr. HARPER can't make it.

Douglas, Hamilton. Name of character in a play put on by the Raccoon Lodge. Young, devil-may-care, poor but desperately in love with Rachel. When Joe Hannigan gets the flu and can't go on, Norton gets the role. *See* FREDERICK.

Douglas, Kirk (Issur Danielovitch Demsky). Was a soda jerk before he was discovered by Hollywood. To Ralph, who also wants to be discovered, this means there's a chance for him. To Alice, it means that somewhere there's an opening for a soda jerk.

Doyle, Tommy. Neighborhood boy who is jailed for passing counterfeit money. And who passed it to Tommy? Ralph, of course, when he was sole claimant on a suitcase full of the stuff. Tommy was running an errand for Ralph at the time of the arrest. *See also* ZIGGY.

Dowsers on DeKalb Avenue. Where you can buy a defective second-hand VAC-UUM CLEANER for $4.95.

Dragnet. Many's the week that this show was number one in the ratings. *Dragnet* was noted for changing names to protect the innocent, and for a theme song (dum-duhdumdum) that meant mystery afoot. The music was so closely associated with its sponsor, Chesterfield cigarettes, that other shows—for instance Lucky Strike's *Your Hit Parade*—chose not to play it on the grounds that it was free advertising (despite the fact that it was a top-rated tune for weeks). Ed hopes that when Ralph blasts him for helping himself to a turkey leg, his name will be left out to protect his innocence. But Ralph reassures him on that score: where he's going, his story won't be on *Dragnet,* it will be on MEDIC.

DuMont. (1942–1955). For years, Channel Five was New York's fourth major TV network. Its featured programs included *Cavalcade of Stars, Life Begins at 80* Fulton Sheen's *Life Is Worth Living, Captain Video,* and, in 1954, the *Senate Army-McCarthy Hearings.* By 1955, it was skeletonized to five hours of live telecasting per week. The DuMont network's parent corporation, the Allen B. DuMont Labs, introduced ELECTRONICAM in 1955, hoping not only to lease the process within the industry but also to give the failing DuMont a strong competitive position with regard to SYNDICATION. All efforts failed in 1955, when the DuMont network folded for lack of outlets.

Dunellin. The Irish village known for its beer (until a curse was put on it) and the Kramden ancestral castle (in which Ralph must spend the night if the curse is to be broken). *See* O'TOOLE, SHAMUS.

Dynamite Moran. The boxer Ralph wants to manage, until Norton knocks him out.

Ebsen, Buddy. Another of the real-life actors in the alleged *Rhythm on Ice,* who also had a role as Georgie Russel in *Davy Crockett, King of the Wild Frontier.* *See also* CROCKETT, DAVY.

Eden, Anthony. Prime Minister of Great Britain from 1955 to 1957 who, Norton points out, could never be a Raccoon because he has not been a U.S. resident for the last six months. Proving (to Norton, at least) that the Raccoons' entrance requirements are too stiff.

Egg Foo Yung. *See* CHINESE RESTAURANT.

Eighteenth Amendment. Made Prohibition the law of the land from 1920 till 1933. Ed suggests that Ralph explain the irregularities on his income tax by standing on the Eighteenth Amendment—and telling the IRS that he was drunk when he filled out his taxes.

elbows. *See* HUCKLEBUCK; RACCOON HANDSHAKE.

electric bill. Alice wants to buy a TV. But Ralph wants to keep the electric bill as low as it's always been: thirty-nine cents.

Electronicam. The "bifocal camera" developed by James L. Caddigan in association with DUMONT engineers, which made headlines in 1955 when the Allen B. DuMont Labs announced that Electronicam would render KINESCOPES obsolete by providing higher quality film at lower production costs. In essence, it combines simultaneous live TV with a filming process. *Captain Video* was filmed with the Electronicam process as a test. But it was with *The Honeymooners,* for one season of thirty-nine episodes from mid-1955 to mid-1956, that it came into its own on nationwide TV. *See also* KINESCOPE.

Elks. Fraternal order, something like the RACCOONS. *See* BRADY, FRANK.

Emily. The guy who wrote the golf book must have really liked her when he wrote "to Emily, whose slice inspired me. . . ."

Emperor of Japan. Either he owns the world's largest collection of boxes made out of 2,000 matchsticks glued together—or Ralph's been conned for Christmas. *See also* STEVENS, MRS.

Enston, Duke. *See* "MELANCHOLY SERENADE."

Esquire Magazine. Ralph polishes his shoes as he prepares to go to the reading of Mary MONAHAN's will. He insists to Alice that he's calm, and she, observing his preparations, agrees: "Of course you are. You just read in *Esquire* where the well-dressed man always polishes his socks." Ed's reaction to *Esquire,* in other surroundings (the barbershop), is somewhat different: *"Vavavoom!"*

Ethel, Aunt. Alice's maiden aunt, whom Ralph marries off to Krausmeyer the butcher.

Evans, Miss. Mr. Marshall's secretary at the GOTHAM BUS COMPANY where Ralph works.

Fain, Sammy. *See* "I'LL BE SEEING YOU."

Fantasyland. *See* DISNEYLAND; OLD MAN GROGAN'S LONG UNDERWEAR.

Farouk, King. *See* COOPER, GARY.

Farquard, Gaylor. The London TV show host whose program closely resembles *The Jackie Gleason Show.* Only his Glea Girls are aging British matrons. And his commercials can be strange, particularly if they feature the Kramdens and the Nortons making a pitch for FLAKEY WAKEY.

Farthing-Gay, Lord and Lady Chumly. Titled Earl (Ralph) and Duchess (Alice) of Rathbone in Ralph's made-for-British-TV FLAKEY WAKEY commercial.

Fat Man's Shop. Where Ed buys Ralph's Christmas spats.

Fatso. The prearranged signal to be used on the night Ralph is going to stage a fight for HARVEY the bully. The wrong guy uses the signal (somehow, the name just fits) and Ralph decks him. *See also* DAVIS, BILL; PROCE, JIMMY.

Faversham, Mr. Organizes the play for the Ladies' Auxiliary of the RACCOONS and flatters Ralph into taking the lead.

FBI. *See* AMERICAN WEEKLY.

Fensterblau, Joe. In German his last name means "blue window," but it means trouble in any language when Ralph bets Joe $10 that Alice will cook dinner for him on command. Alice is such a good sport that she lets Ralph win the bet. Ralph is so moved that he doesn't take Joe's money. On the other hand, Joe also bet Norton $10 on the outcome of Ralph's command . . . and one would just love to know what Norton does about it.

Festa l'Uva. The Italian wine festival to which Ralph and Ed go in disguise to determine whether Alice is two-timing Ralph with Harry VERDERCHI. Not to be confused with "Vesti la giubba," the operatic aria, although Ralph does feel like the clown in *Pagliacci* when he thinks he's lost his wife to another man.

Fight of the Week. One of the shows that Ralph and Ed fight over when they jointly purchase a TV. *See* ROSENBLOOM, MAXIE.

Finch, Clem. *See* BRATTON, CHARLIE.

Fink, Morris. The GRAND HIGH EXALTED MYSTIC RULER of the RACCOONS. He works next to Ed in the sewer.

FioRito, Ted. Bandleader of the 1920s and "big band" '30s, whose style went from tricky rhythms to society swing and who has a number of hit tunes to his credit, including "Toot, Toot, Tootsie." *See also* SONS OF ITALY HALL.

Flakey Wakey. The diet breakfast cereal for which Ed and Ralph write the jingle that wins them a trip to Europe: "Flakey Wakeys add to the taste but take away from your fat little waist."

Flushing. Neighborhood in the New York borough of Queens. The Kramdens and Nortons briefly share a Flushing apartment to save on living expenses.

Fogarty, Mr. When he moves out, Carlos SANCHEZ moves in—and Sanchez's good manners and great mambo nearly wreck Ralph's marriage. *See also* PROCE, JIMMY.

Fomeen, Basil. Accordionist and bandleader of the "big band" 1930s and '40s. *See also* SONS OF ITALY HALL.

Fortune. The parrot Ralph inherits from Mary MONAHAN when she dies.

Forty-second Street. See "SHUFFLE OFF TO BUFFALO."

Foster, Stephen. *See* "SWANEE RIVER."

France. Where Hamilton DOUGLAS, who doesn't possess a string of POLO-PONIES, doesn't possess a villa. And where the Kramdens and Nortons are jailed for unintentionally passing counterfeit money.

Frazee, Jane. American singer and leading lady of '40s movies, who appeared in *Rhythm Inn* (1951) but not RHYTHM ON ICE.

Fred's Gasoline Station. Where Ed has to take his baths when the water in his apartment isn't working.

Fred's Landing. A real place in Jersey, and one of Ralph's favorite vacation spots, despite the occasional appearance of snakes in his tent. Ralph plans on going back for two weeks there with Alice when he gets his $42 tax refund.

Frederick. In the play sponsored by the Ladies' Auxiliary of the RACCOONS, Ralph stars in the role of Frederick, the self-made rich man who can have anything he wants but the love of the lovely Rachel (Alice), who wants Hamilton DOUGLAS (Norton), even though he can't give her a string of POLOPONIES. Eventually Hamilton loses Rachel to Frederick—and Alice is offered a contract by a famous Hollywood agent.

Freitag the Delicatessen's. That's how they say it on *The Honeymooners,* and that's how they said it in the old Bushwick neighborhood where Jackie used to stand in front of it (on the corner of Chauncey Street and Saratoga Avenue), in his black chesterfield and white scarf, swinging his keychain and looking sharp.

Frolics. Rumor has it that Ralph got all the laughs in the 1949 Bus Drivers' Frolics. He did a comedy routine in a ballet dress.

Frontierland. *See* DISNEYLAND.

Gable, Clark. As in Ed's observation that "before I started eating Trixie's cooking, I was a regular Clark Gable." But Ralph also feels *he* has something in common with Gable who, Ralph says, played a bus driver in his first movie.

Gallagher, Mrs. A neighbor of the Kramdens who owns a cat, on occasion mistaken by Ralph for his coonskin RACCOON cap.

Galloping Ghost of Mystery Gulch. *See* CHAN, CHARLIE.

game show. Ralph has managed to be on quite a few in his time, including THE $99,000 ANSWER and BEAT THE CLOCK; however, it is not likely that Ralph will ever win one. It is only his nature to be attracted to sudden windfalls; it is not in the nature of sudden windfalls to befall him.

Garrity, Mr. Ralph's grumbling upstairs neighbor, named after a friend of writer Walter Stone. *See also* COUGARS.

gas bill. Ralph's ninety-three-cent gas bill (printed on a postcard) breaks the record for all-time low established by the COLLIER BROTHERS in 1931.

George. Pipsqueak pool-hall pal of HARVEY the bully.

Gersch, Dick. Publisher of *American Weekly*. The real-life Dick Gersh was a neighbor of writer Marvin Marx.

Gibson, Agnes. Alice's sister, who marries Ralph's lodge brother Stanley SAXON.

Gibson, Mrs. Alice's mother. *See also* MURDER STRIKES OUT; ASTORIA.

Gilanza, Teddy. A Gleason pal from the old neighborhood, his name (and actual physical presence) occasionally appeared in JOE THE BARTENDER sketches, but not in other Gleason segments. He was Gleason's office manager for a few years in the early 1950s. *See also* BADURNDURN.

Ginger. Mrs. GIBSON's collie. *See also* ARTERIAL MONOCHROMIA.

Gladys. A named (but unseen) friend of Trixie and Alice.

Gleason Player. Actors like George Petrie and Frank Marth, whom Gleason could cast and call in on a few hours' notice, were known as "Gleason Players." They did dialects, they wore scars, they played everything from racketeers to RACCOONS, and they usually didn't know until the night before a given show that they were even going on.

Gleason roles. There is a little of each of the Gleason characters in Ralph Kramden, who is alternately a loudmouth and a pitchman, a neighborhood philosopher and a poor soul; and there is nothing like Ralph Kramden trying to adopt the airs of an ostentatious swell à la Reggie Van Gleason III. *See* BRATTON, CHARLIE; KRAMDEN, RALPH; SOGG, STANLEY R.; JOE THE BARTENDER; POOR SOUL; VAN GLEASON, REGGIE III and WILBUR.

glove. In costume as Pierre Francois de la BRIOSKY, Norton knows only one way to defend the honor of his boyhood hero when Ralph besmirches Briosky's name—he slaps Ralph with his glove, demanding a duel. Ralph throws him out, leaving the matter of the duel unsettled. *See also* CHURCHILL, WINSTON.

"Good Night, Irene." Written by Lomax and Leadbetter, and correctly identified by Ralph during his practice sessions for THE $99,000 ANSWER.

"Good Night, Sweetheart." Written by Rudy Vallee and Ray Noble and correctly identified by Ralph as he practices with Norton for THE $99,000 ANSWER.

Gotham Bus Company. The company for which Ralph works. The offices are supposedly on Ninth Avenue and Forty-eighth Street in Manhattan.

Gowanus Canal. Brooklyn landmark. A heavily polluted body of water used mainly for commercial purposes. *See* BRATTON, CHARLIE.

Grand High Exalted Mystic Ruler. The head of all Raccoondom. Unlike mere Raccoons, he wears *three* tails on his coonskin cap and his uniform is coat-length. The man named Raccoon of the Year gets to run for the post of Mystic Ruler. *See also* FINK, MORRIS.

Great Fatchoomara. In order to get enough money to go to the RACCOONS' convention, Ralph has the Great Fatchoomara hypnotize Alice. But even when she's under, Alice comes out on top. Fatchoomara was also the name of a cheese which Stanley R. SOGG often touted.

Grogan. The cop on the beat around Chauncey Street. Kramden gives him a counterfeit bill when he becomes sole claimant on a suitcase full of them, and believes the entire $50,000 to be strictly legit.

Gruber, Herman. Raccoon bowler who sets up a three-variety pizza victory feed after the tournament, with Neapolitan knockwurst, pig's knuckles, and sauerkraut on the side.

Guggenheim, Crazy (originally "Googenham"). A character from the JOE THE BARTENDER sketches, who was discussed but who did not appear in the early days of the *Jackie Gleason Show;* who, in the 1960s, did appear and was played by Frank Fontaine; and who, when Ed and Ralph are lost at sea in a lifeboat, Ed chooses to impersonate to while away the time. Based on a real-life character called "Puke" from Gleason's old neighborhood.

Gunther, August. Millionaire-producer of Ralph's favorite doughnuts. He and his wife lived in the Kramdens' apartment before Alice and Ralph. His brother is in the doughnut business too.

Halsey Street. Real-life street in Gleason's old neighborhood in Bushwick. It was on an amateur night at the Halsey Theatre on Halsey Street that Jackie got his start in show business.

Handy Housewife Helper. For ten cents each, Ralph and Ed buy 2,000 of them and try to sell them for a dollar apiece by means of a TV commercial in which Ralph enacts the CHEF OF THE FUTURE and Ed enacts the CHEF OF THE PAST. The Handy Housewife Helper can sharpen knives, core apples, open cans, grate cheese, remove warts, and double as a skate key. But old-fashioned implements can do the same things better and faster. Ralph is so nervous that the Handy Housewife Helper, in his hands, becomes lethal. The commercial is a failure and Ralph and Ed are out $200 plus the cost of the TV time.

Hannigan, Joe. *See* DOUGLAS, HAMILTON.

har-dee-har-har-har. An expression introduced into Brooklynese by Jackie Gleason. Things like it had been said before, but the particular phrase and inflection (which in very short order swept the country) are unmistakably his own.

Harper, Mr. The traffic manager at the GOTHAM BUS COMPANY who doesn't know Ralph is alive until Ralph talks to him about golf. Then he invites Ralph to join him for an important tournament, and Ralph starts wishing Mr. Harper had never heard of him.

Harry. Runs the pool hall.

Harvey. The bully Ralph has to fight until he stages a fight for Harvey to see. When Harvey sees Ralph getting the best of a guy even bigger than he is, Harvey takes off. *See also* WOLHSTETTER, HARVEY.

Havemeyer. The bus driver laid off because his nerves couldn't take the bus route he was assigned to. Also, the Raccoon who brings the knockwurst on the Raccoons' annual fishing trip.

Henry VIII. The $10 costume Ralph almost gets to rent so he can win the RACCOONS' annual costume party first prize.

Hesitation Waltz. At the turn of the last century, the king and queen of ballroom dancing, Vernon and Irene Castle, claimed it to be a new variation that "has crowded out the old-fashioned waltz." Needless to say, it is one of the "new dances" Ralph wants to learn when Alice persuades him to start acting young.

Himrod Street. Street from Gleason's old neighborhood. As a young man, writer Syd Zelinka met a girl at a party in Brighton Beach and had to take her all the way home to Himrod Street where she lived. Then he had to return to his home. The entire trip took him at least four hours—on subways, trolleys, foot, among a wild and woolly assortment of New York's night people—and he never forgot the journey. He immortalized it the night Ed gets an emergency call from the sewer on Himrod Street. It explodes, and a manhole cover lands on Norton's head. Naturally, no damage is done.

Hollywood Canteen. *See* "DON'T FENCE ME IN."

Home Pride. Brand name of Kramden's stove.

Hong Kong Gardens. The Chinese restaurant to which the neighborhood folk go on special occasions. It even has a floor show. (The Hong Kong Gardens was *not* a real place, but a real-sounding one created by writer Syd Zelinka.)

house. If you are a resident of inner-city New York, you may use the term as though it were synonymous with "home." In Kramden's neighborhood, a one-room apartment is still a "house."

Hucklebuck. Popular 1950s fad dance featuring oscillating elbows and walking like a duck. Norton does it better than Ralph; he has the elbows for it (although *he* insists that Ralph has the walk).

Hudson River. On the RACCOONS' annual boat ride up the Hudson, the RACCOON OF THE YEAR has the honor of piloting the boat as it passes Raccoon Point.

Hurdle, Judge Lawrence Norton. "Hollering Hurdle," the traffic court judge noted for his $50 fines and 50-minute lectures. He has an accident with Ralph just before he is to present Ralph with a safe bus driver award. But, when he realizes the accident was all his fault, he fines himself $50 to keep the records straight. The writers' choice of the name "Hurdle" was no accident; Jack Hurdle was the producer of *The Honeymooners.*

Hurricanes. The name of Ralph's bowling team.

ice box. The early-model icebox with the drip pan underneath is the single most eloquent visible expression of Ralph's refusal to acknowledge progress (the absence of a telephone in the Kramden apartment is its invisible expression). If he considered a modern refrigerator a necessity he could easily take advantage of installment buying, as Norton does. Obviously, he doesn't see the need. Once Gleason was actually approached by a major manufacturer of refrigerators; they were anxious to sponsor *The Honeymooners* if he would get rid of the icebox. He turned them down. If they didn't understand Kramden, he reasoned, their judgment hardly inspired confidence. At times, there has been real ice in the icebox, and sometimes food in it for use on the show. It is possibly the oldest, shoddiest piece of furniture in the Kramden apartment. Yet when Ralph tells Alice he is going to die and she laughs (because he has jumped to conclusions again), he explodes. "We'll see how much of a riot it is when you got to finish the payments on the icebox." *See also* KETTLE, MA AND PA.

iceman. He complains about coming all the way across town to deliver exclusively to the Kramdens, but it could be worse. Unlike Mr. MURPHY, at least Ralph gets his ice.

Ile de France. Elegant French ocean liner of the 1930's, '40s, and '50s. When it looks like Ralph can no longer avoid admitting to Bill DAVIS that he's not a big shot, Norton comes up with a solution: Tell Bill you can't meet him. You've just changed jobs. Now you're the captain of the *Ile de France*, and the ship is sailing in twenty minutes.

"I'll Be Seeing You." Written in 1938 by Irving Kale and Sammy Fain. One of the songs correctly identified by Kramden during rehearsals for THE $99,000 ANSWER.

"I'll kiss you later, I'm eating a potato." One of the "new expressions" Ralph is going to learn when Alice complains that he doesn't act young anymore.

International Order of Friendly Raccoons. *See* RACCOONS.

Italian-American Social Club. Kramden can see it from his back window.

"It's All Over Now." Words and music by Bazzy Simon, 1927. One of the songs correctly identified by Ralph while practicing for The $99,000 ANSWER.

itsy bitsy. *See* TEENSY WEENSY.

Jackson, Miss. "Old Hatchet Face." The first grade teacher Ed and Ralph both had when they went to grade school together.

James, Harry. Ralph says he might have been another Harry James if he'd stuck to playing his cornet when he was a young man. But actually, there's already another Harry James (see dedication of this book).

Joe the Bartender. One of the basic Gleason roles, essentially a monologue in which Joe philosophizes with the unseen Mr. Dennehy about neighborhood regulars. The names used are the names of friends from Gleason's old neighborhood, and the bar is based on Jimmy PROCE's bar, also from the old neighborhood.

Johnson, Mr. Ralph's landlord.

Jones, Bobby. One of the all-time greats of golf, R. T. "Bobby" Jones won American and British titles throughout the 1920s. When Ralph despairs of ever mastering the game of golf in a few days, Norton reminds him that Bobby Jones never gave up.

Jones, Isham. Jones' band was number one in the Chicago area in the 1920s, caught on nationwide till the end of the Depression. *See also* SONS OF ITALY HALL.

Jose. The piano player on THE $99,000 ANSWER.

Judy. *See* WALLACE.

June Taylor Dancers. These precision dancers (known for their kaleidoscopic routines filmed by overhead cameras) have been identified with *The Jackie Gleason Show* in all its phases since the early 1950s and became a regular part of *The Honeymooners* in the Trip-to-Europe musical episodes of the 1960s.

Kale, Irving. *See* "I'LL BE SEEING YOU."

Karloff, Boris. Something like a mother-in-law, Ralph warns Stanley SAXON. "Boris Karloff seems like a nice guy when he's dancing on the *Red Skelton Show* too, y'know. You ever seen him in *Frankenstein?* That's the real Boris Karloff."

Kelly, Grace's father. Rated by Ed as one of the world's great chefs, right alongside Oscar of the Waldorf and Pierre of the Ritz, because "he cooked up a pretty sweet dish."

Kelsey's gym. The scene of Ralph's victory over a stranger, his victory-by-default over HARVEY the bully, and his own eventual defeat by a punching bag. Not to be confused with Kelsey's Bar of *All in the Family.*

Killer Cuoco, Heavywieght contender who takes an off-the-record dive for Dynamite Moran. Phil Cuoco, his namesake, is now the associate producer of *The Honeymooners.*

Kinescope. The receiver tube of the television set; hence a Kinescope film ("kinnie") is one that has been photographed from a TV picture. The end product is predictably inferior. Before the advent of ELECTRONICAM, which simultaneously films and broadcasts live action, kinnies were the means by which live programs were preserved.

King of the Castle. *See* MALE SUPREMACY.

Kinnies. *See* KINESCOPE.

Klein's on Fourteenth Street. Manhattan's famous multi-story bargain basement. Easily reached from Brooklyn on the Canarsie subway, this department store closed in the mid-1970s. *See also* BUCKINGHAM PALACE.

Kettle, Ma and Pa. Hillbilly couple from the 1947 movie *The Egg and I* and later films. *See also* ANTIQUES.

Knuckles Grogan. The thug whom Ralph gets arrested twice: once when he identifies him from a newspaper description, and once when Grogan escapes and comes after Ralph . . . making Ralph the ideal police bait for his recapture.

Kosciusko Street. When Mrs. GIBSON doesn't live in Astoria, she sometimes lives at 33 Kosciusko Street.

Kosciusko Street sewer. Runs roughly parallel to DEKALB in Brooklyn. When Ed sleepwalks, this is where he goes on Thursday nights.

Kramden, Alice Gibson. Ralph Kramden's loving, long-suffering, (but rarely silent) red-haired wife, who gave up a good job in a laundry to marry him.

Kramden, Patrick. Ralph's ancestor who ran off with Shamus O'Toole's daughter in 1827. *See* O'TOOLE, SHAMUS.

Kramden, Ralph. Brooklyn-born bus driver whose early jobs included delivering groceries for the A&P and shoveling snow for the WPA. His uncle wanted him to study architecture, but he gave it up to learn the Charleston. He met Alice Gibson while working for the WPA, and subsequently married her. His Social Security number is 105-36-22 (and may be the only seven-digit Social Security number in the entire country).

KramMar's Delicious Mystery Appetizer. Name that Ralph and Ed think up for what turns out to be dog food. Ralph, not knowing Alice is dog-sitting, discovers it in the icebox, thinks it's delicious, and decides to market it. He tries to persuade Mr. MARSHALL, his boss, to finance the venture. Not until he has fed it to Marshall and a few company executives does he discover his boner.

Kraus Market. Where Alice can buy chopped meat for fifty-eight cents a pound.

Krausmeyer. The butcher who marries Alice's Aunt Ethel.

Krausmeyer's Bakery. Where Alice briefly works as a career girl, stuffing jelly into doughnuts. Years later, on television's *Odd Couple,* it was a Krausmeyer's Bakery that served as Oscar Madison's campaign headquarters when he ran for local office.

Lady Godiva. After Ralph's disastrous commercial on British TV, the London FLAKEY WAKEY representative surprises Ralph by telling him how well it went over. It was, in fact, ''the greatest thing to happen to Britain since Lady Godiva.''

LaRosa, Julius. One of *the* singing sensations of the 1950s. According to Norton, they served together in the navy.

Launslit, Sir. *See* SHAGGY-DOG STORY.

Lavinsky, Kingfish. *See* ROSENBLOOM, MAXIE.

Leadbetter. *See* ''GOOD NIGHT, IRENE.''

Leo, Uncle. Ralph's uncle, variously from Utica and Schenectady. His wife's name is Sarah.

Lewis, Charles. London FLAKEY WAKEY representative.

Liberace, Wladziu Valentino. There are those who say Liberace is the world's greatest entertainer. Also, a ''Liberace'' is Norton's name for a toothy smile. Alice tells Ralph he had better buy a TV or else. For fourteen years, she has had nothing to look at but the icebox, the sink, and the four walls while Ralph goes out bowling, shooting pool, or hanging around the RACCOON LODGE. ''Well, I don't wanna look at that icebox, that stove, that sink, and these four walls. I wanna look at Liberace.''

Little Buttercup. What Alice called Ralph before they were married.

Little Jack Little. Radio favorite, singer and pianist, even before the ''big band'' days when he won new fame as a bandleader. *See* SONS OF ITALY HALL.

Little Sugar Plum. What Ralph called Alice when they were dating.

Lomax. *See* ''GOOD NIGHT, IRENE.''

Luigi. Ralph's totally guessable disguise at the FESTA L'UVA.

Lulu. The beloved dog of Ed's childhood, whom he lost in the Coney Island Tunnel of Love, and for whom he calls when he walks in his sleep. Ralph buys him a new dog, Lulu the Second, to cure his sleepwalking. Now Ed takes Lulu the Second with him when he walks in his sleep.

McClosky. The ladder on McClosky's fire escape comes down when you jump up and pull it. Or, if you're Ed and you're sleepwalking, it comes down on your head without anybody touching it.

McGillicuddy, Frank. The guy who beats out Ralph for the job of convention manager the year the RACCOONS go to Chicago.

McKeever, Jim. Ed's foreman in the sewer, affectionately known as ''Old Muck and Mire.'' As Ed observes, ''He started at the bottom and today, only twenty years later, he has worked his way up to the street.'' He gave Ed his start in the sewer—his "first push, so to speak." He is also the guy for whom Ed buys the ring that Ralph gets stuck on his finger. *See also* COOPER, GARY.

Madison Avenue. Kramden's bus route for the GOTHAM BUS COMPANY. Also, a kind of jargon spoken by advertising men like the one who meets the Kramdens and Nortons when they arrive at the pier for their FLAKEY WAKEY trip to Europe. It is quickly mastered by Ed and Ralph, who approach the conversation with their usual aplomb: Ed—"Let's run it down the manhole and see if it floats." Ralph—"Let's punch him (Ed) in the nose and see if it bleeds."

Madison Square Garden. In real life, Manhattan's famous all-purpose arena was on Forty-ninth Street and Eighth Avenue when the ELECTRONICAM *Honeymooners* were filmed. (The Garden is now located at Seventh Avenue and Thirty-second Street.) When Ralph runs into Bill DAVIS outside Madison Square Garden, it looks remarkably like the entrance to the GOTHAM BUS COMPANY; such is the versatility of *Honeymooners* sets. *See also* ANTIQUES.

Malone, Bugsy. A *Honeymooners* sinner, candy-coated, long before Paul Williams immortalized him in film and music. Only this Bugsy Malone was a grown-up—the big-time mobster out to exterminate Ralph in a case of mistaken identity, with Ralph a dead ringer for Bugsy's syndicate rival.

male supremacy. Something Ralph believes in despite all evidence to the contrary. The basis for Ralph's philosophy that a man's home is his castle, and in his castle, man is king. *See also* Columbus, CHRISTOPHER.

Mambo. A dance that swept the nation in the mid-1950s, but chances are that if no one had ever danced it outside of Cuba, Ralph Kramden would have popularized it single-handedly. Whenever there was a dance to do, chances were that it would be the mambo. It even makes the news the time "Your Questioning Photographer" raises the knotty question: Which is more authentic, the Canarsie or Weehawken style of the mambo? And the RACCOONS hold national mambo contests. *See also* AMERICAN WEEKLY; SANCHEZ, CARLOS.

Man from Space. What Ralph tries to look like by wearing parts of furniture for the RACCOONS' costume party. He almost wins the $50 first prize (for his "impersonation of a pinball machine") when Ed arrives late from an emergency in the sewer and his work togs win him first prize as the Man from Space.

Man in the Gray Flannel Suit. Sloan Wilson's novel about a Madison Avenue executive is Norton's inspiration as he steps out of the sewer in full gear, terrifies Ralph, and asks, "What did you expect to come out of the sewer—the man in the gray flannel suit?"

manhole cover. *See* PIZZA; HIMROD STREET.

Manicotti, Mrs. Ralph's upstairs neighbor, played by Zamah CUNNINGHAM. There is also a Mr. Manicotti, but he rarely appears on screen. Likewise Tommy Manicotti, their son. *See also* COUGARS.

Marciano, Rocky (Rocco Marchegiano). The world's only undefeated heavyweight champion. *See* RING MAGAZINE.

Marshall, J. J. President of the GOTHAM BUS COMPANY, with a new apartment on Park Avenue and a new pool table from his wife. He almost joins Ralph in the KRAMMAR venture until Ralph realizes that he's been barking up the wrong tree . . . and that the ambrosial product he has fed his boss is dog food. *See also* MARSHALL, JULIE.

Marshall, Julie. Formerly Julie DENNEHY, Gleason's first girlfriend (and secretary in his early show business days). She married J. Marshall and found her name and his—J. & J. Marshall—converted into the name of Ralph's boss at the Gotham Bus Company.

Marth, Frank. *See* GLEASON PLAYERS.

Martin, Mr. *See* UNIVERSAL MAGAZINE.

Marty. The thug waiting in the car when DANNY and Bibbo break into the Kramdens' apartment.

Medic. Sophisticated hospital drama starring Richard Boone, and making its debut in 1954. *See* DRAGNET.

"Melancholy Serenade." Gleason's theme song. Also, the unidentified melody played in Kramden's apartment during his warm-up for THE $99,000 ANSWER. Words by Duke Enston, music by Jackie Gleason.

Mercer, Johnny. *See* "TOO MARVELOUS FOR WORDS."

Miami Beach. Scene of one of the later RACCOON CONVENTIONS, and a few other things besides. Once Gleason moved his facilities to Miami Beach, it made good sense to promote its pleasures to the TV viewing audience.

Miguel. ROSITA's partner in crime.

Mildred. A named but unseen friend of Alice and Trixie's.

Minneapolis. Scene of a RACCOON CONVENTION.

moax. In Brooklyese, a dope, a jerk. Ralph often admits that he is one, usually in connection with confession to his jealous streak or to his big mouth.

Molloy, Eddie. The Raccoon whose engagement may be wrecked if Ralph doesn't bowl in the Raccoons' championship tournament.

Monahan, Mary. The old lady Ralph helped on and off the bus, not knowing her estate was worth $40 million, or that he would one day be mentioned in her will.

Monahan, Mr. Another of Ralph's big bosses at the GOTHAM BUS COMPANY.

money matters. It does to Ralph and Alice, which is why so many fiduciary details creep into *Honeymooners* shows. Ralph's salary as a bus driver is a weekly $62; his short-lived janitor job pays $150 a month plus free rent; Alice baby-sits, briefly, for fifty cents an hour; Ralph owes Ed $176.30 for phone calls from the Nortons' phone; it costs sixty-five cents an hour for Ralph and Norton to play pool; Ralph and Alice used to get a whole Chinese dinner for sixty cents when they were dating; Ralph is offered $5,000 by the AMERICAN WEEKLY, but he doesn't get to keep it when his story is canceled; his electric bill is thirty-nine cents; his ninty-three-cent gas bill breaks the all-time low record set by the Collier Brothers in 1931; his rent is $33.33 a month in early episodes (calculated on the basis of the fact that a 15 percent increase is only $5), but with all the subsequent $5 increases, must be way up around $50 by now; his savings account fluctuates between $75 and $3-and-change. When Ralph discovers that he and Alice have only $3.31 in the bank, he explodes at Alice: "What do you do with all the money, Alice?" Alice replies, "I put it in the bank."

Monroe, Marilyn (Norma Jean Baker). Has something in common with Ralph: they've both been in UNIVERSAL MAGAZINE. And when Ralph compares Alice to Marilyn Monroe (to con her into giving up her job at the bakery so she can do housework again), Alice knows he's up to no good.

Moo Goo Gai Pan. *See* CHINESE RESTAURANT.

moon. Where Ralph, in a pique, frequently threatens to send Alice—occasionally Norton as well. "Bang zoom" is a snappier version of the same threat. *See also* VIDEO, CAPTAIN.

Morgan's Department Store. Where Alice almost wins free interior decoration for her apartment until Ralph jumps to the wrong conclusions and throws the free interior decorator out. *See also* ANDRE; CURTAINS.

Morgan's Furniture Store. Whence Norton is going to buy Ralph and Alice's surprise anniversary present, a dining room set, on time. And whither Ralph sends Norton's credit reference (having jumped, again, to the wrong conclusion) reading: "The applicant is a bum."

Morton, Dr. The vet who treats GINGER for ARTERIAL MONOCHROMIA.

mother-in-law. Ralph's is Mrs. GIBSON, with whom he does not, did not, and never will get along, although just after he married Alice, he wrote a very sensitive letter about mothers-in-law and the difficult position they must hold. In Ralph's defense, it is not all his fault. Mrs. Gibson is a mean lady. *See also* KARLOFF, BORIS; RING MAGAZINE; "STRIKE IT RICH."

Muldoon. The RACCOON who brings the beer on the annual fishing trip.

Muller, Freddie. Assistant bus dispatcher (emphasis on *assistant*) at the GOTHAM BUS COMPANY. Ralph borrows his car to go to the Safety Award ceremony and the fishing trip and entertains him every time there's an opening for traffic manager. Freddie is chairman of the play sponsored by the Ladies' Auxiliary of the Raccoons. The part of Freddie is played by George Petrie in the ELECTRONICAM episodes of *The Honeymooners* and is one of the few non-lead roles to recur with any frequency on the show.

Muller, Mr. In charge of promotions at the GOTHAM BUS COMPANY.

Munsey, Joe. An executive member of the *Raccoons* who votes against Ralph as convention manager when he buys his wife a faulty VACUUM CLEANER on Ralph's recommendation, and whose name is distorted to Joe Rumsey by episode's end.

Murder Strikes Out. A suspense play on Broadway to which Ralph gets two tickets when his boss can't use them. He can't take Alice, because she has to stay home (her mother is coming for a visit). And even when he decides to go with Norton, his worries aren't over, because Alice's mother isn't in his apartment three minutes when she reveals the surprise ending to Ralph just to needle him. *See also* THURSDAYS.

Murphy, Mr. and Mrs. When Mrs. Murphy ran off with the iceman, Mr. Murphy had to drink warm beer for months.

$99,000 Answer, The The TV show (modeled after the real-life $64,000 QUESTION) on which Kramden first appears on January 28, 1956, to make a fool of himself and to win no money at all—but to win the "Best Half Hour Television Situation Comedy Award" from the Writers' Guild of America for its writers, Syd Zelinka and Leonard Stern.

Noble, Ray. *See* "GOOD NIGHT, SWEETHEART."

no-cal pizzeria. Cited by Norton as Ralph's great money-making scheme.

Norfolk, Virginia. It's the other direction from Minneapolis and nowhere near the Raccoons' annual convention.

Norris, Herb. Emcee on THE $99,000 ANSWER.

Norton, Edward L. Went to grade school in Oyster Bay, majored in arithmetic in vocational school, and made a few dollars caddying during the Depression. When he chased a golf ball down the sewer, he got his first real job. Today he's an engineer in subterranean sanitation and a ranger third class in the Captain VIDEO Space Academy. He's Ralph's best pal and Trixie's husband.

Norton, Trixie. Formerly a burlesque queen, now Mrs. Edward L. Norton. She can't cook and Ed says it's because of her that he doesn't look like Clark Gable anymore. She's blonde (always has been) and is Alice's best friend.

Nutsy. He hasn't missed a night in the pool room in his entire life, not even on his wedding night. But he does take a night off to watch Ralph take on HARVEY the bully.

O'Donnell, Mary. Mary MONAHAN's maid, who inherits $25,000 at the reading of the will.

Oglethorpe, Miss. "Old Hatchet Face." Ralph and Ed's grade school arithmetic teacher.

"Old Hatchet Face." A name applied by Ralph and Ed to most of their grade school teachers and by Ed to Trixie when they were dating. *See* JACKSON, MISS; OGLETHORPE, MISS.

Old Man Grogan's long underwear. Hanging gaily on Old Man Grogan's line, it's part of the view from the Kramdens' front window. *See also* DISNEYLAND.

"Old Muck and Mire." *See* MCKEEVER, JIM.

Orphan Annie. The little chatterbox with auburn locks who has eyeballs but no pupils furnishes Ralph with an excuse for not bringing the newspaper home the night he tells "YOUR QUESTIONING PHOTOGRAPHER" that he's boss in his own home. When Alice asks why he didn't bring the paper home, he barks that he doesn't approve of their editorial policy. "They just cut out Orphan Annie."

Oscar of the Waldorf. *See* KELLY, GRACE'S FATHER.

O'Toole, Shamus. When Ralph's ancestor Patrick ran off with O'Toole's daughter in 1827, O'Toole put a curse on the village of Dunellin, Ireland, which can only be broken when a Kramden spends a night in the ancestral castle which Shamus haunts.

Overman, Teddy. When Ralph and Ed quarrel over the Jim MCKEEVER incident, Ralph ditches Ed to pal around with Teddy Overman. Overman has all the bad habits Ralph accuses Ed of having, and is monumentally rude besides.

Oyster Bay. Long Island, New York, where Edward Norton attended P.S. 31.

Paramount Theatre (Broadway at 43rd Street). Where Jackie Gleason and his entire CBS-TV cast appeared for two weeks beginning November 17, 1954, performing six complete deluxe stage shows a day in addition to their usual *Jackie Gleason Show* television duties. Cast members included Art Carney, Audrey Meadows, Joyce Randolph, Zamah CUNNINGHAM, the thirty-two JUNE TAYLOR DANCERS, and the "Music For Lovers Only" orchestra of fifty musicians, conducted by Sammy Spear. Sharing the bill with the live shows was the movie *Drum Beat* (starring Alan Ladd and Charles Bronson) in Warnercolor and Cinemascope. If it seems odd today to imagine an elaborate stage show almost gratuitously thrown in with the price of a movie admission, it must be remembered that it used to be standard practice in the great cinema palaces of yesteryear. The *Honeymooners* portion of the program was a shorter version of the ARTERIAL MONOCHROMIA sketch.

Park Avenue. New York City's classiest residential avenue, where Ralph wants to move when he wins The $99,000 ANSWER; where Norton always catches a cold working in the sewer (because it's air-conditioned); and where Mr. MARSHALL lives with his wife and pool table. *See also* VAN GLEASON, REGGIE III.

Park Sheraton. The New York hotel in which jackie gleason enterprises retained a sixteen-room duplex apartment consisting of living quarters, offices, and rehearsal halls (which, on rare occasions, were actually used for rehearsals).

Parker, Mr. The $99,000 ANSWER winner who precedes Kramden, and who is going to come back next week to try to win again.

Paris. Where the Kramdens and Nortons are arrested for passing counterfeit francs. *See also* BRIOSKY, PIERRE FRANCOIS DE LA.

Peck, Gregory. Was an usher at Radio City Music Hall before he was discovered by Hollywood. To Ralph, this means he can be discovered too. To Alice, this means that somewhere there's an opening for a Radio City Music Hall usher. *See also* DOUGLAS, KIRK.

Pentothal. The truth serum given to Ed Norton by the psychiatrist trying to determine why Ed sleepwalks. (Also used, on another TV show of the mid-1950s, to determine whether Clark Kent was Superman. The scene is best remembered for the line which introduced it, "Finish your ginger ale, Kent.")

Perkins, Pat. The brand-name rack dresses that Alice Kramden wears in the ELECTRONICAM *Honeymooners* episodes. But head-of-costumes Peggy Morrison didn't buy them off the racks; she bought them in the wholesale district.

pet names. Generally applied to pets but occasionally to people (see "Old Muck and Mire," "Old Hatchet Face,") and once to Ralph when Rita WEDEMEYER tells Alice to choose a pet name for him that best reflects his most prominent feature. Alice chooses "Tubby." *See also* BUNNY; GINGER; LITTLE BUTTERCUP; LITTLE SUGAR PLUM.

Petrie, George. *See* GLEASON PLAYERS.

Philbin, Jack. Long-time executive producer of *The Honeymooners*, whose name has also appeared on the membership roster of the RACCOON LODGE.

Pierre of the Ritz. *See* KELLY, GRACE'S FATHER.

pinball. *See* SALVATORE'S PIZZERIA; MAN FROM SPACE.

pizza. Only Ralph and Norton can think of sure-fail ways to get rich quick from pizza. For instance, Norton's scheme to sell pablum on pizza, and Ralph's short-lived plans for no-cal pizza. Occasionally, pizza saves the day, as when Alice's recipe for anchovy pizza lures Jackie Gleason to the RACCOONS annual dance. And always pizzas are great fun. As Ed observes, "If pizzas were manhole covers, the sewer would be a paradise."

"Please." Sung by Bing CROSBY in *The Big Broadcast of 1933*, written by Robins and Rainger. One of the songs correctly identified by Kramden during practice sessions for The $99,000 ANSWER.

Pluto. *See* VIDEO, CAPTAIN.

polo ponies. *See* POLOPONIES.

poloponies. In rehearsals for the RACCOONS' Ladies Auxiliary play, Norton as Hamilton DOUGLAS is too poor to offer a string of them to Rachel. ("That's *polo ponies*," Ralph explodes.) Norton gets his lines straight by show time. But Ralph, with poloponies on the brain, manages to make the same mistake on stage. The line is attributed to writer Syd Zelinka.

pool room. Has no name but a very important function: setting up Kramden and Norton for key encounters with the rest of the world. Also, a showplace for Kramden's tantrums, Norton's exaggerated gesturing . . . and Gleason's championship-caliber pool-playing skills.

Poor Soul. One of the most popular characterizations in the Gleason repertory. He wears a benign puppy-dog expression and has a knack for getting stepped on by the world . . . usually for the very best of intentions. It is not uncommon for Kramden to end a *Honeymooners* episode in a Poor Soul frame of mind. In such cases, Kramden, like the Poor Soul (always done entirely in pantomime) wipes his mouth, lets his head sink back into his shoulders, and lets us know by his facial expression alone that things have not turned out the way he planned.

popular songs. Ralph's ill-fated category on The $99,000 ANSWER.

Porter, Cole. *See* "DON'T FENCE ME IN."

potato pancakes. *See* WEDNESDAY NIGHT.

pratfalls. Strictly speaking, Gleason doesn't fall squarely on his prat. He maneuvers slightly to cushion the landing. Nonetheless, his Ralph Kramden spills are a wonder to behold, both for their timing and for the risk involved. In vaudeville days, every comic had to have a few falls up his sleeve; that's no longer true today. And even in the 1950s, Gleason's staff viewed his athletics with some concern. As his former office manager, Teddy GILANZA, recalls, "We never wanted to see him do it, just like a coach doesn't like to see his quarterback running with the ball."

Prescott, Dick. "Your Questioning Photographer," who runs man-on-the-street columns for a local paper (reminiscent of the *New York Daily News*), and asks such controversial questions as: "Which is more authentic, the Canarsie or Weehawken style of the mambo?" and, of an overly garrulous Ralph Kramden, "Who is head of your household?"

Proce, Jimmy. His Park View Tavern in Brooklyn was the model for Gleason's JOE THE BARTENDER sketches; the names used in the sketches were names from the old neighborhood: Mr. DENNEHY, Fatso Fogarty, Bookshelf Robinson, Teddy GILANZA, Duddy Duddelson, Julie DENNEHY, Henry Apollo, Paddy Noto the alderman, and Crazy GUGGENHEIM. When Ralph loses $200 in Raccoon treasury funds, at Dennehy's Bar, it is again Jimmy Proce's tavern that inspires the setting.

Proving Grounds, Aberdeen. In Maryland, the U.S. Army tests new equipment at the Aberdeen Proving Grounds. In New York, according to Ralph, the whole world can count on the subways as the Aberdeen Proving Grounds. The doctor gives him a cure for aggravation and it withstands the subway test.

Puder, Richard. The IRS officer Ralph goes to see when his taxes are questioned. Though Gleason pronounces it "Putter" on the ELECTRONICAM episode, the correct pronunciation is "Pooder." This can be confirmed by the real Mr. Puder, who was the accountant of writers Walter Stone and Marvin Marx.

questionable taste. When you write for Gleason, avoid using it in jokes and scripts. *See* BENSONHURST BUNNY CLUB.

Raccoons. The International Order of Friendly Raccoons (at other times, the Royal Order of Raccoons) is the lodge to which Ralph and Ed belong, and which provides the writers with any number of opportunities for comic situations and sight gags. The Raccoons hold annual dances, fishing trips, costume parties, picnics, boat rides, and no telling what else, all for annual dues of about $15. *See also* RACCOON CONVENTION; RACCOON HANDSHAKE; RACCOON LODGE; RACCOON OF THE YEAR; RACCOON UNIFORM.

Raccoon convention. Held in Chicago one year, Minneapolis another, Miami Beach still another. An annual event, although some years do not commemorate the event with specific episodes about it.

Raccoon handshake. Touch elbows and bounce your Raccoon tails.

Raccoon Lodge. According to Section Two of the rules and bylaws, the entrance requirements are as follows: (1) Applicant must have earned public school diploma, (2) must have been a U.S. resident for the last six months, (3) must pay a $1.50 initiation fee. Norton has been known to feel that the entrance requirements are too stiff. (*See* EDEN, ANTHONY) It is at the Raccoon Lodge that Ralph and Alice celebrate their twenty-fifth anniversary with a second wedding.

Raccoon of the Year. An honor which Kramden wants and Norton gets. Along with the title go the following privileges: (1) opening the first clam at the annual clambake, (2) steering from the bridge of the boat on the annual ride up the Hudson as Raccoon Point is passed, (3) free burial (with spouse) at the Raccoon National Cemetery in Bismarck, North Dakota, (4) a chance to run for GRAND HIGH EXALTED MYSTIC RULER. *See also* SHAGGY-DOG STORY.

Raccoon Point. *See* HUDSON RIVER.

Raccoon Uniform. An usher's uniform (usually dark, sometimes light) topped with a Davy CROCKETT coonskin cap. If you're the GRAND HIGH EXALTED MYSTIC RULER, your Raccoon hat has three tails and your jacket is coat-length. The standard-issue uniform comes with gold braid; the Raccoon of the Year wears platinum braid. If you're Alice, you consider the whole ridiculous "Admiral Dewey sport jacket" overpriced at $35.

Rachel. *See* FREDERICK.

Rainger. *See* "PLEASE."

Ranger. *See* "PLEASE"; VIDEO, CAPTAIN.

Ready, Willing and Able. *See* "TOO MARVELOUS FOR WORDS."

Red. Unseen friend of Ralph's, referred to on the evening that he is to fight HARVEY the bully.

Reynolds, Miss. Secretary at the STELLAR EMPLOYMENT AGENCY.

Rhythm on Ice. One of the movies Ralph and Ed attempt to see when they jointly purchase a TV. The cast is given as Kenny Baker, Jane Frazee, Buddy Ebsen, Jerry Colonna, and Frankie Darro. But in all probability, the movie is about as real as something from a Stanley R. SOGG spiel.

Richard the Chickenhearted. *See* RICHARD THE LIONHEARTED.

Richard the Lionhearted. Ralph tells Ed he's king of the castle, and just like Richard the Lionhearted, he rules with an iron hand. Alice appears, and Ed asks Ralph for a little demonstration. Ed talks too much . . . just enough to give Alice what she needs to needle Ralph: "Tell me, oh Richard the Chickenhearted . . . the peasants have a right to know."

Richardson, Mr. Rome representative for FLAKEY WAKEY.

Riley. The Raccoon who wears a sheet to the annual costume party year in and year out, as Julius Caesar most years and once as Mark Antony.

Riley, Chester A. Gleason's first role. A West Coast blue-collar worker who bought the American Dream hook, line, and sinker, got hooked on the line, and has been treading water not to sink ever since. Similar to Ralph Kramden in some ways (jealous, gullible, battling poverty) but different in one very important respect: Kramden still believes, almost blindly, in the American Dream.

Ring Magazine. Popular boxing magazine in which, says Ed, his mother-in-law is number two contender for the MARCIANO title.

Ritz. *See* KELLY, GRACE'S FATHER.

Robins. *See* "PLEASE."

Rockefeller Center. Privately owned New York City business and lively-arts center, home of the skating rink and the giant Christmas tree, Radio City Music Hall (*See* PECK, GREGORY), and concrete benches where people meet for brown-bag lunches. It is for such a lunch that Ralph and Ed meet when they decide to take up part-time jobs as sidewalk Santas.

Roseland. As in Ralph's immortal statement, "I was interested in songs even when I was a little kid. And when I grew up I didn't waste my time like the other guys. While they were bumming around street corners and pool rooms . . . I spent every night of the week up at Roseland.'' But immortalized even before that as the ballroom dance center of New York. *See also* POPULAR SONGS.

Rosenbloom, Maxie. Slapsie Maxie was the world light heavyweight champion from 1930 till 1934, a movie comedian, and namesake of the nightclub (Slapsie Maxie's) where Jackie Gleason scored some of his greatest pre-TV hits. On the night that Ralph and Ed jointly purchase a TV set, Ralph talks Ed into watching the *Fight of the Week,* Slapsie Maxie Rosenbloom versus Kingfish Lavinsky.

Rosita. The ''Spanish kindergarten teacher'' who is half the con artist team of Rosita and Miguel of Madrid. She's the half who tricks Ralph into embracing her; Miguel's the half who snaps their picture in a compromising position. Together they try to blackmail gullible *turista* Ralph, who would go to great lengths to keep Alice from seeing the incriminating photo.

Round Table. There's one in Ralph's apartment, and another in his horrible SHAGGY-DOG STORY. It's only fitting that his kitchen table should be round. Ralph is, after all, king of his castle. *See* MALE SUPREMACY; RICHARD THE LIONHEARTED.

Royal Order of Raccoons. *See* RACCOONS.

Russell, Jane. Long before she was known to today's TV audiences as the ''full-figure gal,'' she was still the best-known full-figure gal around. Hence Ralph's statement (on the night of Jim MCKEEVER's party) expressing his exhaustion, from working double shifts, in the strongest possible terms: ''You couldn't get me out of this house if you told me Jane Russell was running a party upstairs and couldn't get started till I arrived.''

Salvatore's Pizzeria. Where Ralph wins a ceramic horse with a clock in its stomach for being high scorer in a pinball competition.

Sanchez, Carlos. Manly, gentlemanly bachelor who moves into the apartment next to the Kramdens, teaches the wives to dance the MAMBO and the husbands to be more courteous, and generally upsets the routine at 328 Chauncey Street.

Sarah. *See* LEO, UNCLE.

Saturday. One of Ralph's pool-playing days. He plays both with and without Ed. Guess when he plays better.

savings account. *See* MONEY MATTERS.

Saxon, Stanley. Ralph's lodge brother in the RACCOON LODGE and, since Ralph fixed him up with Alice's sister Agnes, his brother-in-law too.

schemes. What Ralph comes up with to get rich quick that keeps him so hopelessly poor, like building a parking lot across from the new movie house going up (which turns out to be a drive-in) and investing $200 plus television expenses in the HANDY HOUSEWIFE HELPER. *See also* KRAMMAR.

Schultz. He can't bowl, but he's almost called in to replace Ralph the night of the championship tournament. Ralph bowls after all, winning the tournament, but wrenching his back the night before his company physical examination.

Schwartz, Mrs. The building blabbermouth of 328 Chauncey Street.

Seiffer, Dr. Treats Norton when a manhole cover lands on his head, then presides again when Ralph gives blood to a total stranger thinking it's Norton. Seiffer was the name of writer Syd Zelinka's own doctor.

sergeant-at-arms. Norton's post, at least for a while, with the RACCOON LODGE.

sewer. *See* HIMROD STREET; KOSCIUSKO STREET SEWER; SEWER WORKER; PARK AVENUE.

sewer worker. According to Norton, something like a brain surgeon: they're both specialists. Ed is one. So is Jim MCKEEVER. So is the GRAND HIGH EXALTED MYSTIC RULER of the Raccoons, Morris Fink.

shaggy-dog story. A whole narrative genre derived from a series of intentionally forced attempts to conclude a long, boring story with a twist on an old saying or proverb. In preparing his acceptance speech for the RACCOON OF THE YEAR award, Ralph (erroneously) believes that he has invented the original, which concerns Sir Launslit (Ralph's conception of Sir Lancelot), Sir . . . uh . . . King Arthur, a message . . . uh, mission . . . uh, trip, and a shaggy dog that can make the necessary journey when no horse is to be found. The punch line? "I wouldn't send a knight out on a dog like this." The humor? Certainly not the story; but Ralph's botched delivery of the yarn is a model of comic timing and characterization.

Shakespeare, William. Actor, sonneteer, and playwright of Elizabethan England, whom Norton quotes as having said that of the three moments in a man's life when he wants to be alone, the ultimate moment is when he's in the isolation booth of The $64,000 QUESTION.

Shaw, George Bernard. English critic and playwright whose observation that youth is wasted on the young is recalled by Ralph as Ralph vainly tries to be young again. In *Back to Methuselah* Shaw says that "Everything happens to everybody sooner or later if there is time enough"—a notion that establishes his credentials as one of the first modern authorities on the situation comedy.

Shaw, Jerry. An executive member of the RACCOONS.

Sherman tanks. What Ed mistakes Ralph's MAN FROM SPACE costume to be.

Shifty. Unseen friend of Ralph's and Ed's, mentioned the night Ralph is due to fight HARVEY the bully.

Shirley. She works for AMERICAN WEEKLY.

Shor, Bernard. "Toots" Shor was one of New York's foremost restaurateurs (he preferred "saloonkeeper") for more than thirty years. Among his closest drinking buddies and frequent customers were Jackie Gleason, Frank Sinatra, and Joe DiMaggio. The name *Shor* has appeared on the membership roster of the RACCOONS.

"Shuffle Off to Buffalo." By Warren and Dubin, from *Forty-second Street*. One of the songs correctly identified by Ralph as he practices for The $99,000 ANSWER.

Silver Oaks. One of the golf courses where Mr. HARPER plays and Ralph pretends that he does to impress Mr. Harper.

Simon, Bazzy. *See* "IT'S ALL OVER NOW."

sink. In the Kramdens' apartment, it looks like a sink, it works like a sink . . . until you try to draw water. Then it blows up in a burst of steam on Ralph. On the other hand, its faucets can be used for making MAN FROM SPACE costumes, and by sabotaging the pipes, it is possible to ruin Norton's bath or Trixie's dishwashing. *See also* DISNEYLAND.

$64,000 Question, The. Mid-1950s super-giveaway show, where money was given away hand over fist to contestants who could demonstrate their expertise in specific categories. As the questions became harder, contestants moved into the "isolation booth" while maddening music played in the background to keep the TV audience in suspense. Until the quiz show scandals hit (1959) an expert on *The $64,000 Question* was considered an expert indeed. Hence Ralph's crack, directed to Alice, that he qualifies for *The $64,000 Question* as an expert on aggravation; and Norton's, that his mother-in-law could win big money if her category was "nasty." *See also* THE $99,000 ANSWER; SHAKESPEARE.

Skelton, Red. *See* KARLOFF, BORIS.

Slop. *See* BRATTON, CHARLIE.

Social Security. *See* KRAMDEN, RALPH.

Sogg, Stanley R. Gleason's fast-talking TV pitchman for the *Late Late Late Late Late Late Late Late Show*, who combined his cast announcements for each late movie (a fictitious movie with a fictitious, often rhyming, cast) with outrageous TV offers like the informative best-seller, *How to Slide Downhill on Your Little Brother*, and for hillbilly musicians, a combination slide trombone and shotgun. For hints of Stanley R. Sogg in *The Honeymooners*, *see* HANDY HOUSEWIFE HELPER; *Rhythm on Ice*.

Sons of Italy Hall. Facing death together on a lifeboat lost at sea, Ralph and Ed reminisce about the get-together dances where they met Alice and Trixie. In their day, the Sons of Italy Hall featured such top, real-life bands as Little Jack LITTLE, Isham JONES, Ted FIORITO, and Basil FOMEEN.

Spear, Sammy. Gleason's conductor in the days of *Cavalcade of Stars* and for many of *The Honeymooners* years. He appears on the London TV show of

Gaylor FARQUARD as Sir Samuel Spear, a character very much like himself. *See also* PARAMOUNT THEATRE.

Spiffy iron. Norton tries to sell it door-to-door when he loses his job in the sewer, and Ralph threatens to sell it to pressure the bus company into giving him a raise. Both attempts fail miserably. So does the Spiffy iron.

Stanley. Ralph's brother-in-law, Alice's brother, who tries to get Ralph interested in a hotel deal. Not the same as Stanley SAXON.

Stellar Employment Agency. Where Ralph and Alice are offered jobs as domestics when they go to hire THELMA.

Stevens, Mrs. For Christmas, she buys Alice a present so cheap she's embarrassed by it. It's a box made out of 2,000 matchsticks glued together. Unfortunately, Ralph has bought Alice the same present for much more money, believing it came from "the Emperor of Japan's house." Because of Mrs. Stevens' untimely arrival, Ralph is forced to hock his bowling ball on Christmas Eve so he can buy Alice another present. Mrs. Stevens' sister lives in BAYONNE, New Jersey.

"Strangers in the Night." Ed offers to play it on his nose for FLAKEY WAKEY on British TV.

Strike It Rich. In the early 1950s, Warren Hull and the "Heartline" on *Strike It Rich* had TV audiences in constant suspense and tears. The people who appeared on the show had been evicted, wiped out by flood and fire, forced into debt by disease or by fate. One by one, they would sit on the sofa with Hull and pour their hearts out . . . hoping that the phone (the Heartline) would ring. Hoping that the person calling would offer them help, farm equipment, medicine, whatever they needed most. When the phone didn't ring, guests were offered the sponsors' products for their trouble—usually detergent or toothpaste. According to Norton, his mother-in-law watches the show for laughs.

Studio 50. Now The Ed Sullivan Theatre on Broadway and Fifty-third Street in Manhattan, Studio 50 was the theater where all but the ELECTROICAM episodes of the early *Honeymooners* were performed. *See also* ADELPHI THEATRE.

Sunday. THELMA gets them off, along with Thursdays.

Suzie Q. Popular dance of the late 1930s. One of the "new dances" Ralph is going to learn when Alice wants him to act young again.

"Swanee River." Norton's warm-up song whenever he plays the piano. As often as he warms up with it during practice sessions for Ralph's appearance on THE $99,000 ANSWER, Ralph never bothers to learn its name or who wrote it. Naturally, his first question on THE $99,000 ANSWER is: " 'Who wrote Swanee River?' " The correct answer is Stephen Foster. Ralph guesses Ed Norton, and is led off stage in defeat.

syndication. System by which filmed or taped programs (most commonly half-hour reruns) are broadcast directly by local stations rather than by networks, and sponsored by regional advertisers (who would be unable to afford even a minute of air time on network TV). Syndication was launched in 1948 with *Yesterday's Newsreels,* followed by *Sports Album* and *Cisco Kid,* the first truly successful syndicated program. *See also* VIACOM.

"Take Me Back to Sorrento." The script and most sheet music reads "Come Back to Sorrento," written by Ernesto Dicurtis in 1898. However, "Take Me Back to Sorrento" by Ernesto Dequista is the way Ralph identifies it (correctly, we are told) when Mrs. MANICOTTI helps him practice for THE $99,000 ANSWER. It's the one that goes "*Guarda il mare come bello, spira tanto sentimento . . .*"

team names. *See* COUGARS; HURRICANES.

teensy weensy. As applied to pizzas by Ralph, a small slice; as applied by Ed, a sliver, somewhat smaller than the piece Ralph has in mind, which Ed would describe as *itsy bitsy.*

telephone. You won't find one in the Kramdens' apartment most of the time, unless it's the one Trixie lowers from her apartment down to the Kramdens' fire escape. Ralph says it's a waste of money; Gleason says it's the DEUS EX MACHINA of situation comedy. When you *do* see a deus ex machina on *The Honeymooners,* it has to walk through the door like everyone else. *See also* BENSONHURST; ICEBOX.

television. An instrument designed for the bedevilment of Ralph and Ed, whether they buy one, win one, or appear on one in some crazy commercial produced and directed by Kramden himself.

Templeton, Bill. *See* "YOU'RE MY GREATEST LOVE."

Thelma. The maid hired by the Kramdens (and later, by the Nortons) from the STELLAR EMPLOYMENT AGENCY.

"There's Nothing I Haven't Sung About." Lyn Duddy and Jerry Bresler wrote this song for Bing Crosby to sing when Ralph and Ed go to Hollywood convinced that they should be writing songs professionally. Bing sings them out of it, with a tune that has since become closely identified with him.

Thursdays. THELMA gets them off, along with Sundays. Ralph bowls on them. And on Thursday, August 5, 1942 (a Friday, by the calendar) Ralph promised Alice that one day he would take her to a Broadway show—a promise that is almost realized a mere fourteen years later with two tickets to *Murder Strikes Out.* *See also* KOSCIUSKO STREET SEWER.

"Tippy Tippy Tin." Ed offers to play it on his head with a knife for British TV, courtesy of FLAKEY WAKEY on the Gaylor FARQUAD show.

Tommy. The neighborhood youth whose water pistol gets Ralph in a lot of hot water the night the killers DANNY and Bibbo show up.

Tony. Alice's pre-teenaged guide through Rome who Ralph assumes, sight unseen, to be her lover. Also Alice's handsome boss, Tony Amico (the real-life name of one of Gleason's closet friends), when Alice gets a job.

"Too Marvelous For Words." Written by Johnny Mercer and Richard Whiting for the film *Ready, Willing and Able,* 1937. One of the songs correctly identified by Ralph while practicing for THE $99,000 ANSWER.

Tracy, Dick. The familiar Chester Gould comic strip (dating from Prohibition days) is Ed's ultimate wisdom for all matters of investigative deduction. However, when Ralph sleeps on a key to prevent Ed's sleepwalking escape, Ed admits that even Dick Tracy would be stymied.

traffic manager. Ralph is more anxious to get promoted to this job than to any other in the world. *See also* MULLER, FREDDY.

Tubby. *See* PET NAMES.

Tugboat Annie. Rowdy waterfront lady created by Norman Reilly Raine and played by Marie Dressler in the 1933 movie of the same name. *See* CASSIDY.

Tunnel of Love. On separate occasions, Ed fixed the pipes and lost a dog there. *See also* LULU.

Twinkles. What Rita calls Bert WEDEMEYER.

uniform. What Ralph wears more than any man alive. *See* RACCOONS; GOTHAM BUS COMPANY; HURRICANES; CLAM SUIT.

Universal Magazine. Ralph wins the Safest Bus Driver in the City award and they do a three-page spread on him. Mr. Martin, their reporter, covers the story. Another issue featured Marilyn MONROE on the cover.

Utica. *See* LEO, UNCLE.

vacuum cleaner. Ralph buys one at DOWSERS on DeKalb. Because it's defective, it gets him in trouble with Norton, Alice, and Joe MUNSEY.

Valentino, Rudolph (Rodolfo Alfonzo Raffaelo Pierre Filibert Guglielmi di Valentino d'Antonguolla). The first, and to date, the most unforgettable, of Hollywood's "Latin lovers." When Ralph throws Carlos SANCHEZ out of his apartment for introducing Alice to good manners and the MAMBO, only seven words seem to fit the occasion: "And as for you, Rudolph Valentino, out!" The comparison fits; Valentino had the same effect on America in the 1920s, when even the matinee idols were homespun American boys. And the average red-blooded U.S. male felt threatened by some kind of foreign invasion.

Vallee, Rudy. *See* "GOOD NIGHT, SWEETHEART."

Van Gleason, Reggie, III. Philandering ne'er-do-well Park Avenue playboy and one of Gleason's best-loved characterizations. He is a carry-over from Gleason's days in burlesque. Van Gleason considered his parents (played by Zamah CUN-NINGHAM and Art Carney) and his brother (played by Gleason as an occasional double role) inconvenient, and usually told them so. He parted his hair down the middle because he was usually too drunk to do otherwise. He mixed his drinks on a bar counter that faced the audience; the counter moved, conveyor-belt fashion, as he mixed. And, drunk as he was, he always managed to catch his drinks before they came to the end of the belt. Kramden has his occasional Reggie Van Gleason moments, whenever he tries to act like a big shot. He doesn't have to have a drink in his hand to be an arrogant, insufferable, blowhard; all he needs is that insecure feeling he gets when he fears being outclassed, for instance, at the reading of Mary MONAHAN's will, or at the STELLAR EMPLOYMENT AGENCY.

Van Gleason, Wilbur. Reggie VAN GLEASON's e'er-do-well brother, who collected butterflies and did his parents proud. Both Wilbur and Reggie would be played by Gleason in the same sketch.

Vavavoom. *See* ESQUIRE MAGAZINE.

Verderchi, Harry. In more than one episode, Ralph has heard Alice say *"ar-rivederci"* over the phone and assumed it to be the name of his rival. Once he even makes the mistake of confronting Alice with a point-blank "Harry Verderchi," to which she replies, "If that's the way you want it, Ralph, good-bye." And then he jumps to another conclusion, that his marriage is ruined, as Alice walks out on him. In time, his marriage is saved. But does he learn his lesson? Does he ever?

Viacom. One of the leading SYNDICATION outfits, controlling distribution of such top-rated programs as *Hogan's Heroes, The Andy Griffith Show, I Love Lucy, The Beverly Hillbillies, The Dick Van Dyke Show,* and the ELECTRONICAM episodes of *The Honeymooners.*

Video, Captain. Hero of TV's first space show (beginning in 1949), played by Al Hodge, who testified before Congressional committees in the 1950s that many television shows (his, for example) were positively beneficial to impressionable young minds. Among the young minds impressed by Captain Video is Ed Norton's. Video's most notable exploit in terms of *The Honeymooners* occurs when Ralph and Ed jointly purchase a television set, and Ed has to lock Ralph out of his own apartment in order to blast off with the Video Rangers for "Pluto and the Moon." It is, to say the least, a mixed itinerary. And surely, with Ralph angry at him, Ed doesn't need Video's help to get to the moon. See also DUMONT; ELEC-TRONICAM.

Video Ranger. The name applied to a member of Captain Video's team. Ed Norton is a Video Ranger third class.

voh-doh-dee-oh-doh. An expression that dates back to the 1920s. Ralph decides to learn it and other "new expressions" when Alice wants him to start acting young again. *See also* "I'LL KISS YOU LATER, I'M EATING A POTATO."

Waldorf. *See* KELLY, GRACE'S FATHER.

Wallace. Ronnie Burns' interpretation of a souped-up 1950s teenager, who has a date with Judy (he's her "atomic passion") at a local bop contest.

Wallace's Department Store. Uncle Leo gives Ralph and Alice a $25 gift certificate from Wallace's as a Christmas present. *See* LEO, UNCLE.

wallpaper that glows in the dark. One of Ralph's unsuccessful get-rich schemes.

Warner Brothers. Film company that began in 1923, and another of Gleason's references to his early days. It was Warner Brothers that gave him his first film roles in Hollywood. *See* "DON'T FENCE ME IN."

Warren and Dubin. *See* "SHUFFLE OFF TO BUFFALO."

Wedemeyer, Bert and Rita. Rumor has it that Bert Wedemeyer is going to be the new general manager at the GOTHAM BUS COMPANY. Ralph wants to get on his good side by making a fuss over Rita, Bert's attractive but egotistical new wife. The Wedemeyers "live on love." Roughly translated, this means that Bert does the doting and the cooking, Rita makes cooing noises and calls Bert "Twinkles."

Wednesday night. When Norton's regular meal is Chicken Chow Mein (*See* CHINESE RESTAURANT) and potato pancakes. It is also on a Wednesday night that a telegram arrives from "mother," saying that she is coming to the Kramdens' to visit. It is not Alice's mother, but Ralph's, who arrives—after Ralph has made a fool of himself by steadfastly refusing that no mother-in-law of his is setting foot in his apartment.

Weehawken. City in New Jersey, across the river from Manhattan via the Lincoln Tunnel. Formerly famous for its ferry and, according to Ed Norton, for its MAMBO.

Whiteside, Herbert J. Hollywood producer and Mr. FAVERSHAM's friend. When Earl Wilson reports in his column that Whiteside is in town to scout new faces, Ralph is sure that his role as FREDERICK will skyrocket him to fame. But when Whiteside approaches Alice to offer her a part in his new picture, Ralph is deflated . . . until he learns that Alice would rather stay in Bensonhurst with him.

Whiting, Richard. *See* "TOO MARVELOUS FOR WORDS."

Wiggams, Sam. Ed's idea of "the best lawyer in town." He specializes in eviction cases. But Ed's not sure he can be reached or even located; Wiggams has just been evicted.

wisenheimer. Brooklynese, popularized by Gleason outside of Brooklyn, but even before him, by Walter Winchell.

will. When Ralph thinks he's going to die of ARTERIAL MONOCHROMIA, he starts to write his will. He realizes instantly that he has nothing to leave Alice; but he has no trouble deciding that he will leave Norton his bowling shoes. *See also* MONAHAN, MARY; AMERICAN WEEKLY.

Wilson, Earl. *See* WHITESIDE, HERBERT J.

window, back. Now that the laundry has been torn down, you can see the kitchen of the Chinese restaurant from it. Also, the Italian-American Social Club.

window, blue. *See* FENSTERBLAU, JOE.

window, front. From Kramden's, you can see a Chinese restaurant, the pizzeria, and Old Man Grogan's long underwear. *See* DISNEYLAND.

Wolhstetter, Harvey and Helen. They live on Van Buren Street in Gleason's old neighborhood. They have a son, Harvey, Jr., and they are out celebating their tenth wedding anniversary the night Alice baby-sits for them (and Ralph becomes violently jealous). The name Wolhstetter comes from Charles Wolhstetter, a friend of writer Syd Zelinka.

Woodrum, Pete. The Raccoon who wins second place in the annual costume party for his costume as a playboy of the Roaring Twenties.

World of Tomorrow. *See* DISNEYLAND.

WPA. (Works Progress Administration). A government agency created by the New Deal to provide employment during the Depression. It gave Ralph one of his first jobs; it was while he was shoveling snow for the WPA that he met, and later married, Alice Gibson.

"Yes, We Have No Bananas." According to the most recent *Honeymooners* (Valentine's 1978) special, Ralph and Alice's song.

"Your Questioning Photographer." *See* PRESCOTT, DICK.

"You're My Greatest Love." The *Honeymooners* theme song. Music by Jackie Gleason, words by Bill Templeton.

Yucca Flats. Testing site for the atomic bomb, as when Alice complains: "I am the only girl in town with an atomic kitchen. This place looks like Yucca Flats after the blast."

Zamah. *See* CUNNINGHAM, ZAMAH.

Zelda, Madame. *See* CONEY ISLAND.

Ziggy. A counterfeiter with "the Syndicate," who leaves a suitcase stuffed with $50,000 in funny money on Ralph's bus. When Ziggy doesn't claim it (for fear of legal reprisal), Ralph gets it. Then the Syndicate traces Ralph to his apartment. And Ralph really gets it.

INDEX